GOLDSMITH

GOLDSMITH

MONEY, WOMEN & POWER

CHRIS HUTCHINS
AND DOMINIC MIDGLEY

MAINSTREAM
PUBLISHING

EDINBURGH AND LONDON

First published in Great Britain in 1998 by
MAINSTREAM PUBLISHING COMPANY (EDINBURGH) LTD
7 Albany Street
Edinburgh EH1 3UG

ISBN 1 84018 093 5

A catalogue record for this book is available from the British Library

Typeset in Esprit Book
Printed and bound in Great Britain by Butler and Tanner Ltd

Contents

Acknowledgements

THE first thing that any subject of an unauthorised biography is likely to do is to ask his family and friends not to speak to those embarking on the project. And Sir James Goldsmith was no different. But while some refused to speak under any circumstances, many others did, often on the understanding that they were not identified.

Particular thanks are due to Goldsmith's eldest daughter Isabel for breaking ranks and for devoting so much time to interviews with the authors, and to Goldsmith's step-daughter, India Jane Birley. And while Goldsmith's older brother Teddy refused to be interviewed he did sportingly offer tea and agreed to read the chapter on his brother's early years.

Of those other sources who can be named, the authors would like to thank Eton contemporaries Tom Stacey, Philip Goodman and Sir John Hall for their insights into Goldsmith's early life; Charles Raw for his kind permission to reproduce passages from his exhaustive investigation into Goldsmith's business activities in the '60s and '70s; Bill Ofner, Bruce Page, Walt Paterson, Tom Burke, Donald Trelford, Peter Hope Lumley, Jill Rushton, Claudia Cragg, Paul Mercer, David Dearle, Beryl Meier, Maureen Zisserman, Robert Couturier, Bill Lovelace, the Duke of Hamilton, Christopher Wilson, Charles Benson, Richard Ingrams, Lord Healey, Frederic Mullally, Peter Townend, Philip Townsend, Lord Rees Mogg, Tiny Rowland, Alan Sked, the Hon. Sarah Daniel, Robin Leach, Cathy Seaton, Taki Theodoracopoulos, Margaret Luddington, Lady Cosima Somerset, Kathryn Ireland, Sandy Mitchell, Sarah Standing, Professor Hugh Stephenson, Joe Haines, Andreas Whittam Smith and Balendu Prakash.

In France, Olivier Todd, Peter Stephens, Chris Lafaille, Benno Graziani, the Duchess of Durcal and Adnan Khashoggi.

In Mexico, Tony Dillon and his wife Eva for their invaluable local knowledge and advice; the staff of Las Hadas in Manzanillo and Las Alamandas near Careyes; Manuel Sanchez de la Madrid, editor and publisher of *El Mondo desde Colima*; the Colima tourist office and Leopoldo Sahagun Michel.

In Pakistan, Salmaan Taseer, Rao Amjad Ali, Kamran Shafi, Nilofer Shahid, Embesat Salahuddin and Mohammed Osman.

Thanks are also due to our translators Alison Mudge and Mirea Mangual (Spanish) and Philip Benedictus (French).

Prologue

THE letter was short but relatively sweet. 'Sir James [*Goldsmith*] regrets that his commitments at present mean that he will not be able to meet you to discuss your forthcoming book,' it ran. 'He is appreciative of your approach to him.' The interesting thing about the missive is that it was not written on Goldsmith's letterhead but on that of Britain's leading firm of libel lawyers, Peter Carter-Ruck and Partners. It was vintage Goldsmith: the iron fist in the velvet glove.

In his lifetime he did everything he could to prevent publication of this unauthorised biography. The authors were warned at the outset that one of his first moves would be to assign private detectives to delve into their backgrounds and political affiliations. Members of his family were instructed not to speak, with the perceived threat that to do so would mean being left out of his will. And friends were warned not to co-operate. The pressure eventually told on the publishing house which had commissioned the book in the first place. Citing its fear of a costly libel action that publisher pulled out of the deal, paying the writers their advance in full.

What no one but Goldsmith and a handful of confidants knew at this stage was that he had only a matter of months left to live and he was determined that a work over which he had no control should not turn out to be his epitaph. According to one member of his circle, there was even talk of paying the authors half a million pounds to lay off. In the event, Goldsmith died a month before the book's planned release date in August 1997, satisfied that he had resolved the matter.

But, by now, the writers had an intriguing book on their hands. They had travelled the world to investigate their subject in his various habitats and, despite pressure from Goldsmith, scores of friends and enemies, associates and rivals, had spoken out about the workings of the Goldsmith empire. Even a handful of independent-minded relatives had broken ranks and told their stories of life within the family. What emerged was an extraordinary portrait of a remarkable man. Suddenly publishers were interested anew. In the wake of Goldsmith's death, an updated manuscript was completed and this book is the result.

The man who made a fortune from a spate of company takeovers in the US was used to having things his way. His new career in politics may have brought him back into the limelight but it made him, if anything, even more sensitive to unauthorised probing. And with good reason. Few public figures led a more colourful existence than Goldsmith. In Britain, he attracted controversy in the '70s for a ruthless approach to the companies he acquired in his bid to become the housewives' favourite in the supermarket sector. At one stage his Cavenham holding company dwarfed Tesco and Sainsbury's. In the '80s, he sent tremors through many an American boardroom on his way to becoming one of the most feared corporate raiders in the US. Meanwhile, his high-profile private life was proving equally fascinating. In the years following his first marriage in 1954, he produced eight children by four different women.

It is a maverick style that was obvious from his very earliest days, when even his school friends realised that he was no ordinary mortal. 'There was a kind of precocity to Jimmy,' says Tom Stacey, who was in the same house at Eton as Goldsmith. 'I was at university with Rupert Murdoch later and I had exactly the same feeling about him. Their stage was bigger than ours.'

The Brylcreem bounce evident in Goldsmith's leaving photograph from Eton was replaced in later years by a bald crown ringed by distinguished grey and first diabetes, then cancer, robbed him of the prodigious energy that had seen him through many an arduous boardroom battle. At six feet four inches, he had considerable physical presence but it was his force of personality that left the biggest impression. Few who were fixed by the icy stare of his piercing blue eyes ever forgot the experience. It reminded one of the P.G. Wodehouse character whose gaze 'could open an oyster at 50 paces'. Friends recall bellowed greetings from the other side of the room at parties; television interviewers testify to his slash and burn approach to questions; and business associates still marvel at his grasp of a balance sheet.

Almost to the end, there was no sign of a waning in his legendary sexual powers. 'My father's idea of complete heaven was a harem,' wrote his daughter Isabel, shortly after his death. While remaining married to his third wife, Lady Annabel, he continued to conduct a very open affair with Laure Boulay de la Meurthe, an aristocratic Frenchwoman 18 years his junior, and even these relationships did not preclude outside dalliances. There was the occasion at a party held by Lord Rothermere in the Austrian city of Salzburg when he took a fancy to a Greek soprano who was entertaining the guests. The next day she awoke to the heavy scent of flowers: Goldsmith had bought practically every red rose in the city and had them delivered to her room. During his Paris days he frequented an establishment run by the notorious Madame Claude and such was his prowess that he gained a reputation among her girls as a 'bon coup' (loosely translated as 'good lay'). Screenwriter Laline Paull, who was once a house-guest of Goldsmith's, certainly found him a man of appetites: 'I believed him when he said that if he should find himself alone, in a strange town, unmarried, it would be a matter of a few hours before he would remedy that terrible situation and that he honestly could not imagine existing without a woman.'

Goldsmith's life has been public property since the '50s, when his elopement with Isabel Patino, a teenage Bolivian heiress, made headlines around the world. Her tragic death just four months later and the subsequent high-profile custody battle over Isabel, their daughter, only confirmed his image as a popular hero. He went on to earn international renown as a risk-taking tycoon. As he himself once said, 'If the next takeover comes off, I could be as rich as Croesus, or I might be as poor as Job.' But his reputation took a battering thanks to his polygamous lifestyle, his predatory business practices and a bitter legal feud with the satirical magazine *Private Eye*.

Having made his pile, Goldsmith turned his energies away from his commercial interests. First he resolved to change the world as an environmental activist but, rebuffed by elements of the Green establishment, he decided to concentrate on another cause, making the politics of the European superstate his battleground. To promote his views, he founded political movements on both sides of the English Channel. He sat as a member of the European Parliament for a French constituency from 1994 till his death and, in the UK, he used his own vast resources to establish the Referendum Party in an attempt to force the government's hand on a plebiscite on European integration. He clearly felt the need to prove himself on the greatest stage of all. 'There are certain families who bring up their children with leadership presumption,' says Tom Stacey. 'In that respect they are natural movers and shakers and if they see something they care about being messed around with they will do something about it.'

Following her marriage to Imran Khan, the former Pakistani cricket captain, Jemima Goldsmith has emerged as the star of the younger generation of Goldsmiths. But a question mark hangs over which of Goldsmith's sons has inherited his potent brand of drive and flair and is best qualified to take on his mantle in the financial sphere.

His oldest son, Manes (by his second wife Ginette Lery) who, in the normal course of events might have been tipped for the succession, was running a tobacconist's in Twickenham at a time when he might have been expected to be being groomed to take over. Goldsmith was always fiercely protective of Manes (known to the family as Frank) who was diagnosed as a severe dyslexic and sent to the sports-oriented Millfield School.

While no one doubted Goldsmith's devotion to his first born son, it is clear that the boy was not considered dynasty-perpetuating material. And the creation of a dynasty is something that was very close to Goldsmith's heart. For centuries, the Goldschmidts – as they once were – had been poor relations to the Rothschilds, Europe's leading banking family. By the time Sir James's branch of the family arrived in England at the turn of the century, however, they were wealthy enough to buy a 5,000-acre estate at Cavenham in Suffolk. But it was Goldsmith's success that represented the best chance for generations for the family to emulate the Rothschilds' achievements. Indeed, by 1974, Goldsmith had earned a much-coveted place on the board of the Rothschilds' French bank. What he sought then was a successor from his own bloodline with the wherewithal to follow in his footsteps.

In choosing the name Zacharias for the baby presented to him by his then mistress Annabel in 1975 – one year after the birth of Jemima – Goldsmith made no secret of his expectations: the name means 'a boy with a future'. He was at pains to make him a legitimate heir and to this end, three years later, he divorced Ginette and married Annabel, his lover of 14 years. She went on to have a third child but if Annabel thought his birth would mark an end to her husband's breeding, she was to be proved wrong.

Goldsmith went on to father another two children, by Laure, a relative of the Comte de Paris, the pretender to the French throne. But while Goldsmith showered her with all the perquisites of a rich man's consort, there was one area in which he clearly felt unable to give way. He may have been a man who had little time for marital propriety but there was a fascinating clue to his attitudes in his entry in the European Parliament directory of members. Here he took the strangely old-fashioned approach of not acknowledging his children by his mistress. He admitted to only six offspring, one by his first wife, two by Ginette and three by Annabel.

For all his fondness for women, Goldsmith's greatest muse turned out to be his elder brother Teddy, a man who shared none of his preoccupations with international wheeler-dealing. After being eclipsed in the commercial sector as a young man by the brother he knew as Jimmy, Teddy devoted his life to championing environmental issues. There were signs of these instincts early on. Indeed, Dagonal, the French pharmaceutical company which formed the platform for his younger brother's early success, was named by Teddy after the god of crop fertility. It was Teddy who passed on to his brother an apocalyptic vision of the future of the world and remained, to the end, the keeper of his conscience.

Goldsmith's love of power and his fascination with ideas were a potent combination which helped change the face of modern business, and the war chest he amassed in the commercial arena put him in a strong position to promote his political agenda in much the same way as Ross Perot did in the United States.

Goldsmith stood at the head of a family which has already made its mark in countries spread across four continents. But it is in the years to come that the younger generation of Goldsmiths will have the chance to prove whether they are equipped to exploit the fabulous wealth he accumulated and expand what he has left into a vast empire. One thing is certain: as we approach the new millennium, no dynasty is better placed to rise to power and influence or descend into profligate oblivion. Are they up to the challenge? Did he rear them for greatness or condemn them to gilded obscurity? To answer these questions we need to examine the extraordinary story of Sir James Goldsmith and the lives of those who have inherited his fortune and the expectations that go with it.

Chapter One

The rake's progress

THE pin-ups on young Jimmy Goldsmith's study wall at Eton said it all. Even at that early stage a craving for wealth was matched only by his fondness for beautiful women. It was then, and remains, one of the features of Eton that boys have their own rooms rather than sleep in dormitories. But no one adorned their walls quite like Goldsmith and it did not escape the notice of his housemaster, Nigel Wykes. 'I don't think Wykes made too much of a fuss,' says Philip Goodman, a contemporary of Goldsmith's, 'but I think he was a bit surprised to find half-clad young ladies on the wall. Jimmy liked the ladies from the age of ten, I would say.'

Goldsmith, who, even then, spoke French as naturally as he did English, cut a glamorous figure in the drab surroundings of an English public school. His juvenile red-blooded heterosexuality also made him stand out at an institution where *le vice anglais* was a recognised part of many a pupil's adolescent rites of passage. 'He was one of the few pupils who was normal in that house, I must say,' recalls Goodman. 'When I say normal I mean he liked girls as opposed to boys. Little boys tend not to be very normal but Jimmy was very normal. He'd been introduced to the facts of life at a very early age. His father ran the Carlton in Cannes and he went down there for his holidays and he would regale us with long stories about life on the Riviera. We all loved that. He certainly had a wild time during the holidays. I don't think he broke out of school to go to dances or anything but he gave us all the impression that he came back to Eton more for a rest cure than anything else.'

The Eton of the mid to late '40s was an unlikely nursery for millionaires. Rationing was still in force and conditions were spartan. In the absence of radiators, the boys had to content themselves with small coal fires and visits from parents were relatively rare thanks to petrol rationing. 'Life in England after the war, in the late '40s was, in some ways, tougher than in England during the war,' recalls Goodman. 'We didn't suffer badly but it wasn't a life of luxury.'

More uncomfortable was a disciplinary regime based on fagging and the cane. All first form boys underwent a rigorous initiation procedure. Within two or three weeks of their arrival they would be tested by 'the library', a charmed circle of the most senior six to eight boys in the house. These tests were normally scheduled for nine o'clock at night, a time when the younger boys would be dressed for bed in pyjamas, dressing gowns and slippers. They would line up and be interrogated about various aspects of the school. One common line of questioning related to house colours, not an easy topic as Eton has no fewer than 25 houses. 'They would scream at you,' recalls one old Etonian. 'They wanted you to fail.' Any mistakes in Goldsmith's day were rewarded with a sound beating.

A far worse ordeal for a young pup like Goldsmith would have been carrying out the duties of a fag. Each first former was allocated a fagmaster, a senior boy for whom they were expected to act as manservant. Chores ranged from polishing shoes to making tea and preparing boiled eggs, with any departure from the highest standards of performance earning a beating. Perhaps most humiliating of all was the 'boy call', whereby the last fag to come running in response to a shout from a senior boy would be given whatever assignment he had in mind.

Under such a system, life was particularly difficult for the rebellious young Jimmy. His relationship with his housemaster 'Tiger' Wykes ranged from poor to intolerable. Wykes, who had played county cricket for Essex, was a sympathetic master to boys who shared his interest in sport or who had an academic streak. Since Goldsmith fell into neither category, their relationship was doomed from the start. Goldsmith took little interest in sport beyond the odd game of tennis and was more interested in organising dinner parties for his friends in Windsor and trips to the races than reading Virgil.

Indeed one of the few occasions he did take an interest in the classics was when he cornered the market in the crib to the *Electra* of Sophocles one summer. Cribs – or potted guides to books – were banned by the masters who obviously wanted their charges to read the original work but they were, nevertheless, much sought after. By the time term started, Jimmy had bought up the entire stock – up to 20 books – at two shillings and sixpence (12½p) a copy and went on to sell them to boys in the form above him for five shillings apiece. 'It was what you might call his first financial coup or corner,' says the baronet Sir John Hall, one of those who willingly shelled out for one of the cribs.

This is exactly the sort of cheek that would have enraged his housemaster. 'Nigel Wykes and he were at daggers drawn from the beginning,' says Goodman, whom Goldsmith knew as 'Puff-Puff'. 'I think he was a bit of a rebel even in those days and Wykes didn't like rebels.' Another contemporary of Goldsmith, Tom Stacey, adds: 'He wasn't like Douglas Hurd [later to become Foreign Secretary under Margaret Thatcher], who was an amazing grafter who got the top marks. But I think he was certainly bright and able if not naturally scholastic, which I don't think he'd claim to be. He was too impatient for that.'

As a young man, Wykes had been considered rather dashing but he grew 'cantankerous and egocentric', according to one obituary, due to 'the bitter sadness he felt about his mentally handicapped son'. His humour cannot have been helped by a stroke of spectacular good fortune that came the way of one of his least favourite scholars. Goldsmith had been a gambler since he was a toddler, on one celebrated occasion winning the jackpot on a slot machine in the drawing-room of the Hotel de Paris in Monte Carlo when he was just six. It took two waiters to gather up his winnings from the investment of a single franc. At Eton, he refined and expanded the art in the face of official disapproval, placing bets by postal order and sometimes using other boys to deliver them. Nor did he limit himself to his allowance of £1 a week in the belief that his father would make good any shortfall. He was just 16 when he pulled off a mammoth win after wagering £10 on an accumulator bet at Lewes races. When Bartisan, Merry Dance and Your Fancy all came in first, he picked up an astonishing £8,000 – equivalent to £145,000 today – a betting coup which has gone down in gambling history. 'I remember him showing his winnings to me,' says Philip Goodman, 'because it was hidden under his bed in a suitcase. It was all in the old white fivers.'

Mystery has long surrounded the circumstances of Goldsmith's premature departure from Eton to a crammer in Kent but the possession of such wealth must have made his position at school even more difficult than it already was. Wykes certainly thought so. 'I suggested to his father that it would be better if he went elsewhere,' he said years later. 'He was not suitable for my house.'

In line with school tradition, Goldsmith went in search of a suitable leaving present for his soon to be late and unlamented housemaster. Aware of Wykes's love of classical music he called in at Dysons in Windsor High Street and bought a set of nine Beethoven symphonies recorded on old Bakelite 78s. He duly presented them to his housemaster but, just as a touched Wykes began to thank him, Goldsmith asked for them back and, in an act of calculated vandalism, smashed the records one by one. When asked in later years what he remembered about Goldsmith, Wykes said: 'Nothing good.' Wykes died in 1991 at the age of 85 and when a well-attended memorial service was held for him a few years later at King's College Chapel there was at least one notable absentee. Goldsmith was not a man who forgave easily.

Wykes was not the only schoolmaster to find the young Goldsmith impossible. The stint at the crammer in Kent ended abruptly after Goldsmith – even then well over six foot – got into a fight with one of his teachers. He left in such haste that he abandoned a 1928 Singer that he had yet to learn to drive. It was only recovered months later when it was used to pay off a gambling debt for Teddy.

By this time, Goldsmith had certainly packed more into his young life than any of his schoolmates. Born James Michael Goldsmith in Paris on 26 February 1933, he was the son of Frank Goldsmith, a successful hotelier known as the Major, and his wife, Marcelle, who was 30 years younger. Through his father, Jimmy could trace his Jewish origins back to the Frankfurt ghetto of the 16th century, when the Goldschmidts – as they then were – lived alongside the Rothschilds and the Salomons and other Jewish banking families who made it big in the 19th century. The

English branch of the family was established in 1895, when Adolph Goldschmidt and his wife Alice settled in London with their three sons and a fortune estimated at £1 million. Adolph went on to buy a 5,000-acre estate at Cavenham in Suffolk, which included ownership of the local village of the same name.

Frank, the most talented of Adolph's sons, took a degree from Oxford and became a barrister before entering politics by winning a seat as a councillor in Westminster. He went on to stand as a Municipal Reform Party candidate, supporting the Conservative Party at national level, and beat the socialist playwright George Bernard Shaw to a seat on London County Council.

In the general election of 1910, he stood for his home constituency of North West Suffolk and won the seat from the Liberals by 645 votes.

By now a Freemason, Frank looked set for a brilliant career in British public life. The First World War, however, changed all that. Soon after the outbreak of hostilities, his brother-in-law, Ernst von Marx, a senior civil servant in Germany, sent him a telegram from Hamburg, openly asking him how he could consider fighting for anyone other than the Fatherland. The content of the telegram caused a wave of anger and disgust at the Post Office and news of its contents created a furious backlash against the unfortunate Frank. There were riots in the constituency and demands for him to be stripped of his army commission and thrown out of Parliament.

Frank went on to fight on the beaches of Gallipoli and in Palestine and rose to the rank of Major but he never recovered from the rejection he had suffered. At the end of the war he informed his party he would not stand for re-election and moved quietly to Paris. His son's authorised biographers made much of this episode and it might be said to have laid the foundations of a sense of being an outsider, compensated for by an excessively pugilistic attitude, that Goldsmith retained to his dying day.

If Frank was scarred by the experience he did not show it. In France he soon built a hotel empire and by 1928 his chain, Hotel Reunis, ran 48 of the finest hotels in France, including the Hotel Scribe in Paris and the Carlton in Cannes. It was on the train to Cannes that Monsieur le Major, then 50, met his wife to be, a 23-year-old blonde, Marcelle Moullier. They married in London in

June 1929, shortly after the birth of their first child, Edward – now universally known as Teddy – in Paris. Jimmy arrived six years later. His infancy was spent in the grandest suites of Europe's finest hotels as his father travelled from city to city, using private rail carriages for long journeys and his chauffeur-driven Rolls Royce for shorter ones.

It was not the sort of environment likely to produce a well-adjusted child and Jimmy grew up with what some might call a self-assurance which belied his years but which others might describe as arrogance. Either way, it nurtured a level of self-belief which was to serve him well in the years to come.

At the outbreak of the Second World War, Frank was 61 and too old to be accepted into the Army Officers Emergency Reserve. With German troops marching into northern France and the prospect of an Italian invasion in the south, he evacuated his family to England where they took a suite at Claridge's. But, even at the most luxurious hotel in London, it was impossible to escape the bombing and guests spent most nights taking cover in the cellars. Frank decided to move his family to the safety of the Bahamas where he had taken a lease on the Royal Victoria Hotel in Nassau. There he and Marcelle renewed their acquaintance with the Duke and Duchess of Windsor, the former Mrs Wallis Simpson, who had been despatched to one of Britain's most remote colonial outposts to sit out the war. The Goldsmith parents dined occasionally with the Duke and Duchess, who, ironically, given Frank's Jewishness, have since been exposed as Nazi sympathisers.

Jimmy and his brother Teddy started school in the Bahamas, first at Belmont School and later at the Queen's College, run by the Methodist Missionary Society. While his older brother thrived, Jimmy soon fell behind. Nobody doubted his intelligence, it was a capacity for hard work that seemed to be lacking. When Teddy took his seven-year-old brother to task about his unwillingness to learn to read, Jimmy uttered the now famous reply: 'When I grow up, I'm going to be a millionaire and hire someone to read for me.'

Two years later, both boys were sent to a boarding school in Toronto and Jimmy's rebellious streak was honed further. The school had a strong sporting tradition but the more he was pushed to participate in games, the more obstreperous he became.

At the end of 1944, with victory in sight, Frank sent his children back to England to be educated at Millfield School in Somerset: Jimmy to study for the common entrance exam for Eton and Teddy to prepare for Oxford.

Eton and Goldsmith, as we have seen, did not get on and he was certainly not qualified to go on to university. But with his formal education over, Goldsmith nevertheless headed for Oxford where his brother Teddy was in his final year at Magdalen College. It was there that he formed a tight-knit circle of friends, many of whom remain close to this day, and indulged his love of gambling. It was during a game of *chemin de fer* at his brother's college room that he earned the respect of a friend of Teddy's, John Aspinall. Aspinall recalls 'a tall young man with piercing eyes and a commanding presence' walking into the room and standing behind Teddy's chair. He was smoking a cigar and called out a bet. As there was about £400 in the pot, a mixture of cash, cheques and IOUs, I turned to the young man and said, no doubt in the patronising tone of a 24-year-old to a 17-year-old: "Do you realise there is £400 in the pot?" Without a word or a glance at me, he threw a wad of white fivers on to the baize and took up the cards. He lost and paid, and I quietly made room for him at the table – he appeared to be a young man of ample resources.' It was to be the start of a lifelong friendship.

From then on, Goldsmith settled easily into a life of Bohemian excess. With no academic study to distract him, he engaged himself full-time in the serious business of poker-playing, partying and chasing women. According to Noel Whitcomb, the *Daily Mirror* journalist who was later to play an important part in the coverage of his wedding, he was popular 'in his circle of profligate young roués but, to disapproving observers, he was nothing but a philandering libertine with the mind of a bookie and the morals of a tomcat'. It was too good to last, however. His Eton windfall soon went and his gambling losses began to mount. As his luck ran out, so did his parents' patience.

On one celebrated occasion, Jimmy invited a group of friends from Oxford to spend the weekend at the Carlton in Cannes, where they proceeded to gamble away all their funds on the first night. As the son of the proprietor, Jimmy exercised his *droit de seigneur* over the head waiter to borrow more stake money. Even that was almost gone and things looked black when, all of a sudden, Jimmy recovered his winning streak. He went on to recover all the money they had lost and, after three days of high drama, during which none of them had seen daylight, they emerged solvent. It was a vivid illustration of Goldsmith's taste for life on the edge and his capacity for keeping his nerve in a crisis.

News of such episodes, however, filtered back to his father who ordered him back to Paris and put him to work as a waiter and cook at the Luce restaurant in Montmartre. When this failed to have the desired effect on his errant son's lifestyle, Monsieur le Major drafted him further south to the Palace Hotel in Madrid. But Goldsmith had little appetite for life in the *hors d'oeuvre* department of the hotel's kitchens and he soon joined a local gambling circle. After a disastrous losing streak, he returned to London and, with bookmakers and other creditors pressing for repayment, he sent his friend, Digby Neave, to lobby his father for cash to pay them off. It transpired that Goldsmith's debts were now of the order of £2,000.

By this stage, Goldsmith senior had had enough. A gambler himself in his youth, he had been prepared to adopt an indulgent attitude to his son's excesses, but debts of this magnitude went beyond the bounds of youthful exuberance. He was even minded to take the advice of one friend and consign his younger son to Australia to become a fireman. In the event, he decided to be merciful. He would settle Jimmy's bills, but at a price. In return, Jimmy must sign on for his National Service with a provincial regiment based far from the temptations of the capital. The prematurely cosmopolitan 17-year-old, who had cruised the capitals of Europe staying at their finest hotels, found himself billeted in the Shropshire town of Oswestry with the Royal Artillery.

Goldsmith later claimed the army 'made a man of me'. He certainly appears to have knuckled under to an extent that he never had before. He became a training officer charged with reforming the habits of the most rebellious recruits, a task he came to relish. He even gained a reputation as something of a disciplinarian. Not that he was a completely changed man. In the absence of the customary supply of willing debutantes, he contented himself with an affair with a contortionist who worked at the Butlins holiday camp in Pwllheli, north Wales.

By the time he left the army in 1953, at the age of 20, the outside world had changed. The feckless students he had known had begun to revert to type. After their brief flirtation with the good life, they were all starting to settle into careers. For his part, the new, improved Goldsmith decided to return to Paris, where his father gave him a room in what used to be the servants' quarters on the seventh floor of the Hotel Scribe.

By this time, Frank Goldsmith had set up Teddy as the French agent for a London-based company which was marketing a cure for rheumatism called Lloyd's Adrenalin Cream. The venture got off to a flying start when Teddy hit upon the idea of treating a mildly arthritic racehorse, which was entered for the 1952 Prix de l'Arc de Triomphe, with the cream he had renamed Adremad. He planted the story through two journalists he knew on *France Dimanche* and, while Worden II failed to win the race, it ran well to finish second. On the back of this public relations coup sales took off but it was going to take more than one successful product to cover the overheads of the company he had called Dagonal.

He duly branched out into electrical plugs, with another colourfully named subsidiary, Lucifer. But profitability remained elusive. At this point the French Army took a step which was to prove decisive in the formation of the Goldsmith family fortunes: it arrested Teddy for failing to fulfil his National Service and jailed him as a deserter. The family have always maintained that this was caused by his call-up papers being sent to the wrong address and the mix up was resolved when Teddy persuaded the French authorities to allow him to serve out his military service in England. In his absence he needed someone to run the business. As the enterprise was essentially a one-man operation at this stage and run on a shoe-string, Jimmy, then just 20, was the only feasible caretaker. Teddy handed over the reins with no great confidence but it was to prove just the opportunity that the young Jimmy had been looking for in his quest to become a millionaire.

Chapter Two

Elopement of the century

IT was no place for the offspring of a South American Catholic. The Stork Room was famous for many things: East End wide boys and West End aristocrats; gamblers and hustlers; resting showgirls and talent-hungry impresarios. More thin on the ground were the convent-educated teenage daughters of millionaires. But it was to the Swallow Street club that Maria Isabella Patino made her way from Claridge's on the night of her 18th birthday in 1953 after a lavish dinner party thrown by her father. After all, London's most prestigious hotel may offer dining in the grand manner but to a lively young woman, the louche attractions of the night spot run by Al Burnett and Bill Ofner were more seductive.

It was there that she came face to face with Jimmy Goldsmith. Goldsmith would have known something of Isabel's background from Teddy, who, unlike his younger brother, had been invited to the Claridge's dinner with his then wife Gill. He was immediately struck by her dark-eyed beauty but felt a little self-conscious about being in a blue lounge suit while the other men were in black tie. Despite this, he monopolised her for the rest of the evening, much to the chagrin of Julian Plowden, a friend from Eton who is said to have been the one to invite her to the Stork along with Teddy, Gill and their friend Dominic Elwes.

Nights at the Stork tested the endurance of the most seasoned clubbers. Officially licensed till 3.30 a.m. it would often stay open another two or three hours to serve breakfast to the most constitutionally robust. An army marches on its stomach and, in those days, the *demi monde* tottered home fortified by a 6 a.m. plate of smoked salmon and scrambled eggs.

The Stork may have been a novelty to Isabel but James Goldsmith was an habitué of the London club scene. Another of his favourite haunts was the Casanova. A vision in green, lit by candles surrounded by mounds of their own dried wax, it was run by the notorious Rico Dajou. The club's hallway was lined with photographs of famous people, especially American film stars, many of whom had never even been to Britain. This did not stop Dajou. With characteristic *chutzpah* he would scrawl across their pictures: "Best wishes to Rico. Love your club, it's the best in London".

Bill Ofner recalls his rival as a shrewd host. 'Rico had a line that whenever you went in there and asked if anyone famous was in, he would look you in the eye and say, "The Queen's just left,"' he says. 'It was a favourite haunt of the old Duchess of Kent but Rico drove her mad, as he did every customer, by walking up to her and offering her some *kasha* from a hot pan he had just taken off the stove in the kitchen. It was a sort of Russian peasant dish and nobody liked it. But the duchess least of all. She would say to Rico: "Take that awful stuff away."'

None of this was likely to endear Goldsmith to his new girlfriend's family. Isabel was the younger daughter of the multimillionaire Bolivian socialite, Don Antenor Patino, who had largely inherited his wealth from his father, Simon, a former debt collector from La Paz who made his fortune in tin mining. Antenor had then added nobility to riches by marrying the daughter of the Duke of Durcal, a relative of King Alphonso XIII of Spain.

Patino was no greenhorn when it came to seeing off unsuitable young men in pursuit of his daughters. He had already successfully put an end to one romance between his older girl Christina and a young American. When they fled to Madrid, he had them followed and his daughter was returned to Paris shortly afterwards. In his eyes, Goldsmith was no more than a plausible fortune hunter, with no title and barely visible means of support.

According to Goldsmith's brother Teddy, speaking to the *Daily Express* in 1954, Patino had altogether loftier social ambitions for his daughter. 'They wanted her to marry into royalty,' he said. 'There were half a dozen royal marriages lined up for her ... The royal descendants who were considered for Isabel are all good friends of mine. They are all French, they are all in the circle of

Prince de Beauvau-Craon, who is married to Isabel's sister, and they all have castles.'

But Jimmy Goldsmith was to prove a formidable adversary. By the time Patino had realised that Isabel's romance with the young Anglo-French businessman was getting serious their relationship was so strong that prising them apart was never going to be easy. His first move was to threaten Isabel with every Catholic heiress's nightmare: banishment to a convent. He soon discovered that this was having no effect on his daughter's behaviour, a fact he gleaned from the two servants he had instructed to send him daily written reports detailing her movements. It was time to confront the young upstart.

But if Patino thought the angry father's equivalent of calling the miscreant into the headmaster's study would do the trick he had not reckoned with Goldsmith's determination.

No account of Isabel and Jimmy's clandestine romance is complete without the following exchange that is said to have taken place when the young suitor met the exceedingly rich father of his sweetheart. 'Young man,' said Patino, 'we come from an old Catholic family.' Goldsmith replied: 'Perfect, we come from an old Jewish family.' Patino fired back: 'It is not in our habit to marry Jews,' to which Goldsmith claimed he responded: 'It is not in our habit to marry Red Indians.'

By this time, news of the romance had filtered through to Noel Whitcomb, the author of the *Daily Mirror*'s Nightlife column. No contemporary journalist could match the profile he enjoyed in the '50s. His *Mirror* column was read by more than 14 million people and gossipy young men could make handsome fees by passing on tales about the rich and famous. One such informant was Mike Mordaunt-Smith, a socialite and freelance publicist, who was also a friend of Goldsmith's. It was he who fed Whitcomb the first details of the Goldsmith-Patino romance in the bar of the Hotel Crillon in Paris one autumn day in 1953. Mordaunt-Smith even took him to the Hotel Scribe where they walked in on Goldsmith holding a council of war in his father's suite. Whitcomb recalled Goldsmith's first words as: 'Do you know my dear fellow that Señor Patino has actually spread a rumour that I am a *pederaste*? Me! He is a wicked man, but I will not have him making a *maquereau* (pimp) out of me.'

Whitcomb quickly became convinced that he had been brought

to the Scribe at Goldsmith's instigation because the young entrepreneur realised the value of exposing Patino's snobbery in a mass-circulation newspaper. In his book, *A Particular Kind of Fool*, Whitcomb continues: 'I had a strong feeling that he was, in a curious way, enjoying the drama that he had precipitated and revelling in the sensation of being an equal adversary of one of the world's richest men. There was no doubt at all in my mind from the first time I met him that Jimmy was mesmerised by money and took pleasure from being at daggers drawn with a mega-millionaire.'

Isabel, herself, had even succeeded in eluding the minders employed by her father on the pretence that she was taking her dog for a shampoo at a canine beauty parlour on the Avenue Georges V. 'Poor little chap, he is the most shampooed dog in France,' she told Whitcomb with a smile. She appeared to have a refreshingly irreverent attitude to her own antecedents. 'We're not really an old Spanish family at all,' she said. 'My grandfather was a Cholo Indian from Cochabamba in Bolivia, a poor and humble man who became very rich because, by chance, he stumbled upon an abandoned tin mine and, through his own hard work, turned it into a great fortune.'

Here Isabel was being a little disingenuous. By the time Goldsmith met her, the rigours of the pampas were far behind the family Patino. Her father was reputed to be worth $200 million, an unimaginable sum in those days, and her childhood had been gilded to say the least. She attended a variety of schools in the United States where she was a bright, if not particularly conscientious, pupil. She did, however, become an accomplished skier. One instructor in New Hampshire even told her doting mother that she had the talent to qualify for the Olympics if she took the sport seriously. 'She loved it, she was absolutely fantastic on skis,' recalls her mother Christina, Duchess of Durcal. 'She just whizzed around, oh she was fantastic. I used to ski too in America and Switzerland, wherever there was snow. But the years have gone by now and I'm a very old lady and nearly blind.'

Today the duchess lives in Paris, the city where her daughter is buried. Despite her age and infirmity, she retains a lively sense of humour, sprinkling her conversation with charming, if incongruous, Americanisms such as 'Holy smoke'. In certain cultures, for a mother to outlive her daughter is considered the most painful fate imaginable and it is clearly one the duchess feels keenly. Her memories are poignantly sharp. 'She was more fun than a cricket,' she says. 'It's easy to say that now she's dead but I don't say that because she's dead. She was like a cricket, full of life, *full* of life.'

Once a would-be movie actress herself, the duchess recalls that it was one of Isabel's childhood dreams to see her fulfil that ambition. 'She wanted to watch my opening night sitting in the front row,' she says. 'It was her idea of heaven. She wanted me to have been an actress and then she could have gone to opening nights and sat in the front row with me. It was a wonderful ambition wasn't it?'

Diplomacy having failed, Patino resolved to do everything in his power to keep the couple apart. He despatched Isabel to Chateau d'Haroue, the country home of her sister Christina who had married Prince Marc de Beauveau-Craon, himself a former suitor of Isabel who had been seen off by Patino on the grounds she was too young to marry. If anything, de Beauveau-Craon had been a more impoverished version of Goldsmith. At the time he courted Christina, he was even a junior employee of Frank Goldsmith, earning £10-a-week at a travel agency controlled by Hotel Reunis, and his family pile was in such a state of disrepair that only three rooms were in use. But he had one thing that Goldsmith lacked: a title. And nothing meant more to Patino, who was conscious of being one generation removed from the nouveau riche.

By the time Isabel was despatched to the Chateau d'Haroue, Patino money had transformed it out of all recognition. She was accompanied by a chaperone, Princess Maria Windisch-Graetz, who proved to be no match for the young lovers. Isabel wrote to tell Jimmy of her whereabouts and he immediately travelled to the nearby town of Nancy where she could visit him.

By December, Patino had decided that more extreme measures were called for. He knew his daughter was still seeing Goldsmith regularly, what he didn't know was that his daughter was pregnant. In a bid to dampen their ardour, he put Isabel and the princess on a flight to Casablanca for a lengthy tour of North Africa. But he had reckoned without her stubbornness and Goldsmith's initiative. When Goldsmith received a note from

Isabel giving her whereabouts he immediately called Croydon Aerodrome and chartered a de Havilland Dart which would fly him to Morocco for £1,000. On this occasion, however, it was Patino's turn to outwit the star-crossed lovers. When one of his spies intercepted a note from Goldsmith arranging a rendezvous at Casablanca airport for dawn the following day, Isabel was immediately bundled onto a Comet airliner bound for Paris.

According to romanticised accounts, Goldsmith's take-off from Le Bourget was actually delayed by the arrival of the Comet bearing Isabel and his Dart was revving up for take off as she disembarked. But Operation Elopement was not about to be stalled by this setback. With Goldsmith heading for Africa, Isabel had called Mordaunt-Smith in Paris and told him she was ready to flee to England at a moment's notice. Whitcomb, with great presence of mind, advised him not to put her up in a hotel, where she would quickly be traced by her father's aides, but to bring her to his London home. This would also have the happy consequence of providing him with a ringside seat at what the *Daily Express* was to call 'the elopement of the century'. Isabel, Mordaunt-Smith, Whitcomb and his wife were having dinner when Jimmy returned his call from Casablanca. Whitcomb records the following exchange: '"Noel," he shouted. "Isabel's in Paris." "No, she's not," I said. 'She's here."'

While Goldsmith made his tortuous journey back to London, Mrs Whitcomb took Isabel shopping. The heiress had left Paris in such haste that she had only the clothes she stood up in, including a fur coat and a pearl necklace. She picked out a marked down skirt and a blue woollen twin-set at a local shop, but as she paid her £7.25 bill, she dropped the £50,000 necklace. Fortunately for Isabel, honesty prevailed and the pearls had been returned by the time Goldsmith arrived at Whitcomb's house that evening to whisk her away in a chauffeur-driven Rolls Royce.

First they headed for Chester, where Goldsmith's brother Teddy was doing his National Service at the officer cadet training school based at Eton Hall. There they stayed with Teddy's wife Gill at the Grosvenor Arms Hotel at Aldford. 'They were roaring with laughter and Jimmy told me they were off to Scotland to get married,' Teddy said later. Sir John Hall, a fellow National Serviceman and friend of Teddy's and one of the boys who had bought the Electra crammer from Jimmy at Eton some years earlier, was roped in to advise on a discreet route north. As a Scottish property owner, Sir John was well-qualified to brief them on a tour of back roads that would enable them to avoid discovery on the way.

Once in Edinburgh, the runaway couple had to wait 15 days to establish residence and then a further seven days before they could get a marriage licence. This delay must have been purgatory for someone as impatient as Goldsmith, whose own mother once said the only time she could pin him down for a chat was when he was in the bath. The couple spent the time flitting around the lowlands of Scotland in an extended game of hide and seek with the private detectives Patino had engaged to find them. New Year's Eve, for example, was spent at the Golden Lion Hotel in Stirling. Here there were signs that the man who had borrowed money from his firm, Dagonal, to fund his romantic endeavours, was having to husband his resources. Two double rooms with baths, at £3 apiece, were turned down in favour of single rooms at 21 shillings and sixpence each. The Rolls Royce had also given way to a more discreet Standard Vanguard, which Goldsmith had borrowed from his lawyer, and in a further attempt to confuse pursuers, he told staff: 'If anyone telephones or calls for me, say I am at Dundee.'

The enforced three-week lull also gave the Patinos a chance to catch up with their errant daughter. The first sighting of the Patinos in Britain came on 3 January 1954, when the hall porter of a West End hotel called Whitcomb to inform him that they were booked on the night train to Scotland. At that stage, Goldsmith had no idea that his father had received a visit from his prospective father-in-law. Marcelle Goldsmith revealed that her husband had told Patino that he was not against the wedding but considered the couple too young and that they should wait. And it appeared that Patino had moderated his opposition. Marcelle said that all he wanted was to hear from his daughter's own lips that she was in love with Jimmy and wanted to marry him.

The news never reached Goldsmith or Isabel, however, and in the absence of any such reassurance, Patino established a 'war room' in his suite at the Caledonian Hotel in Edinburgh. One of the many intriguing aspects of the saga is that it effected a temporary truce in the legal feuding between Antenor Patino and his estranged wife, the Duchess of Durcal. The couple had separated in 1944 when the duchess went to live in America on the strength of an initial settlement of half a million dollars. But the case was to drag on for another 22 years as suit and counter-suit clogged up the courts in five countries. The marriage had always been something of a mismatch. Patino was a short, self-effacing multimillionaire and the duchess was a strong-willed and glamorous woman who, in the spring of 1940, had been voted the best-dressed woman in the world by Parisian fashion designers – beating the Duchess of Windsor into second place. When her husband obtained a civil divorce, she refused to recognise it on the grounds they were Catholics. She was further enraged when he moved in the Countess Beatriz de Rovasenda, taking out a writ which accused him of 'living in a state of concubinage in the marital home'. It was against this background that they suspended hostilities to save their daughter from the clutches of a man they considered a ne'er-do-well.

Their arrival in Edinburgh was the signal for the world's press to descend *en masse* on the Scottish capital. 'Soon there were hundreds of them,' wrote Whitcomb, 'all searching Scotland from their base at the Caledonian Hotel, checking in every hotel, poking into every boarding house, fighting each other, bugging each other's telephone calls, spending mountains of money and becoming more and more frantic as they found less and less information.'

On 5 January, Patino gained an interim interdict from Edinburgh's court of session barring the issue of a marriage licence to his daughter. Goldsmith's lawyers had anticipated the move, however, appealed within minutes and the interdict was lifted within 24 hours. With all legal routes exhausted, Patino admitted defeat, saying he would withdraw his objections to the marriage as long as Isabel would agree to meet her mother before the ceremony, something to which she readily agreed.

With parental disapproval now a spent force, the Press became the problem. Naturally, Whitcomb was more than happy to assist in an elaborate security operation which would not only allow the couple to get married in peace but also protect the integrity of his scoop.

The night before their wedding day, Goldsmith and his bride-to-be spent the night at Prestonfield House, a guest house three miles from the centre of Edinburgh. The first problem to be negotiated the next morning was how to ensure the happy couple's journey from Edinburgh to Kelso, where the ceremony was due to take place, went undetected. It was here that Whitcomb's tabloid instincts were given free rein. A beribboned wedding car would have been an invitation to discovery but was it really necessary to transport the couple in the fashion they finally were? Goldsmith's authorised biographer, Ivan Fallon, spared his blushes by calling the vehicle that was used a delivery van but Whitcomb describes it more colourfully. 'Roddie Oliver [who ran Prestonfield House] had a rusty old green van that was normally used for taking pigs to market,' he recalled. 'We put a couple of deck chairs in it and the bride and groom laughingly took their places.'

Meanwhile, in Edinburgh, the moment the Patinos' petition was withdrawn, one of Goldsmith's lawyers, John Sinclair, collected the wedding licence from the registrar before returning to his office. The difficulty then was that all the pressmen laying siege to the office were aware that wherever the licence went from there would be the location of the wedding. At this stage, a half-remembered story by G.K. Chesterton yielded the solution. In one of his short stories, people watching a building swore that nobody had gone in or out. No one mentioned the postman because he was seen as irrelevant. Taking this as his inspiration, Whitcomb called the lawyers and organised an ingenious charade. The office cleaner was persuaded to make an unscheduled appearance with her mop and bucket, and leave an hour later carrying the licence tucked in her overalls. As anticipated, she was ignored by the waiting pack and after turning the corner at the end of the road she dropped the envelope containing the licence through the window of Whitcomb's car.

As Whitcomb began the 40-mile drive to Kelso, Isabel was in the midst of an emotional reunion with her mother at a solicitor's office in the town. If Madame Patino ever nursed any hopes of changing her daughter's mind, however, they were dashed as soon as she learned that Isabel was pregnant. Abortion was inimical to her as a Catholic and she gave the couple her blessing.

Despite the secrecy surrounding the event, a crowd of 50 had gathered outside the register office by five o'clock when

Goldsmith and Isabel arrived to meet Whitcomb who was to hand over their wedding licence. Isabel was married in the same twinset and pearls she had worn the day she arrived in Britain and the same leopardskin coat, while Goldsmith wore his suit and a clean shirt he had saved for the occasion. Their wedding night was spent in the honeymoon suite at Prestonfield House and the next day they went to the George Hotel for a celebratory lunch and to face the press. There was even more fuss when they pulled in to London's King's Cross station early the next morning and the celebrations were rounded off with a wedding breakfast at the Ritz, with Goldsmith's friend, John Aspinall, one of the chosen few in attendance.

Cut off from the Patino family millions, the new Mrs Goldsmith settled down to married life in Paris in a suite at the Hotel Scribe provided for the couple by Goldsmith's father. In the months that followed, Goldsmith constantly reiterated his determination not to have anything to do with his in-laws' fortune and buried himself in his work. Meanwhile, the couple appeared happy and close.

It was not to last, however. On the morning of 12 May 1954, Goldsmith rose early and left for the office leaving his wife still asleep. She was seven months pregnant at the time and had been growing increasingly tired. She had seemed fine the previous evening when the couple had taken advantage of the unusually hot weather to have dinner outside on the terrace of a restaurant overlooking the city, but that morning something made Goldsmith call his mother, who stayed in the suite below Isabel, to ask her to check on his wife. She let herself in with her own key to find her daughter-in-law still asleep. But she was shocked at the limpness of her hand when she gently lifted it and immediately called for a doctor.

It soon emerged that Isabel had suffered a massive stroke. An ambulance rushed her to the American Hospital at Neuilly where she was put on a life support system. Goldsmith, who had chased the ambulance in his car, began a frenzied ring round of friends and relatives in a bid to come up with the names of the world's most respected neurologists. The American Hospital itself had a number of prestigious brain specialists and, after an anguished meeting that afternoon, it was decided that if she was to receive the specialist treatment she required, Isabel would have to be moved to the Hartmann Clinic, nearby. There Goldsmith was joined in the tiny waiting-room by his parents and the Patinos, who were again thrown together in adversity – the next instalment of their interminable divorce due to take place in court the very next day.

Meanwhile, outside the hospital, journalists waited for news. Among them was Peter Stephens, the *Daily Mirror*'s dapper Paris correspondent. When he spotted one of the brain surgeons on his way home having trouble with his tiny four-horsepower Renault, Stephens offered him a lift in the chauffeur-driven car of a French colleague. As they headed for the garage where the surgeon's own car was being serviced – the lawnmower Renault had been lent to him in the meantime – Stephens asked him if he could tell him what exactly was going on. 'He said to me,' Stephens recalls, '"No, I don't think it will ever come out."'

Following this ominous conversation, Stephens returned to his office to write up his piece for the next day's paper. It was only when he attempted to check one aspect of the story with the surgeons that he realised that events had taken another dramatic turn: all four surgeons had returned to the Hartmann Clinic. Isabel had suffered a relapse. By the time Stephens reached the hospital for the second time that day, Jimmy had been joined by his own parents and the Patinos. It was clear that Isabel was near death. With her life ebbing away, doctors decided to remove her unborn child and a priest arrived at midnight to administer the last rites. An hour later, she was dead. In the space of a matter of hours, Goldsmith had become both a father and a widower.

Stephens was standing in the garden outside and witnessed Goldsmith's reaction to the news of his wife's death. 'He went pounding up the stairs to the first floor and walked to the end of her bed,' says Stephens. 'The blinds were down but I could see everything in silhouette and he just stood at the end of her bed, head bowed for a short while, then turned around and slowly walked out of the room.' The baby, born two months premature and weighing just 5.5lbs, was named Isabel Marcella Olga, after her own mother, Goldsmith's mother and his godmother, Olga Deterding. Isabel Patino's funeral was held four days after her death at the church of St Honore-d'Eylau on the Place Victor Hugo. It was as glittering an event as any funeral can be. Among the 600 mourners, there were one princess, five duchesses, two marquesses and two counts, according to the socially conscious *Le Figaro*. The congregation also included ambassadors from most of the countries of South America and a smattering of Rothschilds. Just as the couple's elopement had captured the popular imagination, so did Isabel's untimely death. The traffic stopped to take in the sight of more than 2,000 people cramming the pavement outside the church and police had to be called to keep order.

After seven weeks in an incubator, baby Isabel was released from the hospital into the çare of her grandmother, the Duchess of Durcal, with Goldsmith's consent. On hearing this news, Stephens's hard-boiled picture editor in London could think of only one thing: the first exclusive photographs of the baby. Stephens duly rendezvoused with a photographer who took the view that the situation was hopeless and who recommended that they retire to the nearest bistro, have a few drinks and inform London that the task was impossible. But Stephens knew that the baby had been taken from the hospital to a large hotel at Versailles, the Trianon Palace, where she was being looked after by a nanny. There, on the pretence that he was working on a piece about the nannies of famous babies, Stephens succeeded in arranging an interview with Goldsmith's nanny and soon had her eating out of his hand to the extent that it was she who offered them the chance to take pictures of the baby.

Goldsmith, meanwhile, was advised by his father to get away from it all for a while. He decided to take a trip to Africa with his friend, the Conservative MP, Geoffrey Bing. They visited Ghana and then Liberia, where Goldsmith, never one to waste an opportunity, opened a small branch of his pharmaceutical company. When he returned to Paris in July he was happy to leave Isabel with the Duchess of Durcal while he searched for a new home. He and his mother would visit on Sunday afternoons and the arrangement seemed to suit all parties. It was to prove a costly mistake, however.

Having never approved of Goldsmith as a husband for their daughter, the Patinos were no more keen on him as the father of their granddaughter. The first sign that they might try to hold on to Isabel came on 13 September when Goldsmith received the first of two registered letters alleging that the home he had organised for himself and his daughter was 'uninhabitable'. The duchess had gone so far as to send a doctor to examine the apartment and he had advised her, she claimed, that Isabel would be better off living with her in the sunnier climes of Spain.

So when the time came for Goldsmith to take charge of his child after finding a three-bedroom flat on the Rue Marbeau, the duchess was not about to give her up willingly. Goldsmith arrived at the Trianon on 14 September at the appointed hour, with an English nanny in tow. After getting no reply at the door of his mother-in-law's suite, in a fit of paternal rage, he smashed the door down. But neither the duchess nor his daughter were anywhere to be seen. His daughter's disappearance was the cue for the third sensational Goldsmith story of 1954 to hit the front pages. Beside himself with fury at his mother-in-law's behaviour, he immediately consulted his lawyers and demanded that the police arrest the duchess before his baby was spirited away to Spain.

To this day, the duchess justifies her action by claiming it would have been Isabel's wish for her to raise the child. 'She would have wanted me to have the baby,' she told the authors, 'and the proof is that she had asked me already to be the godmother.'

It became clear that the duchess and her estranged husband, Antenor Patino, had again put aside their differences to make common cause in the battle to win custody of their grandchild and Goldsmith's next tack was to exploit the newspapers' fascination with the Goldsmith-Patino saga. Mindful of the Patinos' distaste of publicity, he resolved to embarrass them into returning Isabel. In interview after interview with journalists from France, Britain and around the world he repeatedly accused them of kidnap and described them as 'criminals' and the newspapers responded with prominent pieces featuring poignant photographs of the empty nursery. The ferocity of Goldsmith's response may have taken aback the Patinos but they pressed ahead with their legal fight to adopt Isabel against her father's wishes.

A hearing was duly arranged in front of President Ausset, the chairman of the Seine Civil Court. Like every Frenchman of folklore, Ausset had a mistress and Goldsmith reacted to the news with typical enterprise. After obtaining her name and address from his mother, Goldsmith proceeded to send her a single red rose each day with his love. It is impossible to tell what influence – if any – the woman, whose name was Reine, exerted upon her lover, the judge, but she certainly did her best for her young admirer. Goldsmith, who met Ausset and Reine at a dinner party a year later, was told that she had pestered him every day to take his side.

The scene at the Palais de Justice on Friday, 17 September was something to behold. By now Goldsmith had a popular following and the area was swarming with onlookers intent on spotting the protagonists. Goldsmith had arrived early to avoid the crowds, carrying a letter from doctors which he described as his 'certificate of sanity' as he fully expected the Patinos to try to question his mental state.

After a series of vociferous courtroom exchanges between the two sides, Ausset decided that he should examine the flat Goldsmith had prepared for himself. By the time he reached the Rue Marbeau, a crowd had already gathered and the balconies of adjoining apartments were full of curious neighbours. He spent half an hour making a careful tour of the five-room, top-floor apartment and when he left he announced that he would make his adjudication at 2 p.m. the next day, a Saturday.

It was soon clear that the judge's sympathy lay with Goldsmith. He described the apartment as comfortable and 'even luxurious'. He had also been impressed with Marcelle Goldsmith who had promised to occupy herself 'maternally' with the child. He pronounced himself satisfied with Goldsmith's financial status and dismissed criticisms of his behaviour in knocking down the door of the duchess's hotel suite saying it was 'clearly the result of his distress and his anxiety to know the whereabouts of his daughter'. He concluded by ordering the Patinos to return the child to its father by four o'clock the following afternoon.

Fifteen policemen lined the pavement at 3.45 p.m. on Sunday as a black limousine drew up outside 23 Rue Marbeau, where Goldsmith waited, sheltering from the rain in the doorway. The duchess, unable to bear the indignity of defeat in person, had sent her sister, the Marquise Ginori, to return the child with its nanny. She and her son-in-law were never to speak again, their last meeting occurring at Isabel's graveside 'many, many years ago'.

Goldsmith's response to his wife's death and the traumatic events that followed was to throw himself into his business. With

Teddy back in England doing his National Service, the budding entrepreneur was at last in a position to flex his commercial muscles largely unhindered by outside forces. Dagonal, the pharmaceutical company he had inherited the year before, was a tiny outfit, with a turnover of £5,000 a year and one employee. Goldsmith was determined to turn it into something much bigger. There was little scope for expanding the existing lines but, aware that the French pharmaceutical market was lagging behind those in other Western countries, he went on a tour of the US, Britain, Austria and Italy in search of new products. It was to prove a conspicuously successful trip, which resulted in deals to sell a number of drugs, including Lantigen B, a vaccine against colds developed by Australian group, Beast & Gee, and a nasal spray called Rhinosterin.

When Teddy returned to France in 1955, he was understandably impressed with his brother's progress and when Jimmy offered him a 30 per cent share in the company he still effectively owned, he considered it a fair offer. After all, while he was away his younger brother had transformed Dagonal out of all recognition. It was now a flourishing enterprise with a wide range of brands and no fewer than 100 employees.

Teddy lasted a year in the new environment. His handling of the distribution side of the company proved disastrous and both brothers decided it would be better if he left. One story that illustrates the gulf between the two brothers in terms of their entrepreneurial flair goes like this: Teddy was talked into buying a large quantity of artificial lawn by a cousin. When he failed to find a market for it, Jimmy agreed to buy it. Unlike Teddy, he made no attempt to sell it as a garden covering but had it dyed pink, made into gloves and promoted in chemists as a cure for cellulite. Women had only to rub their thighs with their gloved hands and any unsightly scaling would disappear . . . or so Paris's Arthur Daley claimed.

In the absence of Teddy, other names came to the fore. Claude Henri Leconte, a journalist and PR man who was a friend of Jimmy's, helped him write the advertising material. Maurice Lignon, a generation older than his employer but a great fan, became the company's super salesman, regularly breaking bonus targets. In his third year he even won a car. Both men were to become key figures in the building of the first Goldsmith fortune.

In these early years, however, cash flow was an endemic problem. And when one particular demand for back taxes threatened to break the firm, Goldsmith asked Leconte to approach his own bank manager and arrange a loan. Fortunately, the banker already knew Goldsmith by reputation and was more than willing to get in on the ground floor with a likely prospect.

Goldsmith was also stretched by his domestic costs. Thanks to the Patinos' legal challenge to his fitness to care for Isabel he had been forced to maintain not only a nanny but his mother who, under the terms of the custody judgement, had to live with him and his child. Pride also forced him to retain a butler as a sort of badge of status.

One of his few solaces in these stressful times was the company of his devoted secretary Ginette Lery, the daughter of a Paris Metro worker. Ginette had joined the company as an 18-year-old. She was blonde, she was pretty and she was mesmerised by her energetic boss who was just three years older. Working together, often late into the night, neither of them had much chance to meet other partners, and they experienced the highs and lows familiar to anyone who has struggled to make a business work. The constant strain of juggling creditors alleviated, from time to time, by the euphoria that accompanied a successful deal only served to bring them closer together. Romance blossomed over the final demands and, by 1956, their relationship was a sexual one.

The course of true love did not run smooth, however. Ginette later said she found her lover both 'difficult' and 'nervous'. Debts depressed him enormously and the strain of coping with the pressure made him run down. Ugly boils came out on his head and, by his mid twenties, most of his hair had fallen out. By early 1957, Goldsmith was desperate for new capital. He flirted with an Italian company called Lepetit but pulled out of negotiations when it became clear that they would not settle for less than 80 per cent of the business he had sweated blood to build. His next brainwave was to take on the big manufacturers by selling drugs to regional wholesalers at a discount. To this end he embarked on a whirlwind tour of the country, travelling in a chartered plane with Ginette and Lignon. After three days, the trio had set up deals worth £200,000, extracting promissory notes from each wholesaler to present to the bank on the following

Monday in a last ditch attempt to stave off his creditors.

It was always a David and Goliath struggle and when the big manufacturers threatened to withdraw their bestselling lines if the distributors did not drop their new maverick client it was no contest. By now, the situation was desperate. With the deadline of Monday, 10 July looming, Goldsmith spent the weekend in bed at a loss as to what to do next and in a state of near despair.

Goldsmith's saviours were the sort of people he probably despised most: striking workers. France's banking unions had chosen that very weekend to stage their first strike since the '30s. It was only when Goldsmith made his weary way to the newspaper stand and saw the headlines that he realised he might live to fight another day. In fact, the dispute lasted for weeks and by the time the bank staff were back at work, Goldsmith had managed to dispose of his company to his biggest competitor for a small fortune. Not only did Laboratoires Roussel pay £110,000 but they also left him with the royalties on the sales of Lantigen B – then worth around £4,000 a month. Their ordeal over, Goldsmith and Ginette took a well-deserved holiday in Spain.

Goldsmith was not about to enter semi-retirement, however. By the autumn, he had re-established himself in France by linking up with a Dr Laffort, who owned a small manufacturing plant in the Loire valley. Laffort was a boffin in search of a marketing man. In return for royalties on sales, he was prepared to hand over his small laboratory and factory to Goldsmith. The next step was to find a co-operative banker. This time Goldsmith did not have far to look. His introduction came in the form of a circular from a bank based on the ground floor of his own office building on the Rue de la Paix. After a meeting with the branch manager he was introduced to the family bank's Paris chairman, Selim Zilkha. Goldsmith and Zilkha, a 30-year-old Sephardic Jew from Iraq, immediately hit it off and within two years they were not only friends but business partners.

By the spring of 1958, he was again employing hundreds of people and he decided to merge his French interests with a newly created English operation to form a company called SPHAL. He also bought his first public company in the UK, Clinical and General Services. But money continued to be tight and he was eventually forced to sell his royalty rights to Lantigen B to Roussel, arriving for the negotiation after a sleepless night at

Ginette's hospital bedside attending the birth of his first son in May, 1959. Money was so short at this stage that, as patients were not allowed to leave until their accounts were settled, Ginette was forced to stay in hospital for weeks while Goldsmith attempted to raise cash to pay the bill. The official version has it that salvation eventually came in the form of a backgammon win at the Travellers Club. The truth, according to Jean-François Revel, who once worked alongside Goldsmith, is that the man for whom £20 million was later to become loose change was obliged to borrow the cash from his friends.

While this and the income from the sale of his Lantigen B royalties solved his problems in the short term, the long term looked as uncertain as ever. In France, he decided to sell his existing interests and launch a new company, Laboratoires Lanord. Its future prosperity was assured when Maurice Lignon approached his old boss with an American fake tan product called Man Tan and suggested they obtain the French rights. Goldsmith was immediately interested, the only problem was the cash. Zilkha came to the rescue, but this time for a price: he wanted half the company. The agency rights were duly acquired, and the product, renamed Right Tan for the French market, proceeded to sell well.

In Britain, persistent criticism of a cut-price line of cortisone tablets Goldsmith was marketing meant he needed to find new markets to exploit. It was a fortuitous meeting with Charles Clore, one of the most successful businessmen of his generation, in the Paris night club Chez Fred that presented him with the proposition that was to lead him into fresh territory. Clore, pioneer of the art of the hostile takeover, had just completed the acquisition of jewellery-to-cutlery combine Mappin and Webb and was keen to offload Lewis and Burrows, a chain of 28 British chemist shops.

Initially, Goldsmith saw the purchase as a sound piece of what the analysts call vertical integration: the chain would provide him with a captive market for his products. Unable to finance the entire deal himself, Goldsmith again brought in Zilkha as his business partner, with each taking a half share. Part of the deal was that Goldsmith promised to spend two weeks out of every month in London and began looking for a base more permanent than his customary room at the Ritz. He duly rented a handsome house on Regent's Park as home for Ginette, Isabel and Manes. Goldsmith was about to make his mark on London.

Fatherhood the second time around was to throw up Goldsmith's best idea to date. As he joined Ginette in shopping for Manes's clothes he could not fail to notice the paucity of specialist outlets. In France, parents of young children in the '50s flocked to the Pre-Natal departments successfully established in a string of stores. It was not long before Goldsmith had come up with the concept of a dedicated chain of shops targeted exclusively at mothers of babies and young children. Mothercare was born.

The vehicle for this mould-breaking high-street concept was to be the Lewis and Burrows chain but it was not long before Goldsmith and Zilkha had another 50 shops with the acquisition of W.J. Harris, a chain of pram and nursery furniture stores. This swift early expansion was not matched by profit growth, however. In the first 12 months the enterprise lost £140,000 and the second year was even worse, with losses rising to £180,000. It was only the success of Right Tan that saw Goldsmith through these traumatic early stages.

It soon became clear that if Goldsmith was to maintain his 50 per cent holding in Mothercare he was going to need deep pockets. Nor was he prepared to tolerate a partnership in which he was the minority shareholder. The result was that he sold his shares in Mothercare to Zilkha in early 1962 and bought out Zilkha's share of Lanord, a transaction that left him with a healthy surplus. What he lost was a share in a surefire winner. When Zilkha sold Mothercare for £120 million in 1982, he received more than £60 million for his personal shareholding.

Any disappointment Goldsmith may have nursed at missing out on the Mothercare bonanza was soon swept away by a money-making scheme which was to yield him a fortune of his own.

During a reconnoitre of the US market he could not fail to notice the huge success of a slimming product called Metrecal made by the pharmaceuticals giant Mead Johnson. To obtain a European licence for such a massive seller would have been totally beyond his means so Goldsmith decided to make his own copycat version of the appetite suppressant. His first task was to find an established French pharmaceutical company with a name that could easily be confused with Metrecal. The result was Laboratoires Milical, which, fortuitously, had been making slimming products for years. His me-too product was so successful that Mead Johnson soon resorted to litigation. But Goldsmith had prepared the ground well. He counter-attacked by claiming it was the Americans who were exploiting the goodwill of a French company name that had a far longer pedigree than Metrecal. Hopelessly out-manoeuvred, Mead Johnson backed down and Goldsmith proceeded to clean up all over Europe.

Conscious of how close he had come to oblivion in the past, Goldsmith decided to secure his prosperity on this occasion by selling a third of the company now known as Gustin-Milical. The stake went to Baron Alexis de Gunzburg, a cousin of the Rothschilds and a distant relative of Goldsmith. Although he was not in a position to pay cash, Gunzburg did have a large holding in Source Perrier, the world-famous mineral water company which, even then, was growing fast and making a healthy profit. Goldsmith duly accepted a tranche of shares in Perrier in return for his piece of Gustin-Milical.

His business affairs may have been complex and the source of much stress but Goldsmith was a man who played as hard as he worked. He was a regular member of the lunchtime get-togethers at the celebrated long bar – now gone – of the Hotel Crillon presided over by the late Sam White, the *London Evening Standard*'s man in France and the doyen of post-war Paris correspondents. A measure of White's standing came on the occasion the BBC asked to film the journalists assembled in the bar of the Crillon to cover the so-called 'U2' summit between President Eisenhower and Khrushchev in 1960. It was to White that the management of the hotel turned for approval before inviting them in.

Each lunchtime, he would hold court over a 'coupe de champagne' served by the ever attentive Luigi, all the while milking the highly placed socialites he dubbed his 'stringers' or sources. Goldsmith he knew as his 'right-wing stringer'. Another regular at the Crillon bar in those days was a journalist-turned-novelist Frederic Mullally. A former political editor of the *Sunday Pictorial* – now the *Sunday Mirror* – under the late, great Hugh Cudlipp, he had moved to the French capital following the success of his debut thriller, *Dance Macabre*.

One memorable lunchtime in the spring of 1960, he and Goldsmith were introduced. 'He was a young man, tall, good-looking, well dressed and blond,' recalls Mullally, adding, 'with a full head of hair', a description which contradicts Goldsmith's authorised biographer's description of a man prematurely balding through grief and stress. Indeed, Mullally got the impression that Goldsmith was, even then, something of a party animal. He continues: 'Goldsmith asked: "would you like to come to a *maison de rendezvous*?"'

A *maison de rendezvous* was a sort of upmarket brothel reminiscent of the type of establishment portrayed in the film *Love in the Afternoon*, where bored housewives like the character played by Catherine Deneuve found illicit excitement and supplemented the housekeeping into the bargain.

'I immediately said yes,' says Mullally, who now lives in Hammersmith, West London, and continues to write books despite being in his late seventies. He, White and Goldsmith duly repaired to a four-storey town house on the Avenue Hoche, just off L'Etoile, where Goldsmith was received by a high-class Madame who obviously knew him very well. 'The girls came down one by one, did a twirl round the salon and smiled,' says Mullally. After making their choice of companion each man retired to an upstairs room.

'My normal effort would be 20 minutes in those days,' says Mullally. 'I came down to the salon again and presumed I would meet our hostess, Jimmy and Sam, but there was no one there. When I eventually found the Madame, she told me that Jimmy had sent the first girl down and requested another one. When I asked, "Where is Mr White?" she told me he was in the *cabane*, where the ladies relaxed when they weren't working. It was a small room with a large refectory table. Sam was at one end, surrounded by girls in negligées, and there was French bread, cheese and half a bottle of wine on the table. Sam was entertaining them in his impossibly fractured French – he spoke with a very strong Australian accent – but they were hanging on his every word.'

The pair left shortly afterwards. Mullally had enjoyed the novelty of the visit and White had to go back to the office, but Goldsmith remained to sample the delights of girl number three and, sportingly, to settle the bill.

'Jimmy Goldsmith was generous,' concedes Mullally. 'He wasn't very rich at that point. But he loved the women. He was a whoremonger. That much was clear because he was so well known to the Madame. It was all "James" and stuff.'

Alongside this well-established regime of R&R, Goldsmith was also pursuing his own brand of domestic life. After taking the trouble to set up Ginette and his children in a house on Regent's Park in the autumn of 1960, he embarked on what was to become a full-blown affair with another woman, Sally Crichton-Stuart. When she came into his life a little over a year later, she was already one of the faces of '60s London. She had married Lord James Crichton-Stuart, the youngest brother of the Marquess of Bute, in 1959. But the marriage was barely two years old when she met and began her friendship with Goldsmith. By this time she was reputed to be one of the most glamorous women in the world and Goldsmith, smitten by her looks, always referred to her as 'the most beautiful woman of her generation'. She was more than a clothes horse, however. Unlike Ginette, she was a vivacious night-bird and she and Goldsmith had many friends in common. Both loved parties and he felt good to be seen with her on his arm.

Born in India, the daughter of an army colonel, Sally had gone from a girls' boarding school to finishing school before being launched as a debutante by a mother who vetted her romantic career with extreme care. Throughout the '60s she modelled for an agency owned by Peter Hope Lumley and run by Jill Rushton. 'I admired Sarah [she uses Sally's given name] tremendously because she had an amazing classical beauty,' says Rushton. 'She gave out this marvellously cool aura without being cold. It took a bit to get to know her because she had a sort of reserve like a lot of classically beautiful people do, as if to say, "What are people after me for?"'

Her modelling career was hampered by frequent cancellations: 'It was, "Cancel this, cancel that,"' says Rushton. 'Quite honestly you can only do that to *Harper*'s and *Vogue* so many times and not only are you in danger of losing work for that model but also for your others if they think they can't trust you. It was the mother, not Sarah, and the way she did it. Sarah was lovely, very serene, a joy. We often had lunch next to the office. She was so stunning. I mean, fabulous skin, fabulous eyes, just everything.

The epitome of elegance. I was nicknamed the Bunny Mother because of the way I used to guard my little chickens.' By no means all of Sally's admirers were unwelcome, however. Her marriage to Crichton-Stuart was not a success (after nine years it was annulled).

Goldsmith's affair with Crichton-Stuart almost ended in catastrophe when they were on holiday together in 1962 and were involved in a horrifying accident with two members of their party, the racing correspondent Charles Benson and another friend, Mark Watney. The four were passengers in a taxi on the Isle du Levant, just off St Tropez in the south of France, when it turned over at speed. Goldsmith and Sally were largely unhurt but Benson and particularly Watney were very badly injured. One friend of Watney who saw him soon afterwards recalls that, festooned in bandages, 'he looked like a zebra'. Benson, meanwhile, required 86 stitches in his head and a passing hitchhiker was also injured.

It was night-time and the ambulance took some time to arrive. One version of the story that did the rounds of Goldsmith's circle is that it was he, complaining loudly, who was first to be taken into the ambulance despite his relative lack of damage. But Benson says this is a distortion. 'He did go to the mainland before the rest of us but he was going to try to organise help for us, which took quite a long time coming,' he says. The cause of the accident was never established. 'Nobody ever discovered that the driver was drunk,' says Benson. 'It's one of the world's mysteries, what he thought he was doing. He just went down the mountainside with no brakes and no lights.'

By this time, Goldsmith had set up a second household in London for Sally but he had no intention of marrying her without first doing the decent thing by Ginette, the faithful secretary who had stood by him through his darkest days and had borne him a son. His convoluted plan was to marry her to legitimise their son (as his father had done following Teddy's birth), then divorce her and marry Sally. This arrangement was outlined to both women, who were promised all the trappings that go with being a Goldsmith wife and Ginette was reassured that any divorce would be a purely legal matter and would not affect his long term commitment to her and their child. Matters were helped by the fact that Ginette had never really settled in

England and returned to Paris in February 1962, where she moved into a large house on the Rue Monsieur that had once belonged to the composer Cole Porter.

The awkwardness of Goldsmith's position was starkly illustrated when he and Ginette were quietly married in early 1963. At about the same time, he obviously felt compelled to throw a lavish bash for Sally. The party at Maxim's in Paris was such a grand affair that many friends who had flown in from London assumed it was an engagement party.

It was always a rather complicated arrangement aimed at one James Goldsmith having his cake and eating it. The whole package fell apart when, after marrying Ginette, she became pregnant with Alix and any prospect of divorce had to be delayed. Sally, who was after all a woman with options, appears to have had enough. She took up with Philip Martyn, a free-spending man-about-town whose gambling skills were to win him a backgammon world championship title in 1972.

On one thing the friends of Sally Crichton-Stuart, née Croker-Poole, all agree: her socially ambitious mother would never allow her to settle for second best and that Sally finally married the all-powerful and incredibly wealthy Aga Khan probably owed a great deal to Mrs Croker-Poole's shrewd management of her early life. Karim Aga Khan had succeeded his grandfather in July 1957 as Iman, the spiritual leader of 14 million Ismaili Moslems around the world and, ideally, his wife would have been a blushing virgin. But in the case of a woman as beautiful and enticing as Sally, he was prepared to make an exception. The couple met in St Moritz on New Year's Eve, 1968, when Sally was just a month off her 29th birthday. In the grand ballroom of the Palace Hotel they danced into the dawn of 1969 and the Aga Khan was captivated.

And when, in the summer of 1969, she became engaged to the Aga Khan, whose followers take a dim view of promiscuity, he telephoned Peter Hope Lumley and asked him to exercise discretion in talking about her past. 'He didn't want to give the impression that he was marrying a model girl,' says Hope Lumley. The wedding duly took place in October 1969. The reception, attended by Princess Margaret, was held at the Aga Khan's Paris home, No 1 Rue des Ursins on the Ile St Louis, which he had inherited on the death of his playboy father.

Like Hope Lumley, Jill Rushton was invited to the sumptuous nuptials. Her most lasting memory of the event was a typically tart remark from Sally's mother as she made her way down the receiving line: 'She took one look at my clothes and said, "Oh Jill. I nearly bought that outfit, but it made me look too old." I thought, "You bitch."' Rushton also recalls the scene in the ladies' loo when Sally stood with her 'last fag and orange juice, quote, unquote' (the latter a thinly disguised glass of Buck's Fizz) out of sight of the disapproving Muslim temperance crusaders outside. In fact, her attempts to give up smoking and drinking never lasted. The marriage ended in divorce in March, 1995, and eight months later she sold the jewels the Aga Khan had given her for £17.8 million and set up home in Geneva with her French divorce lawyer, Philippe Lizop.

Chapter Three

Un homme d'affaires

HAVING lost one mistress, Goldsmith was not slow in enlisting another. And he did not have to look far. Lady Annabel Birley and Sally Crichton-Stuart were firm friends and both women naturally attended the launch of Annabel's, the basement club on Berkeley Square set up by Annabel's husband, Mark Birley, in March, 1963. The inaugural party, held four months after the opening of John Aspinall's Clermont Club upstairs, has since been described as 'the event of the season'. So select was the guest list that the actor Peter O'Toole found himself having to gatecrash. One man who had no need to sweet talk his way past the doormen, however, was Goldsmith, who had been invited as a friend of Aspinall. As night turned to dawn the morning after that opening night, two couples were left alone on the dance floor, Annabel and Mark and Sally and Jimmy. Within months, Sally would be off the scene and Goldsmith would be casting around for a new lover.

On the face of it, Annabel was not an obvious choice. She has always been considered striking rather than classically beautiful and, at five feet seven and a half inches, she was tall enough to be a policewoman but hardly statuesque. What set her apart was her personality. Her vivacity and sense of fun shone through wherever she went. And it was those qualities as much as her strong features that gave her her powerful sex appeal.

It was typical of Goldsmith, if hardly sporting, that he should take advantage of Annabel while he was in the night club her doting husband had named after her. Goldsmith's first move on his prey is recorded somewhat triumphantly by Ivan Fallon, his authorised biographer: 'Annabel was sitting on her own at a table in the club one night in the autumn of 1963, waiting for Mark to return from sorting out a problem in the kitchen, when Jimmy Goldsmith's tall figure [he was an inch shorter than Birley, incidentally] loomed over her. Could he join her?'

Annabel's and the Clermont were later dubbed 'the two symbols of extravagant '60s hedonism'. As the club gained a reputation as the place to be seen, so Birley was forced to work longer and longer hours and Annabel, who had their three children to think of, liked an early night. Increasingly bored, she had changed her attitude to Goldsmith, the pushy young Anglo-French businessman she had initially considered something of an *arriviste*. If anyone could be said to have played Cupid in their affair, it was the irascible Aspinall. Soon after their respective clubs had opened, he and Birley had a row over the use of the shared wine cellar and the staircase which connected Annabel's in the basement with the casino upstairs was closed off never to be reopened. The pair are said to have hardly spoken since but Aspinall continued to think highly of Annabel and is said to have encouraged her friendship with Goldsmith.

By this time, as we have seen, Goldsmith was a seasoned adulterer and soon Annabel was embroiled in her first affair. They would meet at the Ritz, have dinner in Goldsmith's room and she would be home in plenty of time for her husband's return at four or five in the morning.

These clandestine meetings carried on for more than two years before she told Birley what was going on. Despite his hurt, they continued to live together for several years but some of her aunts refused to speak to her once the affair was made public. Her family, the Londonderrys, were, after all, well-established aristocrats with a reputation to consider.

Annabel's grandmother, Edith, Marchioness of Londonderry – widely known as 'Circe' – ran the most influential political salon of her day from Londonderry House on Old Park Lane. The family grew rich on King Coal, with mining interests in Wales and the north-east of England. The Londonderry air is less grand these days, however. The family did badly out of the nationalisation of the coal industry, and were forced to sell some property. Wynyard Park, for example, a mansion with 70 rooms set in 8,000 acres of County Durham, is now the home of Sir John Hall, the multimillionaire chairman of Newcastle United and, ironically, the son of one of the miners who helped build the Londonderry fortune.

The fruits of this wealth were all around when Annabel was a young girl. The daughter of the 8th Marquess of Londonderry, she was educated by a governess until the age of 11 and is prone to point out that she had a title long before Goldsmith was knighted by Harold Wilson in the notorious Lavender list of 1976. Nor is life in the grand manner anything new to the former Lady Annabel Vane-Tempest-Stewart. She grew up at Wynyard Park at a time when the family also owned Londonderry House and an estate in Ireland.

She was born at home in London on 13 June 1934, the second of three children and named after her mother's favourite song, the '20s hit, *Miss Annabelle Lee*. Her schooldays, when they began, were spent at Southover Manor, a boarding school near Lewes Prison in Sussex. Like her daughter Jemima, she was an enthusiastic, if accident-prone, horsewoman in her youth, breaking her collarbone twice and her left wrist. But while the Londonderrys had all the trappings of wealth, Annabel experienced her share of tragedy as a young woman. Her mother died of cancer at the age of 47, when Annabel was just 17, and her father coped badly with the loss. 'After that my poor father simply didn't want to live,' Annabel recalled later, '[he] virtually drank himself to death, though ultimately, it was his heart which gave out. He was 52.' She became a debutante and, during the season of 1952, her lofty social status was confirmed when she and another deb were invited to dinner by Queen Elizabeth II, an appointment which was the new monarch's first private engagement following the death of her father, George VI.

Her debutante days over, at the insistence of her father, she was sent to work as a journalist for Lord Beaverbrook. At this point, one of English society's most eligible young women departed from the script. It was at a party at the Queen's ice rink in Bayswater that Annabel met her future husband. Each time she slipped and fell on the ice, a dashing young man picked her up. His name was Mark Birley and he was not the sort of suitor her father had in mind.

Birley may have been tall and charming but, as the son of the society portrait painter Sir Oswald Birley, he did not appear to have the wealth or prospects to match Annabel's antecedents.

She, however, was smitten. 'Every girl was in love with him,' she once said. 'To me he was a god, the most glamorous creature I had ever met in my life.'

Despite the objections of her family, the couple married in March 1954, when Annabel was just 19, and spent a two-month honeymoon in the skiing resort of Kitzbuhel. Off-piste, life was to prove rather tougher. Their first marital home was the attic of her mother-in-law's house in St John's Wood, something of a come down for the girl from the country house set. As her husband flitted from career to career, Annabel gave birth to three children in six years: Rupert, Robin and India Jane.

The incident which was to change their lives forever occurred in the early '60s, when gambling entrepreneur John Aspinall took out a 21-year lease on 44 Berkeley Square and opened the Clermont. He needed a tenant for the basement and Birley decided to rent it for use as a night club. His original idea was to call it Black's but, after a change of heart, he resolved to name it Annabel's as a tribute to his wife. Raising money for the venture was no easy task but Birley's lack of cash was more than matched by a level of charm and charisma that many of the couple's friends found impossible to resist. It is an investment none of them will ever have regretted.

But as Birley's club went from strength to strength, his home life was proving a source of great unhappiness as he failed to persuade his wife to give up her lover. He eventually moved out of their home, Pelham Cottage in South Kensington, in 1971 and two years later, though still married to Birley, Annabel was expecting Goldsmith's baby. On discovering that she was pregnant in August 1973, she was faced with a dilemma. Since she was nearly 40, her doctor was concerned for her health. She also had the delicate task of breaking the news not only to her husband but to her children. In the event, she decided to have the baby and Jemima was born in January 1974, at Westminster Hospital. Goldsmith was not present at the birth. 'I never wanted Jimmy around,' Annabel once said. 'He's the sort of father who wants to see the baby for the first time in a basket with ribbons on it, as if it's just been delivered by the stork.' Annabel was to have another child, Zak, before Goldsmith agreed to divorce Ginette and marry her.

If Annabel thought her wedding would be a romantic tying of

the knot at the local register office, with the happy couple walking to their wedding car through a sea of confetti thrown by close friends and family, it was a notion of which she was soon to be disabused. Instead, she was to fly to Paris alone, telling no one of their plans, for a top-secret ceremony at the local *mairie* or town hall. Someone, however, was determined that the nuptials would not go unnoticed.

Two weeks before the wedding took place on 16 November 1978, a mystery person made the first of three calls to the *Daily Express*'s William Hickey diary column. In the late '70s, Hickey was edited by Peter McKay, a bitter foe of Goldsmith through his contributions to *Private Eye*'s scurrilous Grovel column. As a result, the vendetta was carried through to the pages of the *Express*. Goldsmith's antagonism to the column was never made more clear than at the height of the bidding for Beaverbrook Newspapers in 1977. McKay picked up the phone one day to hear Goldsmith's voice saying: 'Ah, Mr McKay, I'm very shortly going to be your proprietor. However, you need not fear for your job.' McKay, one of Fleet Street's saltier characters, refused to be intimidated. If anything, the veiled threat served to exacerbate anti-Goldsmith sentiment at the paper. And so when the anonymous calls about his proposed wedding came through they were greeted with keen interest.

'One day somebody rang me out of the blue,' recalls the author Christopher Wilson, then a Hickey reporter. 'It was a well-spoken woman – they always are – and she said, "I just thought you'd like to know that Jimmy Goldsmith is finally going to marry Annabel." I said that was very interesting. Later I got another telephone call saying he was going to marry her in Paris but when I asked if the caller could tell me any more, once again she hung up. When she rang a third time in a week it was to say, "Annabel is going to Paris tomorrow to marry James," and gave the British Airways flight number. That was all I was told.'

On the appointed day Wilson duly took a cab to Heathrow, bought an economy ticket and boarded the plane. Sure enough, there was Annabel, listed as Mrs Vane on the passenger manifest, seated in the first class section with her sister Lady Jane Rayne and her sister-in-law Nicolette Harrison. 'I'd never spoken to her before,' says Wilson, 'so I thought I'd take the gentlemanly approach and went up to her and introduced myself and said, "I know you're going to Paris and I know what's going to happen next. I just want you to know that I'm not going to get in your way. I'm not going to try to interfere with you but I'm here to report what happens."'

At the airport in Paris, however, good-planning turned to cock-up. Wilson lost Annabel after being delayed at passport control and emerged to find his quarry being whisked away in a chauffeur-driven car. Wilson then did what many a journalist has done in similar circumstances, he headed for the swankiest hotel in town, the Ritz, checked in and reviewed his options over a drink in the bar. 'Just on the off-chance I went up to the concierge and said, "Lady Annabel Birley, elle est ici?"' says Wilson. 'He not only said yes but told me her room number.'

Having relocated the future Mrs Goldsmith, Wilson's next task was to discover where the wedding was to take place. Under French law, the banns have to be posted outside the *mairie* where the ceremony is to take place. There followed a marathon tour of Paris's many *arrondisements*, or districts, by Michael Brown, the paper's Paris correspondent, but despite scrutinising the noticeboards outside every *mairie* he could find no trace of the Goldsmiths' banns. As the men from the *Express* busied themselves in their attempts to discover the location of the wedding, Goldsmith was entertaining nine guests, including his business adviser Gilberte Beaux, to dinner at a Russian night club.

The next morning, Wilson was joined by his photographer, Bill Lovelace, and the pair resolved to tail Annabel as she left the hotel. When she emerged at ten o'clock, the Hickey men were crouched in the back of a taxi on the Place Vendome and as she was driven away they set off in pursuit. 'It was like something out of the Keystone Cops,' he recalls, 'because that day there was some official event taking place and half the streets around L'Etoile were blocked off. So her car was zig-zagging to get around all the road blocks and we kept on losing her.'

The chase ended in gridlock on the Champs Elysées and Annabel, desperate not to be late on her big day, abandoned her car and set off on foot. Bill Lovelace, who left Wilson in the taxi to follow her, takes up the story. 'She was running, stumbling, obviously in a panic, perhaps thinking she was going to be late and was going to suffer the wrath of the great Mr Goldsmith.'

After half walking and half running for half a mile, Annabel arrived at her destination, the offices of Générale Occidentale. As Lovelace took up position outside he was appalled to bump into two agency photographers he knew from a previous stint in the city. After having seen off this threat to his exclusive by pretending he was waiting for a friend, he was startled by the sudden emergence of Annabel and her groom to be. 'I didn't have time to do anything except whip the camera out as they walked towards me,' says Lovelace. 'She was about ten yards in front of him, heading for a car.'

No one could have been more shocked by this turn of events than Goldsmith himself as Annabel, perhaps unwisely, had decided not to tell him about the approach from Wilson on the flight over. Lovelace's snatched shot was clearly not going to be a great picture and may not even have been usable but that didn't matter to Goldsmith. Spotting the photographer, the six-feet-four-inch financier, then a youthful 45, made a run at the 54-year-old Lovelace, who was a good six inches shorter. 'He rushed at me like a madman,' says Lovelace. 'He was red in the face and he grabbed hold of me. I was saying, "Look, don't be silly, this is ridiculous carrying on like this" and he was saying, "I'll have that film, I'll have that film." At that point he was joined by two of his doormen who helped him to drag me inside. There was no point in struggling because there were three of them holding me. He's a big man and he had me in a pretty tight grip. He squeezed me so tight he broke the reading glasses that were in my top pocket. All the time, I was saying, "Look, be sensible," but I knew the game was up. In any case, I knew damn well, as he did, that you can't do what I was doing in France because the laws about taking pictures of people in the street are quite different to what they are in England.

'He wrenched the camera open in their front hall and ripped out the film. I was saying, "I think you are being very silly because this is going to look worse in print than the picture would have." Anyway, the story made a Hickey lead and was picked up by *Time* magazine.'

Happy with a job well done, Goldsmith headed off for his wedding. Unfortunately for Annabel, he had not got her a wedding ring and so she used the same plain gold band her sister Jane had bought her from the Burlington Arcade for her first wedding 25 years earlier.

After he had seen the next day's edition of the *Daily Express*, which carried a full account of the fracas, Goldsmith dictated a self-justifying letter to *The Times*. 'Yes, Lady Annabel and I did marry yesterday in Paris,' he wrote. 'Let me explain why we chose Paris. When a middle-aged couple who have shared their lives for the past 14 years are able to marry, it is appropriate that they should choose to do so with the dignity of silence. That is still possible in Paris because not only is there respect for personal privacy but such privacy is protected by law. The *Daily Express* journalist chose to follow Lady Annabel to Paris and to break this law. Therefore, I carried out a "citizen's arrest" of the journalist and disarmed his camera.' He ended his letter by thanking the *Express* for 'a wonderful wedding present – the legal opportunity to "manhandle" a representative of its gossip column'.

An angry Wilson responded to what he called Goldsmith's 'foolhardy comments' in *The Times* the very next day. 'The "citizen's arrest" to which Sir James refers was, in fact, illegal,' he said. 'When my photographer was taking pictures of the couple in the street, there were several French police at Sir James's disposal standing within calling distance. Sir James ignored them and, with the help of an aide, grabbed the photographer and bundled him inside the offices of Générale Occidentale. There, with the help of employees, Sir James broke the photographer's camera, broke his spectacles, bruised his ribs and skinned his knuckles. Then, while the photographer was still being held, Sir James "escaped" in a cowardly fashion. It seems extraordinary that a man of Sir James's position should then admit to being pleased to engage himself in a public brawl on his wedding day.'

Today, Wilson claims that he learned later that Annabel had insisted Goldsmith marry her because her children were growing up and she wanted to legitimise them, particularly at a time when Zak was going to Eton. 'It was the most grudging act of marriage that has ever been given by a man to a woman,' he says. 'It was disgraceful the way that he treated her. The only bunch of flowers she got was from me. I sent two dozen roses to her room at the Ritz hotel the night before and when I met her at Annabel's some time later she said she was thrilled to get them and always remembered her wedding for the roses that I had sent her. I think she must have been very angry at the way she was treated that day. But certainly she was not allowed to go back to his house that day and that, presumably, was because Laure Boulay de la Meurthe [his French mistress] was there. All he was doing was legitimising his children in about the most snubbing way that he possibly could. That doesn't mean to say that she was any the less enthralled by him. I think she was always in love with him and, to an extent, he was her protector.'

With the Londonderry wealth somewhat diminished, she relied on Goldsmith for a standard of living that would be the envy of her forbears. Since her marriage, home has been Ormeley Lodge, a Georgian mansion in six acres on the edge of Richmond Park. 'It's like a palace,' says one visitor, 'or, at least, a very grand country house with two or three drawing-rooms instead of one. Because it backs on to a golf course, it looks as if it's got thousands of acres, and yet it's only 20 minutes from London. It's very stylishly furnished in a bold and brave and unconventional way, and she lives there like a slightly dippy English country lady with masses of dogs yapping their bloody heads off.'

But while the basement dining-room can seat up to 100 people, entertaining on such a grand scale is fairly infrequent. Annabel is more likely to host Sunday lunch in the kitchen. When Goldsmith was away, which became more and more often the case, she settled down with her dogs – four Norfolk terriers and a rescued mongrel – on a huge four-poster with rose-printed drapes. 'Of course when Jimmy's at home the dogs stay downstairs,' Annabel told the *Evening Standard* in 1995. 'Either way I aim at nine hours and then wake myself up laughing. Both my husbands noticed that.'

Life has not always been so kind to the third Mrs Goldsmith, however. In 1986, her brilliant eldest son, Rupert, disappeared, presumed drowned, off the coast of West Africa. Rupert, then 30, was living in Lomé, the capital of Togo, where the company he worked for was building a grain terminal. Syrian millionaire Wafic Said loaned the Birleys his private plane to help in a huge search operation but no body was ever found. There was even speculation that Rupert had been involved with the American intelligence services and that this had contributed to his untimely end. His death came as a body blow to Annabel. 'He was my first born,' she once said. 'I was 20 when I had him and I worshipped that boy. At first I withdrew into a shell, hardly went out for a year. I couldn't face seeing people. Maybe it wasn't a bad thing. Somehow I worked it out of my system, anyway. I can talk about it now, but for ages I couldn't. He was so much part of my life.'

Rupert's death has not been her only brush with tragedy. She had had a close shave with her younger son by Birley, Robin, 16 years earlier. When Goldsmith was away one weekend in the winter of 1970, Annabel took her three children by Birley to John Aspinall's zoo, Howletts, in Kent. It was Aspinall's habit to take selected visitors inside the tiger cage to mix with the animals at close quarters. Robin, then 12, was stroking one of the beasts, Zorra, when it suddenly turned on him, pushed him over and closed its mouth over his head. Aspinall reacted by desperately pulling at the tiger's jaws to prise them apart while his then wife Min pulled her tail. Zorra then switched its attentions to her, knocking her over before being scared off by her screams.

'They rushed Robin to Canterbury Hospital, his mangled head on Annabel's arm in the back of the car,' wrote Ivan Fallon in *Billionaire, the Life and Times of Sir James Goldsmith*. 'He had a gaping hole where his mouth was and his bottom jaw hung by a thread. Annabel was certain he could not survive but hours of emergency surgery saved his life. However, the bones on one side of his face were so crushed that they would never develop and he grew to maturity with a lop-sided face but no other permanent damage.'

As Robin grew up, the family made an effort to ensure that he spent time with Aspinall so he would not bear a grudge against him in later life. It was a strategy that obviously worked. The two men rubbed shoulders as Referendum Party candidates at the last election. For his part, Goldsmith always got on with Robin Birley, whom he admired as a businessman who made a small fortune from a chain of sandwich shops.

In the other Goldsmith households she is known as 'Patti' after the popular soul singer Patti Boulaye. But there is nothing populist about Laure Boulay de la Meurthe, a niece of the Comte de Paris, the pretender to the throne of France. Although Lady Annabel has never publicly uttered one word against the woman who replaced her in Goldsmith's affections, it is the evident glee she took in referring to her late husband's mistress as Patti that betrayed her true feelings. Annabel may have presented a public face of civilised acceptance of her husband's informal polygamy but, behind the scenes, her behaviour owed more to the backstage manoeuvrings at a Miss World contest than the liberal carelessness of the Bloomsbury Group.

Indeed, Goldsmith's extended family came together under one roof only once before his last days. The occasion was the marriage of Alix Goldsmith, his daughter by his second wife Ginette Lery, and Giofreddo Marcaccini in 1991. This has been presented in the past as a harmonious gathering of mothers and children but, according to one member of the family, the truth is rather different. Annabel, who perhaps had reason to resent Laure, procrastinated over whether she would attend right up to the last moment. In the end, she and Jemima failed to attend the civil ceremony and the lunch that followed it at Montjeu, Goldsmith's chateau in Burgundy, and made only a truncated appearance at the wedding party at Laurent in Paris the next day.

For a long time she refused to visit Goldsmith's estate in Mexico on the grounds that it was Laure's territory and, while she relented in later years, the two women's visits never coincided. Even when Jemima took Imran to Cuixmala for the first time in December 1995 for the traditional New Year party, Annabel insisted on taking Benjamin to Barbados to avoid Laure.

As time passed, Annabel began to adopt a more philosophical approach. One who observed the Goldsmiths at play was struck by her apparent readiness to introduce her husband to younger models of herself. Having reconciled herself to Goldsmith's adulterous ways, she seemed to revel in his flirtatious behaviour to the extent of encouraging him to meet girls who were as much Laure's junior as Laure was hers. 'He sort of fancied them, carried along by Annabel and Jemima, and they all thought it was a jolly funny family thing,' recalls the observer.

If this was Annabel's way of getting at her husband's mistress perhaps we should not be surprised. In the naming of her third child as a respectably remarried woman there was an indication that she felt stability was hers at last. In both Christian and Jewish traditions, the name Benjamin is given to the last born. But if Annabel believed this was the end of her husband's breeding, she was sorely mistaken. Even as they signed the papers legitimising their union in a French *mairie*, she must have known that a younger model was already an almost permanent fixture at her new husband's house on the Rue Monsieur. As Isabel was to put it shortly after Goldsmith died: 'My father's idea of complete heaven was a harem. He saw no reason for discarding any of his relationships.'

In a curious reversal of national psyches, it was Laure who adopted a very English stiff upper lip in the face of Annabel's resentment. The daughter of the twice-married Countess Monique d'Harcourt, she comes from a family which retains a pre-Revolutionary air of aloofness and privilege. Titles proliferate in modern France, with nobility stemming from pre-Revolutionary times – the so called *ancien régime* – the Napoleonic era and beyond. With no authoritative directory to draw on, there are many pretenders but the Boulay de la Meurthes' title is very much the genuine article.

As a child, home was the splendid Chateau Fretay in Loches, near Tours, where she grew up with her two sisters, Jilone and Yseult, and where she developed her lifelong love of horse riding. Jilone, now the Countess of Clairmontiner, is married to Renaud, also a Count, and they have two children. In addition to their home in Paris they own a castle in Brittany.

At 18, already a conspicuous beauty, Laure applied for a job on *Paris Match*, a magazine whose judicious mix of social froth and political bite had turned it into a French institution. 'She was very beautiful, very pretty, very nice and a little bit shy,' recalls Benno Graziani, then editor-in-chief of *Paris Match*. 'She volunteered for everything. She was alone at that time and so she could go to, I don't know, Arabia or India at a moment's notice.'

By the time Laure met Goldsmith in the winter of 1977, she was 26, living with her sister on the Left Bank and a rising star at *Paris Match*. Her first impressions of him were intended for publication as the pair first met when she went to interview him. Alas, the piece never appeared and there is no trace of the manuscript in the *Paris Match* files. Graziani described her relationship with Goldsmith as a *coup de foudre* – a bolt of lightning – and she was soon to become the main woman in his life. Indeed, by the time he married Annabel in 1978, Laure was already ensconced in his home on the Rue Monsieur. Annabel may have made the transition from 'other woman' to wife, but in doing so, she had created a vacancy for the role of mistress.

When Laure moved to New York to work for *Elle* as its bureau chief there, her relationship with Goldsmith was well-established. In November 1980, Goldsmith also decided his future lay across the Atlantic and, while he would spend only 122 days a year in America because of US tax laws, much of the rest of his time would be spent in Central America and so he would be spending comparatively little time in Europe. Annabel, who had given birth to their third child, Benjamin, just five weeks earlier, was faced with a stark choice. She could either uproot her other children from their various schools, leave her beloved Ormeley Lodge and move to America or accept that she would see much less of her husband, who would then be living in the same city as his mistress. After an emotional dinner with Goldsmith in New York and a tearful night, she decided to stay in London.

Laure soon moved into her lover's suite at the Carlyle Hotel but she continued to spend the odd weekend with her colleagues at a house they shared on Long Island and – in a rare exhibition of her racy side – was even known to join them in a spot of skinny-dipping in the Hudson. All in all, there was little indication that she had just embarked on an affair with a billionaire whom no one could describe as thrifty. 'No, she didn't change a lot after meeting Jimmy,' says Graziani. 'She always wore the same clothes. She doesn't like jewellery. She's not interested in those things. She never liked money.'

But she was inexorably moving into a different sphere. By the end of 1982, she had discovered she was pregnant with their daughter Charlotte and Goldsmith, having decided that a hotel-based existence was not conducive to family life, resolved to buy a house. Laure duly found two large brownstones on East 80th Street off Park Avenue and he proceeded to refurbish them in typically extravagant style. From the street, the building was not particularly impressive but it stretched back almost the length of a block and by the time Robert Couturier had finished with it it was one of the most remarkable homes in the city. Couturier was a young French designer who had made his name by designing the chic Paris restaurant La Coupole and building a house for the film producer Dino de Laurentiis in North Carolina. His plan for Goldsmith's house was equally ambitious. He proposed the construction of a three-storey atrium, spanning both properties, at the rear and a sweeping curved staircase leading up to a large drawing-room. For their part, Goldsmith and Laure scoured New York's salerooms buying *objets d'art*, Oriental rugs and antique furniture.

It is testimony to Laure's discretion that even during what must have been an emotionally turbulent time she maintained an iron curtain between her professional and private life. 'She's very petite and slim and nobody in the office knew she was expecting a baby,' says a former colleague of her first pregnancy. 'None of us noticed a thing and we were seeing her in the office every day. Then she disappeared for three or four weeks, so she must have been more than eight months pregnant, and when she came back she'd just popped the baby. It was quite funny. Nobody could believe it at first.'

The couple were still living in New York when Laure became pregnant a second time with Goldsmith's eighth and final child, Jethro. It was 1987, the year of the Great Crash and, after selling everything he owned in the US, Goldsmith spent much of the ensuing three years with Laure in Mexico before returning to Europe to help mastermind the restoration of Montjeu.

That completed, Laure hankered after a return to journalism and Goldsmith bought her the magazine *Point de Vue – Images du Monde*, the *Hello!*-style house journal of the French upper classes. Like Goldsmith at *L'Express*, she was not content to allow things to roll along as they had before her arrival. Over the years she replaced many of the editorial team she had inherited and expanded the magazine's cast of characters from a tired circle of European royalty and irrelevant aristocrats to a wider range of celebrities and politicians. 'She's really efficient, very pragmatic, I should say, and she always knows what she wants,' says Benno Graziani. 'She never hesitates and she's very authoritarian.'

Her hard-nosed approach paid off and *Point de Vue*'s circulation soared. Part of its growing appeal lay in her own ability to net the big interviews. When she accompanied Goldsmith to Pakistan in October, 1995, she persuaded Embesat Salahuddin, the then wife of Youssef, Imran Khan's closest friend in Lahore, to call Benazir Bhutto and arrange an appointment for her to interview the then prime minister. Despite the fact that Bhutto was a bitter opponent of Goldsmith's son-in-law, she agreed. Two months later, Laure flew out to Pakistan once more. She had wanted to spend two days interviewing and photographing the Pakistani leader but, understandably, Bhutto had better things to do with her time and Laure had to content herself with a much more limited audience.

Prime Minister Bhutto and the mistress of the father-in-law of her most bitter political opponent met in the suitably chilly atmosphere of an air-conditioned reception room in her residence in Islamabad. Laure and Bhutto shook hands but the photographer had to content himself with a nodded greeting as he had been warned that, as a foreign male in a Muslim country, he could not expect to shake the hand of a woman. If Bhutto was expecting a grilling from someone who had links to the enemy camp, she was in for a pleasant surprise. Laure's questions were subject friendly to say the least and, on the evidence of the piece published in *Point de Vue*, the prime minister spent a pleasant hour or so acquainting Laure with her life story. Of Imran Khan there was not a single mention.

In addition to widening its scope, Laure has also succeeded in making *Point de Vue's Premier Bal* one of the highlights of the social calendar for a certain kind of French aristocrat. For a crowd-pulling guest of honour she has to look no further than her aunt, the Comtesse de Paris, and, in November 1996, 29 swan-necked debutantes paraded before them in a riot of taffeta and chiffon. Ten fiddlers in white tie and tails serenaded the guests as they walked through the covered courtyard of the Grand Hotel to the Salon Ravel, with its spectacularly ornate ceiling, huge crystal chandelier and ranks of gilt-edged mirrors, each partly obscured by a large bouquet of flowers. There the gilded youth tucked into a splendid dinner accompanied by magnums of champagne. Followers of Goldsmith's business career, which included a stint as the owner of Bovril, were amused to see that the entree was *Marmite de l'Amiral*. Goldsmith himself arrived more than an hour late, modestly sidestepping a pillar to avoid a high-profile entrance between the violinists. Later on, he was to draw on a lifetime's experience of sizing up attractive women to pick the belle of the ball. The siting of the ball at the Grand Hotel had a poignancy of its own for Goldsmith, whose first job was as a receptionist at the Hotel Scribe opposite.

Ironically, home for Laure these days is the house on the Rue Monsieur, where she and Ginette occupy entirely separate parts of the building but use the same front door. Unlike the armed neutrality that persists between herself and Annabel, Laure's relations with Ginette are positively cordial. They will dine together and Ginette has taken on the role of aunt to Laure's two children.

In many ways, however, Laure was one of the most intriguing women in Goldsmith's life. Annabel made it clear when she became pregnant with Jemima that she expected to become Goldsmith's third wife. But Laure appears to have had a more independent bent. Her two children have her surname rather than Goldsmith's and he did not even list them in his entry in the directory of members of the European Parliament. 'It's hard to tell whether she'd have liked to be married,' said one acquaintance. 'She'd never discuss that, of course, but I think she was happy. I think most of his ex-wives or girlfriends were happy. Jimmy was a very generous person, so they all knew that they would be very, very well looked after whatever happened.' Despite her Catholic background, Laure appeared to be under little pressure from her family to end her association with the much-married father of her children. As one rather cynical friend puts it: 'You know, if there is money it doesn't bother anybody. Perhaps if he had been the milkman it would have been different.' One family member even doubts whether Laure would have married Goldsmith if he had asked her. There is some anecdotal evidence, however, that Goldsmith presented Laure as his wife when he was abroad. When Goldsmith and Laure travelled to Pakistan, they met Embesat Salahuddin. 'He introduced her by saying, "This is my wife,"' she recalls.

Annabel may be one of life's great survivors and her public face of charm and vivacity hides a resilient streak. This is hardly surprising in a woman who had her husband's infidelity regularly paraded before her – and the rest of the world – in newspaper gossip columns.

But Annabel has never been the sort to play the victim. While her children were young she devoted herself to their welfare. As they grew up and became more independent, however, she flourished anew. Suddenly she was back in the headlines as the latest confidante of the Princess of Wales. Their relationship dated back to 1981, shortly after Diana and Charles married. In Annabel, a mature woman with plenty of worldly wisdom to dispense, the green young princess found a mother figure. It is testimony to Annabel's powers of diplomacy that she succeeded in cultivating both Diana and Camilla Parker Bowles, the mistress of Prince Charles and a rival, naturally enough, of his wife. Indeed, in 1989, both of Charles's women found themselves attending the same party at Ormeley Lodge. Annabel had arranged the event as a celebration for the 40th birthday of Annabel Elliot, Camilla's younger sister. Folklore has it that while Prince Charles disco danced, the two rivals for his affections found themselves together in the kitchen. Diana turned to her older rival and hissed: 'Why don't you leave my husband alone?'

Following the departure of Lucia Flecha de Lima, the wife of the Brazilian ambassador and Diana's guiding light, it was Annabel who took on her mantle. As the princess went through a hotly contested divorce, it was Annabel who was pictured alongside her in the back of her car as it swept out of Kensington Palace. Diana became a regular weekend visitor to the Goldsmith home and after amusing other guests with what Annabel describes as her ready wit, would take the dishes into the kitchen and get on with the washing-up. After her death on 31 August 1997 Annabel recalled: 'One of my most enduring memories is from her last visit this summer, when she came for lunch with the boys after returning from her first trip with the Fayeds. I can still picture her, sitting on the sofa cuddling Harry – she was always cuddling him – and exchanging quips with William . . . I will miss that fresh little voice on the telephone, always rather humbly asking me if we were busy at the weekend.'

But it was through the new-found fame of her daughter by Goldsmith, Jemima, that Annabel confirmed her celebrity. Just as Jemima supported her husband Imran Khan throughout a high-profile libel case in the summer of 1996, so Annabel was rarely outside the photographers' field of view as the three of them made the daily dash into the courtroom.

One family member, perhaps unkindly, likens Annabel's behaviour to that of Teri Shields, the mother of American actress Brooke Shields, who gained a reputation for living her life through her daughter's fame. 'Annabel behaved just like Teri Shields,' says the relative. 'Even at the Referendum Party conference she managed to secure a photo opportunity for just herself and Jemima. The whole family were sitting together up on the balcony where there were no photographers so those two must have slipped downstairs just long enough to pose for that photograph of them together.' This newly acquired determination is a far-cry from the scatterbrained image of her younger days. The family still recalls with merriment the occasion when Goldsmith was anxiously awaiting an independent adjudication on a business deal which hung on a presentation he had made personally. He and Annabel were holidaying on a yacht in the Aegean on the day the verdict was to be announced. Goldsmith was committed to a trip ashore and so left explicit instructions with Annabel to be sure to write down the precise figure when it came through on the ship's radio. The telephone numbers that Goldsmith juggled with had little meaning for his then mistress, however. When he got back she said: 'It was six million, or was it 16 million or maybe 26 million. Oh, I know I should have written it down.' The true figure, as it turned out, was £18.5 million.

At 63, Annabel remains a handsome woman, who retains a daring dress sense that dates back years. Her fondness for split skirts was her undoing on a day she accompanied Goldsmith to court during the *Private Eye* libel trial. The wind blew up her skirt to expose her underwear and the picture received wide circulation in the next day's papers. Far from being mortified by this exhibition, one who knows her well argues that she would have been disappointed that the picture was not even more revealing. 'That wouldn't have fazed her at all,' he says, 'She's such a funloving sort, I bet she said, "Damn, I wish I hadn't been wearing knickers that day."'

Laughter looms large in her life. Friends testify to her earthy sense of humour and her enthusiasm for practical jokes. A good example of this comes from Bellini's, an Italian restaurant she frequents near her home in Richmond. Lunching with a girlfriend one day, she amused the staff and fellow diners by sending a fruity note to a particularly dull-looking group of businessmen and pulling a face when the embarrassed recipient turned to identify his 'admirer'.

Nor was Annabel the sort to pine in her sitting-room while Jimmy was away in France. She continues to see her ex-husband, Mark Birley, regularly. It was she who went round to Thurloe

Square in Kensington to cook dinner for Mark Birley on his birthday in 1996. Further evidence that their split was a highly amicable one came in October of the same year when she holidayed with Birley's sister Maxime de la Falaise in France. As a friend of one of the Goldsmith brood says: 'It was like the Bloomsbury set. I don't know how they all did it. They were all divorced and married to one another and yet they all gave the impression of living happily together. They didn't seem to mind too much whose mother slept with whose father and what they produced.'

Chapter Four

The making of a tycoon

GOLDSMITH took the name of his grandfather's Suffolk estate, Cavenham, for the company he was to use to cut a swathe through British business. He founded it in 1964 and in many ways he could not have chosen a better time. The Beatles had conquered America. Harold Wilson had become prime minister on the back of a promise to harness the white heat of the technological revolution. And a mood of optimism was sweeping the country.

The success of Right Tan in France, gave Goldsmith the springboard he needed. Inspired by the example of Sir Charles Clore, one of a handful of pioneers of the hostile takeover bid in the '60s, he began researching potential targets. Clore and others, like Sir Isaac Wolfson and Maxwell Joseph, had been demonised for terrorising family companies and breaking down relationships between employers and workers that had been built up over generations. Working on the basis that some of Britain's best-known brand names were undervalued by the stock market and, in addition, held undervalued property assets, these early corporate raiders would surreptitiously build up large stock-holdings to avoid inflating the share price. If, when they swooped, the bid failed they could rely on a substantial gain by selling at the top of the market. No one was more scathing about their tactics than Lord Attlee, the former Labour prime minister, who once memorably referred to the environment they created as a 'jungle red in tooth and claw, and particularly Clore'.

Goldsmith's first predatory move was to buy 60,000 shares in Procea Products, a slimming foods company, best known for its

Slimcea bread. This gave him a 20 per cent stake and made him the biggest single investor. It also tied up much of his capital for what was – initially, at least – an unsatisfactory return. With no conventional bank likely to advance Goldsmith the cash he needed to pursue his high-risk strategy to create a large food manufacturing group, Clore pointed him in the direction of Wolfson, the man who made a fortune out of Great Universal Stores.

Wolfson was specialising in loans to personable entrepreneurs who found it hard to get backing elsewhere. The consequence was that interest charges were high and those who failed to meet their repayments found themselves victims of a different breed of dawn raiders – the bailiffs. Goldsmith happily accepted Wolfson's rationale that high risk lending justified the rates he charged and, as a relative newcomer, was also prepared to turn up for meetings at 5am, the time when the insomniac Wolfson saw his most desperate cases. After negotiations with Wolfson and his partner Harry Recanati, Goldsmith agreed to their bank taking a third share in his new private company Cavenham Foods – which he had the right to buy back at a later date – while he and Baron Alexis de Gunzberg had the remaining two thirds.

One of Cavenham's first moves was to acquire a Stock Exchange listing by buying a small public company called Carsons, an ailing Yorkshire-based chocolate manufacturer. Goldsmith immediately transferred ownership of his Procea stake from Cavenham Foods to Carsons and, with the help of the Wolfson loan, bought the rest of Procea and a small confectionery company called Yeatman. By the beginning of 1965, through a process of piecemeal acquisition, Goldsmith had built up a group with 6,000 employees, sales of £30 million but no profits to show for all the activity.

Behind the scenes, however, some tidy little deals were being made. Soon after the private Cavenham Foods bought Carr & Company of the eponymous water biscuits fame, Goldsmith sold the freehold on its Carlisle factory for £600,000, and promptly leased back the premises for £63,000 a year. This enabled the biscuit company to buy out Cavenham's controlling share in Carsons for cash leaving Goldsmith with a profit of £75,000. This is an early example of a ploy that Goldsmith used a number of times in his business career. He manipulated a company in which he had a controlling interest – and thus the power to set the price – to buy stock from another company in which he had a substantial interest.

The next deal was even more complex. Carr & Company made a bid for J. & A.P. Holland, a confectionery group already acquired by the private company, Cavenham, and then became the effective holding company of his group. Carr's name was then changed to Cavenham Foods.

Goldsmith's next coup was the acquisition of a tobacco wholesaler called Singleton and Cole. It was significant for two reasons. Not only did it furnish him with a substantial windfall at a difficult time but it brought him into contact with a man who was to have a powerful influence on his business development, Jim Slater.

Slater was a grammar school boy who left school at 15 to train as an accountant. By the age of 35, he had become the youngest member of the board of the car giant Leyland Motors and went on to become number two to the chairman Donald Stokes before leaving to start his own investment company in 1963. He chose as his business partner the up-and-coming Tory MP Peter – later Lord – Walker. Walker pulled out in 1970, after being made a minister in Edward Heath's government, selling his shares for £450,000, but the chess-playing Slater ploughed on to create a multinational empire with a market capitalisation of £280 million and through his ruthless attitude towards takeovers changed the face of British business.

In 1965, however, Slater was at the helm of a modest investment business. He had bought 20 per cent of Singleton as a 'strategic stake'. This was Slater speak for a stake of a size that gave the owner effective control of the business and was therefore worth a premium on the market price. Goldsmith and Gunzberg accepted his logic and bought his 120,000 shares for 13 shillings (65p) apiece. The news that a hostile bidder was on the horizon prompted Singleton's chairman, George Waddington, to hire the merchant bank Warburg's in an attempt to repel boarders. Goldsmith eventually triumphed by upping his bid to two Cavenham shares for each Singleton share but he was soon in financial difficulties as interest rates rose and the Labour government introduced a prices and incomes policy. Soon Goldsmith's profit forecast was in tatters.

He had had trouble meeting his targets before, notably when he had told shareholders in 1964 that Carsons' losses would be cut from £68,000 to £8,000. In the event, the company lost £120,000. This time round, Goldsmith and Gunzberg attempted to improve their fortunes by merging Cavenham with Perrier in France to form a joint venture with a turnover of £15 million. Perrier by this time had 55 per cent of the French soft drinks market and had diversified into confectionery. It had little impact, however, and soon Cavenham was heading for a £1 million loss, disastrously at odds with the promise of a profit 'substantially greater' than the £216,000 of the previous year. Goldsmith began casting around for businesses to sell. Salvation came in the form of two small subsidiaries of Singleton and Cole. When Goldsmith forked out the equivalent of £1.4 million for the tobacco wholesaler he had no idea that its portfolio included two snuff companies that between them would turn out to be worth more than what he had paid for the entire group. But as Goldsmith scoured the balance sheets for promising disposals, he noticed they were rapidly increasing their profits. When he approached Conwood Corporation, the kings of the American snuff market who were forbidden by anti-trust legislation from expanding further in the US, he found a willing buyer. The only snag was that Conwood's consultant, John Tigrett, was only prepared to buy half the snuff business. The two men developed an instant rapport, however.

Goldsmith had already developed the sophisticated charm that was to become one of his hallmarks in the years to come, along with a studied ruthlessness. Business associates, whether friends or foes, often found themselves invited to his home. This was not so much a display of intimacy as an act of exhibitionism designed to impress the most sceptical negotiator. After all, Goldsmith's then offices, located in a shabby block off the A4 in Slough, only instilled confidence in the sense that they made the visitor keenly aware that this was a man who was not extravagant with his overheads. On the home front, however, Goldsmith was the man for whom the phrase 'Think champagne and you'll drink champagne' could have been invented. Even when times were hardest, domestic comfort was always the last thing that was going to be sacrificed. Years later, when asked by a TV producer what he would miss most if his empire fell apart, he said: 'The luxury'.

So even John Tigrett, a self-made man who had acted as consultant to big names like the late Armand Hammer and the late Roy Thomson, could not fail to have been impressed when he arrived for breakfast one Sunday morning. Despite sailing close to the wind in commercial terms, Goldsmith lived in some splendour in a house on Regent's Park. The choreography associated with a visitor's arrival and departure also left nothing to chance. Guests were greeted at the door by a butler but, on departure, as if to show how valued they had become after the briefest of interactions, they would invariably be escorted personally to their cars and waved off amiably by the host himself.

The magic certainly worked with Tigrett. Not only did he agree to buy half the snuff companies but he was prepared to introduce Goldsmith to Swiss banking contacts who would be able to lend him the difference. The result was that Cavenham received more than £800,000 from Conwood SA, a Swiss joint venture formed between Conwood and Cavenham, a huge profit of £730,000 on the snuff companies' balance sheet valuation of £76,100.

This was not enough to avert the crisis, however. Goldsmith was still £500,000 short of attaining his profits forecast. Such a shortfall would be nothing short of disastrous. Investor confidence would evaporate, never to return and Goldsmith's business career would be over, at least for the time being. His only course, he was advised by his stockbroker, was to come up with £500,000 and gift it to the company.

Fortunately for Goldsmith, his French interests were doing relatively well. Gustin-Milical, under the prudent management of Maurice Lignon, was returning a steady £120,000 a year and, between them, Goldsmith and Gunzberg were able to raise the sum required from French bankers by putting up their French assets as collateral. The structure of the deal confused some City observers but there were clear benefits in it for Goldsmith and his partner. After all, their private company Cavenham Investments owned 5 million shares in Cavenham Foods and if the English public company went under these shares would have immediately become worthless. This last-ditch manoeuvre may have averted disaster but Cavenham's 1967 accounts hardly portrayed a company in rude health. It made a net loss after interest payments and other deductions, there was no dividend payout to shareholders and the auditors quibbled with the directors' goodwill evaluation of £950,000.

Goldsmith's father did not live to see out his younger son's latest crisis. Frank Goldsmith had died on Valentine's Day 1967, aged 88. It was a desire to impress the father who had been so supportive during his days as a feckless youth that had helped to drive Goldsmith on. And it was one of his abiding regrets that Monsieur le Major witnessed his struggle but never lived to savour his success.

With his latest crisis over in London, Goldsmith's thoughts turned to the other side of the Channel. Gustin-Milical, that one stable outpost of his growing international empire, was expanding, but only slowly and Goldsmith was keen to use it as the foundation of a financial empire.

Their first target was the Union de Transports et de Participations, a subsidiary of the state-owned Union Financière de Paris, that was being auctioned off after its parent got into difficulties and was placed in liquidation. At first sight it was an unpromising acquisition for a company in pharmaceuticals. Union de Transports had been formed in 1896 to run trams in Algiers but by 1967 it was essentially an investment company with substantial assets of £820,000 in the form of investments and property. The people in charge of the sale on behalf of the French government were Count Thierry de Clermont-Tonnere and Gilberte Beaux. Madame Beaux, as she is universally known, was not the sort of woman in whom Goldsmith normally showed any interest. The wife of a half-Russian *parfumier* 14 years her senior, she was 37, short and dumpy. But she had skills that were to prove invaluable to Goldsmith in the decades to come. The daughter of a Corsican banker who had been a victim of the Great Depression of the '30s, she began her career in banking as a typist at the age of 17 and worked her way up the hard way. By the time Goldsmith met her she had wide experience of the banking and financial sectors.

Goldsmith's purchase of the former Algerian tram company, whose name was later shortened to Union de Participations, signalled the start of a series of unorthodox share transactions that were to make Goldsmith a rich man. Just as he had used Carr

& Company to purchase at a premium the Carsons shares held by the then private Cavenham Foods company in 1965, Goldsmith proceeded to use Union de Participations to buy shares in Gustin Milical.

The labyrinthine nature of these deals has been outlined by Charles Raw, a former *Sunday Times* journalist, who probed Goldsmith's affairs more closely than anyone else in the '70s. He completed a 20,000-word, four-part investigation of Goldsmith's finances in January 1981, just as Rupert Murdoch finalised his takeover of Times Newspapers. Senior counsel spent three months going through Raw's findings and eventually gave them a clean bill of health but, by then, Harry Evans, the editor who had commissioned the probe, had gone and the new proprietor decided not to publish. Raw left the *Sunday Times* soon afterwards and it was not until May 1985, that extracts from his opus were published in *Private Eye*. Tellingly, Goldsmith never sued.

Raw's pieces tell a fascinating tale of financial engineering. Goldsmith had paid just £300,000 for a controlling interest in Union de Participations but that stake gave him access to assets worth more than £800,000. One of his first acts was to use these funds to buy 26,600 shares in Gustin-Milical. 'The price it paid was a steep one – £535,000, or about £20 a share,' wrote Raw. 'This was about 70 per cent more than the value at which Gustin-Milical's shares had been quoted only a year previously. For the shareholders in Gustin-Milical it represented an enormous bonus.' And one of those was Goldsmith.

And that was not the end of Goldsmith's profit-taking. According to Raw he followed this up with a £900,000 rights issue to finance the purchase of another 30,000 shares in Gustin-Milical, again at a handsome premium. In this way, Goldsmith's slimming business became a subsidiary of Union de Participations and he made himself a tidy sum in the process.

By this time, Goldsmith had set his heart on becoming a banker and his extended negotiations with Madame Beaux had persuaded him that she was just the sort of person he needed to run it. When she protested that she could not leave unfinished the task of disposing of Union Financière, Goldsmith told her he would buy whatever was left providing she could raise the money to finance the purchase. This she did, and then she turned her mind to finding a bank. One promising candidate was Société Générale Foncière, a bank with substantial property interests. A 30 per cent share which would give the buyer a controlling interest was for sale for £900,000 but this was money Goldsmith did not have. With Beaux and Clermont-Tonnere on board, however, he now had people with the contacts to arrange such a loan. The SGF deal was particularly attractive because a property company, Manera, was willing to pay £2.4 million for the company's prestigious head office at 90 Champs Elysées and other properties.

The problem was how to cover the buying price until the property transaction went through. This was resolved in a way which was typically Goldsmithian. Money was borrowed from two banks using as a guarantee the very SGF shares the loan was being used to purchase. The deal went through smoothly enough and Générale Foncière was merged with Union de Participations and two others to form a new holding company which they called Générale Occidentale.

But the ramifications of the Foncière deal were to rumble on for another seven years. Michel Breton, an assistant director of the banking division who was made redundant in the wake of the takeover, led a shareholder action against the deal, arguing that the company had been bought with its own money. The case dragged on for two years until the two accountants appointed to investigate the terms of the deal by the Police Judiciare produced a 500-page report. While it was not the accountants' place to judge Goldsmith's actions, their findings were damning. Apart from describing Gustin-Milical's share price as 'very overvalued', the report noted that no less than three quarters of Générale Occidentale's profits in 1969 had come from inter-group sharedealing. This had created an 'artificial construction whose birth and development were due more to financial manipulation and cleverly orchestrated publicity than economic reality'.

The report also touched on the existence of a Dutch investment company called Elam. The accountants noted that SGF had guaranteed total loans of £760,000 to the company but concluded that Goldsmith 'exercised no function' at Elam. According to Charles Raw, however, they were wrong. He discovered that Goldsmith was made a director on 2 August 1968, and five months later he was joined by his brother Teddy.

Elam went on to buy six million shares in Cavenham Foods, a massive 40 per cent of its capital. The remarkable thing about all this is that at no time was Elam ever listed as a shareholder in Cavenham's register of shareholdings.

'Goldsmith's passion for secrecy is a basic characteristic of his business dealings,' wrote Raw. 'It has led him frequently to suppress information which shareholders are entitled to have. But in the case of Elam he appears simply to have ignored the requirements of British company law. And by using an international network of companies to ensure that the true facts were almost inaccessible he was developing a method of concealment which he was to refine and use to great effect in the future.'

Elam's existence proved short-lived. Towards the end of 1969 – less than a year after SGF had guaranteed loans of £760,000 – the company was sold to Générale Occidentale. At the time of the sale, Elam's Cavenham shares were valued at 10 shillings (50p) each, three shillings (15p) more than they were trading for on the London stock market. This means the owners of Elam made £1 million between them.

'It would be intriguing to discover where Elam was getting its Cavenham shares,' remarked Raw. 'Directly or indirectly, many of them must have come from Goldsmith . . . [and his] private UK company, Cavenham Investments. This company held a large block of Cavenham Foods shares. Cavenham Investments had disposed of 3.9 million shares before March 1969, and Goldsmith's . . . dealing register at Cavenham Foods reveal that . . . [he] personally sold over one million shares between June and November 1969.'

Despite the incendiary contents of the accountants' report, Breton's pressure group was falling apart. After Goldsmith launched a counter-suit against it in 1970, all but Breton and a friend had pulled out of the case. In June 1974, a judge decided that there were 'no grounds for prosecution' but when Breton took his case to the Court of Appeal, it ordered further inquiries to be made into the takeover. 'The timing could not have been worse,' observed Raw. 'Just one day earlier in Britain, Goldsmith had been appointed chairman of Slater Walker with a brief to rescue that company. News that he was being investigated in France for misuse of company money would have made sensational headlines.' Goldsmith was saved from this ordeal by the fact that, for some unknown reason, the previously indefatigable Breton chose this moment to abandon his crusade. Within two weeks of the judgement from the Court of Appeal he had withdrawn from the battle and the action died.

While Goldsmith was making small fortunes from ingenious manipulation of share prices, Cavenham was emerging from a period of struggle. In 1969, it was a food manufacturer employing thousands of people and with sales of more than £30 million, but it made a profit of just £16,000. Indeed, that year was the sixth in succession that it failed to pay a dividend. But if Cavenham shareholders hadn't exactly prospered, Goldsmith most certainly had. In Paris, he had his house on the Rue Monsieur with a courtyard and magnificent ceilings, while in London he had an equally fine property on Regent's Park. His personal wealth was such that he was even in a position to give £100,000 'out of his own pocket' to promote the European cause. Euroscepticism was much more of a minority interest in those days.

With his personal wealth secure – for the time being at least – and Cavenham's share price riding high after a multinational restructuring that put Union de Participations at the apex of a pyramid of companies in France, Britain and Holland, Goldsmith plunged anew into the takeover game. This time, however, he was ready to take on some of the biggest names in British industry.

His first target was Bovril, a well-established group whose profits had remained stagnant for ten years. When he started buying shares they were languishing at 180p but by the time he launched his bid on 27 June 1971, they had climbed to 247p. He offered 310p a share in Cavenham shares and loan stock, terms that valued the bid at £9.7 million. Fortunately, Cavenham's share price was also benefiting from the Heath-Barber boom and between April and June it had risen from 70p to 85p. Cavenham's status was also helped at this delicate stage by the sale of half of its retailing arm to the Southland Corporation of Dallas for £3.3 million. This meant that a division of the company that had been bought for less than £1 million was now valued at around £7 million and the share price responded accordingly.

It was now clear that for his bid to succeed, he would have to offer a cash alternative to his share deal. The Southland sale would help fund this but it required more fancy footwork by Madame Beaux to raise cash from banks on the Continent. Soon Goldsmith was in a position to send a telegram to every single Bovril shareholder with news of the cash offer.

But Bovril was not about to give up without a fight. Its chairman Lord Luke was replaced by his younger brother and Rowntree Mackintosh was persuaded to make a counterbid of £10.9 million. Beecham began sniffing around too but pulled out over concerns that it would be unable to dispose of Bovril's ranches and abattoirs in Argentina and repatriate the proceeds. By now Goldsmith was in so deep that Jim Slater warned him that if he did not succeed this time the City would never take him seriously again and any future bids would be doomed to failure.

But for a time it began to look as if Goldsmith would have to fall on his sword. After weeks of raiding the stock market for Bovril shares, he had just about exhausted his resources. It was then that he received an unexpected call from Annabel's neighbour Maxwell Joseph, the boss of Grand Metropolitan, who also owned Express Dairies. He was willing to buy Bovril's dairy business for between £5 and £7 million and would pledge the sum if Goldsmith would commit himself to selling in the event of victory. It was just the breathing space that Goldsmith needed. By Wednesday, 18 August he owned 47 per cent of Bovril's shares and was able to announce that the Prudential had offered him their holding, enough to take him over the crucial 50 per cent barrier.

'Bovril was the turning point in Jimmy Goldsmith's career,' said John Tigrett afterwards. Joseph duly bought the dairies for £5.3 million, reducing Goldsmith's outlay for the group to £9 million. By the time he had sold off those parts of the company he had no use for, Goldsmith claimed to have recovered the bulk of the purchase price and yet retained the main brands: Bovril, Marmite, Ambrosia Creamed Rice and the Virol and Jaffajuice drinks. He soon cut overheads by half a million a year, and doubled profits to £2 million. Madame Beaux, who had spent years financing the export of cars to South America and had become fluent in Spanish, even managed to pull off the sale of the Argentinian meat works. When Goldsmith pulled out of the food manufacturing market in 1979, he collected a profit of £36 million from Beecham for the Bovril brands alone. No wonder

Goldsmith himself describes it as 'the most important deal of my life'.

It also marked the start of a period of accelerated growth that took Cavenham into the big league. Four months before Goldsmith closed the Bovril deal, Cavenham reported sales of £35 million and profits of less than £2 million. In January 1972, turnover was running at £400 million.

Acquisitions began to be made at the rate of one a month. In September, 1971, he paid £10 million for Wrights Biscuits. In December, he bought the South African Marmite company followed by the French agricultural and pharmaceutical company, Sanders, for £12.7 million. A month later he made what was by far his biggest bid to date, an £86 million offer for Allied Suppliers, owner of some of Britain's best known high street shops, including Lipton's, Home & Colonial, Maypole and Presto supermarkets.

With his British interests mushrooming fast, Goldsmith found time to make a significant acquisition in France. In April, 1972, Cavenham bought 20 per cent of Générale Alimentaire, one of France's largest food groups, and Générale Occidentale acquired another five per cent. With the co-operation of the Rothschilds, who owned another quarter of the company, he merged it with Cavenham's French subsidiary FIPP.

By the end of 1972, Goldsmith's interests Europe-wide had a stock market value of more than £200 million, according to the *Sunday Times*. Apart from his food and retailing companies in the UK, he still owned Gustin-Milical and other pharmaceutical companies in France, in addition to Anders, a £40 million turnover producer of animal concentrates, Générale Alimentaire, and companies which controlled half the country's mustard and vinegar markets.

Elsewhere he owned a snuff business in Germany, a gin company in the Netherlands and 25 per cent of the Danish Irma chain of food shops.

His romantic life was equally multinational. In Paris, Ginette was esconced with Isabel, Manes and Alix in the Rue Monsieur. In London, Goldsmith was deep into his affair with Lady Annabel Birley and contemplating the possibility of a second family.

At this stage, Goldsmith's momentum appeared unstoppable.

But no one knew better than he the importance of consolidation in a bull market. His share price might have been booming but Goldsmith was well aware that at the first sign of a downturn it was the fast-growing, entrepreneurial groups like his own that would be hit hardest. With this in mind he resolved to build a cash reserve with which he would be in a position to prop up his share price in the lean years he knew were to come. The unlikely vehicle for this exercise was a tiny financial services outfit called the Anglo-Continental Investment and Finance Company.

When he first started buying its shares in September 1971, they stood at 37p. By the following June they were up to 270p. When a group of journalists he was entertaining at the Ritz asked him what Anglo-Continental was all about, he gave them his gloomy forecast of a slump in the offing and described Anglo-Continental as the 'company which is going to be able to protect Cavenham when its shares fall'.

The boom had been stoked by a significant change of policy by the Heath government. Late in 1971, it had done away with the limits on the size of loans that banks could make to private borrowers. The result was a huge inflationary spiral as banks fell over themselves to lend money and property prices soared as speculators moved into the market. The crash, when it came, was correspondingly spectacular. The Yom Kippur War in the Middle East caused the OPEC oil crisis which led to the price of oil quadrupling within a fortnight from $3 to $12 a barrel. Britain's miners took advantage of the energy crisis to strike for better pay and conditions and Heath was forced to declare a state of emergency and to impose a three-day week on industry in a bid to conserve energy. The consequences were disastrous for business. As interest rates increased from five per cent in the summer of 1972 to 13 per cent in November 1973, the *Financial Times* share index slumped dramatically, falling from 544 in May 1972, to 146 in January 1975. When Heath called an election in February 1974, it was no surprise that Harold Wilson recorded his third general election victory.

Among the biggest victims of the slump was Slater Walker, whose share price collapsed from 260p to 35.5p. It rallied at the beginning of 1975 when it trebled in line with the market as a whole but it was clear that it would take a long time to recover the confidence of the City. Slater's problems were of no small concern to Goldsmith, who held eight per cent of his company's stock.

By this time, he was facing problems of his own in France where Générale Occidentale's share price was sagging badly. It fell from £30 a share to £17 a share between 1974 and 1975, according to Charles Raw. This prompted some anxiety among the major outside shareholders, notably the Prudential Assurance Company, which actually began selling shares in 1975. Fearing a run on the shares, Madame Beaux was forced to plead with them to stop.

This was not Goldsmith's only problem, however. Générale Occidentale had borrowed heavily to buy shares in Cavenham and these loans were now due for repayment. To raise the necessary funds, Goldsmith organised a rights issue of 625,000 Générale Occidentale shares in April, 1975. Surprisingly, in the circumstances, the shares were fully subscribed. But closer examination reveals that of the institutional shareholders, only Hambros, Goldsmith's bank, and Union des Assurances de Paris, France's largest nationalised insurance company, took up their share allocation. Nor was the offer a hit with the public at large who took up only four per cent of the shares.

The bulk of the shares, according to Charles Raw, were bought by what he calls 'a remarkable rag-bag of companies'. In addition to the Paris-based Trocadero Participations, a former Slater Walker company Goldsmith had bought at the end of 1974, there were five of them based in Switzerland, Lichtenstein and Panama. Between them they bought just under 365,000 shares, wrote Raw, amounting to a total investment of £6 million. And all, he explained, were linked to Goldsmith: 'The Lichtenstein company was Ligogne, which had been formed by Goldsmith in 1962; on the only occasion its existence had been publicly revealed (in 1970) it was described as "a family trust whose principal beneficiaries are Mr J.M. Goldsmith and his family". Ligogne subscribed for 70,000 shares.

'The Swiss company was called Rila, formed in 1969 shortly after a Dutch company of the same name had become the largest single shareholder in GO. Although the Swiss Rila has never featured prominently in any Goldsmith documents, it is in fact associated with Goldsmith himself and has been used by him as a vehicle to purchase shares on several occasions in some of the group's companies. Rila subscribed for 90,000 shares.

'Then there were three Panamanian companies, Delta, Quiny and Splendor. Delta and Quiny had on their boards Swiss lawyers known to act for Goldsmith as directors. The third – Splendor – appears to have been a family company, for at one time Goldsmith himself was president, his brother Edward was vice president, and an old family friend, John Tigrett, was secretary. Together these companies subscribed for just over 200,000 shares.'

Intriguingly, another subscriber to that rights issue, whose identity was not made known at the time, was Slater Walker. Its banking subsidiary bought nearly 70,000 shares at a cost of nearly £1.2 million. Raw argued that if Slater Walker had collapsed completely or fallen into 'unfriendly hands' this shareholding might have been revealed and with it the precarious state of Générale Occidentale's own finances, with disastrous results for its share price.

As it was, Slater and his friend Goldsmith managed to effect a smooth transition of management. On the morning of Monday, 21 October 1975, Slater telephoned Goldsmith in Paris to warn him that he had decided to resign. At noon he called on the deputy governor of the Bank of England, George Blunden, to tell him he was going and to nominate Goldsmith as his successor. The very next day, Slater's annointed was called in.

By Friday night the rescue bid was in place and Goldsmith's board was announced. It was packed with close associates, including his banker Charles Hambro, his account manager at Hambros, Peter Hill-Wood, Lord (Victor) Rothschild, a Rothschilds banker Ivor Kennington, and Dominique Leca, a member of his board at Générale Occidentale.

Slater's nemesis had appeared in the unlikely form of Lee Kuan Yew, the prime minister of Singapore. Kuan Yew later gained a reputation as a stern advocate of the free market but Slater's 'freebooting style of capitalism' was too much even for him. His anger was first aroused by the Singapore Monetary Authority's eccentric £22.4 million purchase from Slater Walker of Granite House in the City of London at the height of the boom, a deal which gave the British company a profit of more than £13 million. He was further enraged by Slater's break up of Haw Par, Singapore's biggest company. The young British management

Slater installed not only broke up one of Singapore's business institutions but created a culture of kill or be killed that appalled the conservative Kuan Yew. When Haw Par's managers moved their headquarters to Malaysia, a country with which Singapore had a bitter rivalry, it was about the most provocative thing they could have done. It was not long before the Singapore finance minister instigated an inquiry into 'serious wrongdoing' at Haw Par and Spydar Securities, a company set up to operate a management incentive scheme.

Slater sat out the crisis in Britain but was alarmed by threats from Kuan Yew to extradite and jail him and he actually considered fleeing the country. Indeed, he was *en route* to the airport to catch a plane to South Africa when he called at Tiny Rowland's house at Bourne End in Buckinghamshire to lobby for help with accommodation or work when he got there. In the event, Rowland talked him out of leaving and lent him not only enough to cover his personal debts of £1 million but another £2 million to get started again. Slater's number two, Dick Tarling, was less fortunate. He was successfully extradited, tried and sentenced to a year in Singapore's notorious Changi jail.

Most seriously of all, however, the Singaporean government froze £14.5 million that Haw Par owed the Slater bank in Britain. As other depositors lost confidence and began withdrawing their money, the Slater Walker share price plunged from 100p to 50p. It was while Goldsmith was in Singapore on a mission to recover the frozen funds in December 1975, that he was sent a copy of an article from *Private Eye*. It was the first link in a chain of events that was to transform Goldsmith's public image in Britain.

If the 7th Earl of Lucan had not murdered his children's nanny and then gone on the run in 1974, Goldsmith would never have got involved in the most high-profile libel action of the century. The two men were both regulars at John Aspinall's Clermont Club and both keen gamblers. There, however, the similarities ended. While Goldsmith was a hard-working, semi-self-made man, 'Lucky' Lucan was a shiftless individual who had gambled away most of the quarter of a million pounds he had inherited on the death of his father in 1963. As his luck ebbed away and his fortunes declined (he left behind £85,000 worth of debts), his incipient oddness seemed to become more and more marked. In his rooms in Elizabeth Street, Belgravia, he kept a collection of Hitler's recorded speeches and a number of books about psychiatric illness. Hanging in his wardrobe was a row of identical pin-striped suits.

His arrival at Goldsmith's house in Paris the month before his disappearance was totally unexpected, as was his request to borrow £10,000, which he said he needed to pay off his estranged wife and regain custody of his children, Lady Frances, Lady Camilla and Lord (George) Bingham. Goldsmith, who hated lending money in the belief that it ruined relationships, offered to give the hard-up earl the cash. To his credit, Lucan, who had been a guest at Goldsmith's holiday villa in Acapulco the previous year, refused the offer and a compromise was reached. Goldsmith would guarantee a bank overdraft for the amount. And that, according to Goldsmith, was the very last time he ever set eyes on John Lucan.

It was on the night of 7 November 1974 that a man lying in wait in the basement of the house where Lady Lucan was staying with her three children in Lower Belgrave Street attacked the nanny, Sandra Rivett, with a length of lead piping taped with Elastoplast at one end. Her battered body was later found in a US mail bag. The alarm was raised by Countess Lucan who, after coming across the intruder, had been attacked herself and had desperately defended herself with a piece of welded iron banister she had pulled off the staircase. It was widely believed that the intended victim was not the nanny but Veronica Lucan herself and it was equally widely believed that the man who did it was her estranged husband with whom she had been feuding in the courts for weeks over custody of their children.

That night, Lucan called his mother and persuaded her to go to the house where he said 'a terrible catastrophe' had taken place. The police were in the house when he called again to speak to his mother. He himself was last seen at the Sussex home of fellow Clermont member Ian Maxwell-Scott, who had been in the card school Goldsmith had joined at Oxford. In the absence of her husband, Mrs Maxwell-Scott gave him a drink and some tranquillisers before he fled into the night never to be seen again. The following day his car was found in the port of Newhaven with a piece of tape-wrapped lead piping similar to the murder weapon stowed in the boot. (Mrs Maxwell-Scott did not report her midnight visitor until 48 hours after the murder.)

Despite the diligent interrogations of Chief Superintendent Roy Ranson – one of his questions to Aspinall is said to have been: Did you feed Lord Lucan to your tigers? – the missing earl was never found. At the time it was accepted that he had probably jumped to his death from a cross-Channel ferry but that didn't stop Fleet Street from investing hundreds of thousands of pounds over the years following up the most tentative of leads. Several of these suggested that he had re-settled in one of the South American countries following plastic surgery to make him unrecognisable.

Goldsmith was in Ireland on the night of the horrifying events in Lower Belgrave Street. He was still absent when, the following morning, Aspinall summoned those closest to Lucan to his own house in Belgravia. The guests included Dominic Elwes and Charles Benson. Conspiracy theorists wrongly suggested that the gathering was a council of war on how to help Lucan evade justice. In truth it was merely an opportunity for extended gossip on their friend's disappearance and a discussion over what they should do if he ever did contact any of them.

The police called them the Eton mafia and they, in turn, knew the team put on the Lucan case as the Nob Squad. 'They are a funny breed,' says Detective Chief Inspector David Gerring, who worked closely with Ranson in 1974 but has now been retired for 17 years. 'They have been born into a society that tells them from the day they are born that they should be the rulers. They go to the same weddings, funerals, prep schools, public schools, universities and merchant banks. And they never squeal or snitch on their own. It's like hitting a brick wall.'

And getting them to talk to the police was not straightforward. Goldsmith proved particularly elusive, evading the attentions of a team of 50 officers for three weeks before eventually being located and called in for questioning. 'We wanted to see Goldsmith straight after the murder but he was always abroad and seemed unwilling to come forward,' recalls Gerring. 'Goldsmith had this incredible aura about him. He was absolutely charming. When he eventually stepped through the doors of the nick, he was charismatic and courteous. Nothing fazed him. Every alibi he gave for his movements over the three weeks checked out.'

Gerring remains convinced, however, that Lucan is still alive and that Goldsmith had a leading role in spiriting him out of the country. 'Among Lucan's inner circle of friends, only Goldsmith had the financial resources and the worldwide contacts to get him out of the country and set him up with cash abroad,' he says. 'Lucan's contacts would have looked to Goldsmith as someone able to provide funds that could never be traced back to the UK. Goldsmith could organise the others – that's the way the senior officers on the murder squad viewed it. I have said from day one that Lucan is alive and I still believe that to be true. I believe he is living in South Africa and I have no doubt Goldsmith has taken the secret of Lucan to his grave – even though we could never prove his involvement.

'He was the only one who could have sorted out complex issues such as private bank accounts in any one of dozens of foreign countries. Even in 1974, he had unlimited access to private planes and boats and it was the easiest thing in the world to slip out of Britain from some isolated port or airfield at that time. The checks were non-existent. My feeling is that Goldsmith engineered the Lucan escape at a fairly safe distance. James Goldsmith was too clever to get involved in the nitty-gritty of putting him on a boat across the Channel himself.

'When we finally managed to pull him in he told us a grand total of nothing. He said he knew Lucan and that he went to Eton. But, at the end of the day, that was about the end of it. The only thing I could put on him after an hour in the interview room was his overcoat – the most expensive I've ever seen in my life.'

The whole affair was dredged up the following June when the *Sunday Times* magazine published an article on the Lucan disappearance. It not only suggested that Goldsmith had been present at the notorious lunch at Aspinall's Belgravia home, but carried a painting of a gathering in the back room of the Clermont Club in which he and Lucan both figured. Dominic Elwes, it turned out, was not only the artist responsible for the painting but had also helped the *Sunday Times* put the article together, effecting a personal introduction between the writer, an Old Etonian named James Fox, and John Aspinall. As a result, Elwes and Aspinall were quoted in the final piece.

None of this would have pleased Goldsmith but what made him apoplectic with fury was the magazine's cover picture that showed Annabel with one arm draped around Lucan's shoulder as they both smiled warmly.

Goldsmith in a temper was something to behold. 'When Jimmy got angry his pupils dilated,' says Olivier Todd, who once worked for Goldsmith in Paris. 'Those very blue eyes became very, very black and in another culture he would have just put up his sword and gone through you. But he couldn't do that.' What he could do was almost as effective. Elwes was excommunicated, a procedure that was carried out with Goldsmith's customary efficiency. Not only did he ostracise him personally but made sure that Aspinall and Mark Birley banned him from both their clubs.

It was the final straw for Elwes who had a long history of depression and was already on his uppers. Before the damning *Sunday Times* piece appeared, Elwes was spotted driving round Berkeley Square in his clapped-out Mini, which had one door held shut with a piece of string. Suddenly a huge chauffeur-driven Rolls Royce pulled to a halt beside him in traffic, the electric window glided down and out popped the head of his ex-wife Tessa Kennedy, the heiress with whom he had eloped in 1958. After greeting him warmly and pointing him out to their children in the back, her limousine pulled away as the traffic began moving again. Elwes, meanwhile, stalled and was forced to push start his car to get the engine going. It was a poignant incident towards the end of the life of a man who had promised much. Despite his lack of means, he had a reputation as one of the most amusing men in London, with a ready string of anecdotes and an engaging manner in the telling of them. But he never recovered from Goldsmith's sentence of social death. After an unhappy summer in the south of France, he returned to London at the end of August and took an overdose of barbiturates on 5 September. It was later reported that he left two suicide notes, the shorter of which ran: 'I curse Mark and Jimmy from beyond the grave. I hope they are happy now.'

It was after a memorial service for Elwes at the Jesuit church on Farm Street in Mayfair in November, 1975, that an incident took place that set in train a series of events that was to obsess Goldsmith for a full 18 months. Tremayne Rodd, a godson of Elwes' mother, punched Aspinall. Apart from exposing the tensions between those Elwes had left behind, the incident caught the attention of Richard Ingrams, editor of *Private Eye*. In a full-page article headlined 'All's well that ends Elwes', the satirical magazine dissected the politics of Lucan's circle and, most crucially of all, alleged that Goldsmith had organised the obstruction of the law.

At the time the piece appeared Goldsmith's first thought was to do nothing about it. But when *Private Eye* followed it up with a second article linking him with the disgraced T. Dan Smith, who had been jailed for bribing councillors in the north-east, he decided action was called for. In Goldsmith's case, this did not mean a cold letter from his solicitors but a full scale legal assault of a like that the magazine – and the British media in general – had never seen before. There were not only 63 writs against *Private Eye* but a further 37 against its distributors. He also announced his intention to apply to the High Court for permission to bring proceedings for criminal libel, a method by which he could attempt to have the editor sent to jail.

By this stage, Goldsmith had no time for faint hearts. 'Jimmy became wilder and madder whenever I suggested he stop persecuting *Private Eye*,' said Anthony Blond, a director of Pressdram, publisher of *Private Eye*, and, incongruously, an old friend of Goldsmith. '"They have attacked my son," he said. "I will throw them into prison. I will hound their wives, even in their widows' weeds." Then he gripped my arm. It was quite anxious-making.'

By this time there were signs that the Establishment had turned against the *Eye*, which using contacts at the highest levels of the Church, Government, Press and Judiciary, had become a constant irritant to some of the most powerful people in the land. The news that Mr Justice Wien was prepared to allow Goldsmith's petition for criminal libel neverthless came as a source of surprise – and disquiet – to Richard Ingrams, the *Eye*'s editor.

Further proof of Goldsmith's success in penetrating the upper echelons of society came on 26 May 1976, with the publication of Harold Wilson's resignation honours list. It was, by any standards, the most extraordinary selection of candidates for ennoblement ever published. It was soon dubbed the Lavender List as it was said to have been written on lavender-coloured notepaper by Wilson's aide, Lady (Marcia) Falkender, who was the first secretary to a prime minister to be made a baroness by her boss.

The late George Hutchinson, writing in *The Times*, expressed something of the scorn that greeted the publication of the names: 'No honours list, resignation or otherwise, has ever been attended by such farce . . . No individual recipient, however deserving, can feel altogether happy. Who would wish for inclusion in a roll call giving rise to universal astonishment and derision?' The list included the Tory industrialist James Hanson, the crooked raincoat manufacturer Joseph Kagan, and the crooked property speculator Eric Miller. But one of the most surprising names of all to be found on this Labour prime minister's honours list was a man who was not only an avowed enemy of socialism but also a named contributor to Conservative Party funds, James Goldsmith, included for his services to 'exports and ecology'. The reasons mentioned in Goldsmith's citation, were if anything, more bizarre than the honour itself. Cavenham as a British-based retailer had no export trade to speak of and if anyone deserved recognition for work in the field of ecology it was his brother Teddy.

Furthermore, the relationship between Goldsmith and the prime minister dated back only a few months. According to Wilson's former press secretary Joe Haines, it was Lady Falkender who had first introduced the socialist premier to the red-blooded capitalist and she only succeeded in the face of some resistance from Wilson. 'In 1975 Marcia arranged through David Frost for Harold to have lunch or dinner with Goldsmith but when Harold saw it in his diary he blew his top,' recalls Haines. 'He asked the diary secretary how that had got into his diary and he was told that Lady Falkender had put it there. Harold said to me, "All my life I've attacked those who make money rather than earn money," and he said, "I can't be seen," it was Goldsmith and somebody else "I can't be seen to be having lunch with him so cancel it" and it was cancelled.'

That was not to be the end of the matter, however. By October, 1975, Goldsmith was chairman of Slater Walker and, to some extent, Wilson owed him. Mindful of the effect on City confidence if the full extent of the Slater Walker crisis became known, Wilson had blocked a full scale Department of Trade inquiry into the collapse. Perhaps he was grateful for Goldsmith coming to the rescue at a difficult time. In any event, the pair did eventually get together to discuss French planning procedures, a subject on which Wilson evidently found Goldsmith 'very impressive'. The two men also met in February 1976, when Frost invited both to dinner at his home. The guests on that occasion also included Lady Annabel Birley, Wilson's wife, Mary, and Lady Falkender. Goldsmith and Wilson may have found common cause in their antipathy to *Private Eye*. Wilson was no fan of the magazine which ran a feature called Mrs Wilson's Diary, a cruel send up of his poetry-loving wife's humdrum existence.

With Goldsmith in no mood to compromise, *Private Eye* began to respond in kind. Goldsmith's original battery of writs was soon countered by one from *Eye* writer Michael Gillard alleging slander by Goldsmith and John Addey, a City PR man. Then *Sunday Times* writer Philip Knightley joined the fray, issuing a writ for libel against Goldsmith in relation to the contents of an open letter he sent to editors following a piece Knightley wrote about the case. Gillard was to lose his case after pursuing it to the House of Lords. Knightley won his.

Meanwhile, behind the scenes, Peter Cook, the late comedian and owner of *Private Eye*, had decided to approach Goldsmith in a bid to resolve the matter. It got nowhere and Cook was later to say that he found Goldsmith one of the most unpleasant people that he had ever encountered.

On 30 July Richard Ingrams was eventually committed for trial at the Old Bailey on the criminal libel charge. Within a fortnight. Goldsmith had made his first attempt to have him jailed for contempt on the grounds that Ingrams had broken an undertaking not to mention him in the *Eye*. The judge refused, fining Ingrams, Gillard and the magazine £1,000 instead. Goldsmith's image was not helped by the revelation that private detectives employed by him had been ferreting through the magazine's rubbish bins in search of evidence.

The case continued for almost a year, each side fighting charge with counter charge, until in May 1977, it ended almost as suddenly as it had begun. Simon Jenkins, then editor of the *Evening Standard*, was keen to broker a deal which would clear the way to Goldsmith taking over Beaverbrook Newspapers and thus save his newspaper, which would be closed if a competitive bid from Lord Rothermere's Associated Newspapers went through. Given the aggression of Goldsmith's stance to date, the terms Jenkins conveyed to Ingrams amounted to virtual surrender. Goldsmith wanted costs of £30,000, an apology run as a full page ad in the *Evening Standard* and paid for by the *Eye* and an undertaking to meet for lunch or at least shake hands. Ingrams accepted with alacrity and a week later Ingrams and Patrick Marnham, the writer of the Elwes article, were formally acquitted.

Goldsmith never did satisfy his desire to meet Ingrams face to face, however. 'I was prepared to meet him but I had hysterical opposition from my wife who'd been with me throughout the case,' says Ingrams. 'She was absolutely horrified at the idea that I might meet him.' He rejects the suggestion that he was afraid that Goldsmith might assault him, saying: 'I think my wife was more likely to hit me than Goldsmith.' The couple have since parted.

Goldsmith may have extracted an apology from *Private Eye* but both his reputation and Cavenham's share price had taken a battering and he must have begun to consider at this stage the advantages of taking the company private so that it would no longer be vulnerable to the vagaries of public opinion.

In May 1976, Goldsmith made a £100 million bid for all the shares in Générale Alimentaire that it did not own. At the same time he raised Générale Occidentale's stake in Cavenham to just over 50 per cent but said he had no intention of bidding for the remainder of the company. Within seven months, however, he announced just such a bid. The fact that he broke his word so soon after giving it inflamed City opinion against him. His position was not helped by the fact that he was only prepared to offer 120p a share. Cavenham shares may have been trading at 95p at the time but they had stood at 230p as little as four years before and his offer was seen as derisory. 'Stop stamping your feet Jimmy and stump up your money,' said *The Economist*. Goldsmith responded with a tactical withdrawal. In February 1977, he called Peter Hill-Wood, his account manager at Hambros, from Barbados to tell him to drop the bid.

But he had not yet finished. In the months that followed he negotiated long and hard. If Goldsmith's plan was to succeed he needed the support of the Prudential, a key shareholder. After thrashing out a deal with its investment chief Ron Artus, Cavenham's shares were duly suspended and he eventually bid £40 million for 25 per cent of the shares. By now, the resistance had largely been broken and, as Cavenham's share price fell further to 80p, the remaining outside shareholders caved in and Goldsmith, through Générale Occidentale, soon owned Cavenham in its entirety. This made him the proud proprietor of a company employing 60,000 people with sales of £1.6 billion. On the retailing side it dwarfed both Sainsbury (turnover £535 million) and Tesco (turnover £617 million), and on the manufacturing side it was the third biggest food company in Europe, admittedly some way behind Unilever and Nestlé.

The man who had named his company after his grandfather's estate now had assets worth infinitely more than 5,000 acres of Suffolk.

Chapter Five

Citizen Goldsmith

THEY should have known it was a trap. Hugh Stephenson and James Bellini agreed later that the 'smirky smile' playing on Goldsmith's lips was the clue they failed to spot at the time. They had been told he was feeling nervous and as they chatted with the man they were about to interview they even made a special effort to put him at his ease. Stephenson might have been more suspicious if he had had a chance to compare notes with the programme's editor Paul Ellis. Goldsmith's PR man, sitting in the gallery, told him just before the countdown to transmission: 'I think you are going to enjoy this.'

What followed has gone down in history as one of the most notorious performances in the history of broadcasting. In the space of half an hour, two seasoned professionals who had been presenting a live show every week for months were left floundering by a relative amateur who proved himself a master of the soundbite and the crushing putdown.

Ask Stephenson how he remembers that television confrontation with Sir James Goldsmith on *The Money Programme* in November 1977 and he responds: 'Have you ever boxed? It's absolutely like that. You're caught on the ropes and you've got to take the blows. You've got a full round to go and all you can do is duck and weave.'

The genesis of the interview dated back to a private lunch given for Goldsmith at Broadcasting House on 22 June 1977. Present were Paul Ellis, David Graham, his producer, and Goldsmith himself. Cavenham had grown into the third largest food company in Europe in less than 13 years and *The Money*

91

Programme had decided it was time for an in-depth look at its meteoric rise and the man behind it. The lunch was the cue for an elaborate courtship ritual between Goldsmith and the BBC which was to drag on for two and a half months before closing in spectacular fashion. Goldsmith did not like John Roberts, the programme's choice of front man for a filmed report on his business to be shown the week before his own live interview, and refused to allow him access to his factories. He wanted guarantees about the programme's objectivity and, after agreeing to set aside two days for interviews with David Graham, ultimately refused to co-operate personally until the live interview.

The report on Cavenham, shown on 28 October 1977, was a hard-hitting critique of Goldsmith's whole approach to business. 'Sir James Goldsmith doesn't visit his factories much,' said Roberts, who presented the report standing outside one of the Goldsmith factories. 'He has become the financier. He leaves his managers to sort out the brands in the companies he buys. The strong national brands, shop names or products are kept and improved. The others are scrapped or sold.' The programme was screened at a time when 'asset-stripping' was at its height. In its purest form, the practice involved speculators identifying companies whose assets were worth more than the buying price. These would then be broken up, the work force made redundant and sold by their constituent parts, thus yielding a healthy profit to the speculator. Naturally, such behaviour attracted widespread public condemnation. The programme stopped short of calling Goldsmith an asset-stripper but the implication was clear.

Roberts also noted that Cavenham did not 'lavish money on its appearance', patching up old factories rather than investing in new ones. Nor was it innovative, he argued. 'It has grown to its present size without introducing a single major new product,' he claimed. 'It was not an originator or inventor. It is an improver of other people's work.' The programme also said that successful companies were sold to fuel expansion. It was all calculated to goad Cavenham's boss into a furious response but as he and Ellis worked out the ground rules for his response in the following week's programme Goldsmith was strangely calm. What Ellis didn't know was that an ingenious sting was being prepared.

Few knew more about the art of the television interview than

David Frost, who was then at the height of his powers, and it was he who was brought in by Goldsmith to coach him on how to turn the programme to his own advantage. Jim Slater, who had been on the very same programme weeks earlier, stressed to Goldsmith the importance of putting his case regardless of the question he was being asked. During one 'rehearsal', he interrupted Goldsmith saying: 'Don't answer the question, make the points you want to make.' But the most crucial demand of all, according to Frost, was that the programme be live. That way there would be no chance for the BBC to edit the interview in a manner which would favour the interviewers. Goldsmith was reassured that the Sunday repeat would be shown unedited too.

In a letter to Ellis dated 31 October 1977 – four days before he was due to be interviewed – he betrayed none of the righteous indignation he was to exploit to such good effect on the day. He began by saying that he had watched the first programme with 'great interest' and ran through the conditions they had agreed. These included advance notice of the first and last questions that would be addressed to him and that no one but he and the interviewers – Stephenson and Bellini – would participate in the programme. His most esoteric request ran as follows: 'You will attempt to let me have an upright chair rather than the sofa to sit on.'

But while Goldsmith had prepared himself scrupulously, Stephenson, gulled, he says, by a verbal assurance from Goldsmith that he was perfectly happy with the previous week's programme, did not even view Roberts' filmed report on Cavenham. It was a fatal mistake. From the outset, it was clear that Goldsmith intended to use his 35 minutes of air time to nail the criticisms broadcast the week before. He went on the attack straight away and soon two promising TV careers were being ruthlessly demolished. 'In those days none of us had earpieces so Bellini and I were stuck there with a live programme, with the clock going, and this sort of nuclear explosion happening in front of us,' recalls a rueful Stephenson, sitting at a formica-topped table in the common-room at London's City University, where he is now professor of journalism.

However uncomfortable the experience may have been for the interviewers, it made compulsive viewing in the country at large. *The Money Programme* was not a show which attracted a mass audience but the great Goldsmith debate propelled it up the ratings chart. Millions who would normally have dismissed it as a dry financial programme tuned in the following Sunday afternoon to watch the repeat. What made it different was the spectacle of two journalists being ritually humiliated by a charismatic businessman who was determined to give better than he got. The following exchange provides some flavour of how the proceedings degenerated.

> *Goldsmith*: 'The spirit of what you said is that we bought and sold companies, we dealt in companies, you just said it just now, did just that, buying and selling companies, that's what you said, isn't it?'
> *Bellini*: 'Well, at times they call you . . .'
> *Goldsmith*: 'Did you just say that just now? Did you just say it?'
> *Bellini*: 'They call you Mr Takeover in France.'
> *Goldsmith*: 'Did you just say it on this programme?'
> *Bellini*: 'It is my impression, Sir James, that you've made your reputation as a buyer and seller of companies.'
> *Goldsmith*: 'That is your impression. Not only is it your impression but it is exactly what you have just said on this programme. It is just that. Buying and selling companies. Can I agree that you said it?'
> *Bellini*: 'It is part of your . . .'
> *Goldsmith*: 'Can we agree that you said it?'

Goldsmith's approach was based on the premise that the previous week's report had told damaging lies about his company and his methods. First he accused the programme of showing film of the most run-down of all his factories, saying the shots of disused sheds at Colnebrook were 'as representative of Cavenham today as Henry Ford's original shed was of the Ford Motor Company'. The truth was, he claimed, that, far from cheese-paring, Cavenham was in the midst of a £237 million capital investment programme.

Next he turned to the charge that he made his money by buying and selling companies. He argued that in the 12 years Cavenham had been operating, he had sold companies with a combined turnover of just nine per cent of his current sales and retained 91 per cent. In the face of such number-crunching, the interviewers, who had gone into the programme under the impression that they were to have a general discussion about business philosophy, were helpless.

By now well ahead on points, Goldsmith turned to the allegation that he was nothing more than a financier who had never come up with an innovative product. 'I will try and explain to you what a new product is in the food industry,' he said. 'There are fundamental new products every decade in the food industry. After the war there were frozen foods, then there were instant foods, then there were frozen dry foods. These were great fundamental new leaps forward in basic research in food. The remainder is development and that is true for most industries.'

By this time, the temperature of the discussion had soared, and just as Goldsmith had accused *The Money Programme* of lying about his company, so Stephenson returned the compliment. Noting that Goldsmith had taken Cavenham private just seven months after saying that he had no intention of raising his holding in the company, Stephenson asked bluntly: 'I was really interested in why did you lie?'

Goldsmith responded by saying that he had changed his mind in the face of wholesale changes in the state of the economy. Interest rates had fallen from 15 per cent to five per cent in those seven months, he argued. The value of sterling had changed markedly and so had the stock market. It was the closest the interviewers got to pushing Goldsmith on to the back foot but he was not there for long.

One area where the interviewer is usually at an advantage is in knowing precisely how much time there is left to go and so he can tailor the end of the interview accordingly. Indeed, Goldsmith had his back to the studio clock. But here again he showed his shrewdness at the outset by removing his watch and placing it on the table in front of him so that he too knew exactly what the time was. With less than a minute to go he delivered his *coup de grâce*.

Bellini had said that shareholders who had spoken to *The Money Programme* had alleged that he had used their own money to buy them out.

> *Goldsmith*: 'But you know perfectly well that's nonsense

and so does Hugh Stephenson, he wrote it.'

Stephenson: 'I wrote that?'

Bellini: 'He didn't write that, that was an interview with a shareholder.'

Goldsmith: 'No wait a minute, Hugh Stephenson's own article in *The Times*, in which you said – my dear fellow, I'm delighted to quote it to you, I'm sure you haven't got much time, let me just quote it to you. The outcome – by you, that's what you said, this is on the fourth of August 1977 – is that shareholders who were in Cavenham before the partial offer in May "have effectively got a little over 155p for their entire holding. That is a price at which few would quibble." So what the devil are you quibbling about?'

Stephenson: 'The fourth of August, I was on holiday in Ireland.'

Goldsmith: 'You are editor of *The Times* business paper, aren't you?'

Stephenson: 'That's true, yes.'

Goldsmith: 'And this was signed by the Financial Editor of *The Times* and you are responsible for that?'

At this stage, Bellini intervened to bring the programme to an end and, with the credits still rolling, Goldsmith could be seen to get out of his seat and storm off only to be halted by his microphone wire. He stopped, detached it and walked off the set into the night. A job well done.

A letter from one viewer later described the interviewers as 'a couple of innocent schoolboys, who have not done their homework, in the arena with a man-eating tiger'.

Amid all the heat and light of Goldsmith's performance, however, it is tempting to overplay the extent to which he won the argument. Many of the criticisms of his approach to business jar in the post-Thatcherite era. After all, while he may have closed down factories and broken up acquisitions, he nevertheless ran a business with a workforce of 60,000 and sales of £7 million per trading day or £1.8 billion a year. But other points he made do not stand up to scrutiny. Enraged by the observation that he 'patched up' old factories rather than build new ones he repeatedly referred to a £237 million capital

Above: The young Jimmy Goldsmith dining out with the heiress Isabel Patino who was to become his first wife (© Topham)

Left: Goldsmith's leaving photograph from Eton

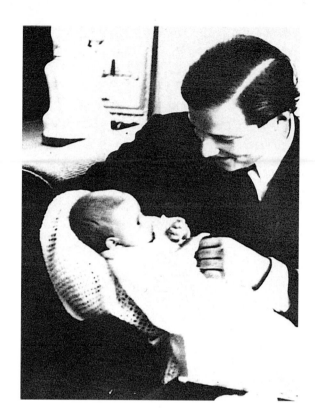

Goldsmith with his four-month-old daughter Isabel after a Paris court had ordered the Duchess of Durcal and her husband to return their grandchild to him in 1954 (© Press Association)

Opposite: The Duchess of Durcal, Goldsmith's first mother-in-law, who once pipped the Duchess of Windsor to the title of the world's best-dressed woman (© Topham)

Goldsmith arrives at the Savoy for the first anniversary dinner of the ill-fated *Now!* magazine in 1980 with Prime Minister Margaret Thatcher (© Press Association)

Opposite: Sally Crichton-Stuart, the mistress Goldsmith described as 'the most beautiful woman of her generation' (© Topham)

Above: A suitably attired Princess Diana arriving in Pakistan with Jemima Khan and Lady Annabel Goldsmith
(© Press Association)

Below: Goldsmith with his 'fan club', Lord Jacob Rothschild (left) and Australian media magnate Kerry Packer, at the launch of their bid for BAT in 1989
(© Press Association/Topham)

Imran Khan, Jemima and their baby son Suleiman with Princess
Diana in Lahore, three months before her death
(© Press Association/Topham)

Goldsmith's long-term mistress, Laure Boulay de la Meurthe (right),
with her aunt, the Comtesse de Paris (© Rex)

investment programme. In a damage-limitation memorandum to BBC bosses, Paul Ellis pointed out that the programme was something of a fig leaf: 'In the last financial year, additions to the fixed assets were £30 million. That is 1.8 per cent of Cavenham sales, low by comparison with most companies and no more than he had invested in each of the last five years *before* the investment programme is said to have started.'

To Goldsmith, however, his *Money Programme* experience only confirmed him in the belief that the media was a haunt of left-wingers and fifth columnists and the only way he could ever really expect to get a fair hearing was to own a newspaper himself. His first tack was to attempt to become a proprietor through acquisition. As a result he was linked with almost every important media sale that occurred in the '70s.

The first opportunity arose in 1976, when the Astor family, tired of throwing good money after bad, put *The Observer*, Fleet Street's ailing dowager, up for sale. The man at the centre of the negotiations was Lord Goodman, chairman of the trust that shared ownership of the paper with the Astor family, but, equally significantly, a close friend of the then prime minister, Harold Wilson. Rupert Murdoch pulled out of the lists early on after his interest was leaked and any interest Goldsmith might have had appeared to be stifled by Goodman, who was reported to have said that he would 'never' get hold of the paper.

Goldsmith, for his part, called Goodman to remonstrate with him, arguing that he had never put himself in the frame in the first place. By the time they ended their conversation, however, they had decided to meet for breakfast with the paper's editor David Astor, one of the owning family. The meeting went as well as it could have done. Astor asked him whether he could guarantee the paper's editorial independence. Goldsmith later claimed he said no but that he would only make a bid if he was invited to by the staff. To this end, he asked to meet a group of senior journalists. They, in turn, were equally keen to meet him to find out 'whether or not blood dripped off his fangs', as one put it to Geoffrey Wansell.

There was one not insignificant hurdle to be negotiated first. Goldsmith, who was in the midst of his libel battle with *Private Eye*, had also slapped a writ on *The Observer* over a front page story by Polly Toynbee that had alleged salt levels in Marmite – a

Cavenham product – exceeded safety levels and so were a danger to babies. 'He sued us for a million pounds, I think, in his usual exaggerated way,' recalls Donald Trelford, the editor at the time. 'When he approached me about meeting the journalists, I said I didn't see how I could meet him until we had resolved this matter and so he withdrew it. So the one permanent gain we got out of Goldsmith's bid for *The Observer* was that he had to drop his libel action.'

This little piece of unpleasantness resolved, a dozen *Observer* hacks were invited to dinner at Goldsmith's house on Tregunter Road, Chelsea. His efforts to charm the journalists backfired badly, however. When they sat down to eat, they found themselves presented by the butler with a bottle of claret apiece. Goldsmith claimed later that this was merely a reflection of his generous nature but many of the journalists saw it differently. 'He had obviously heard that journalists like to drink,' recalls Trelford. 'I actually thought this was rather convenient, as a matter of fact, better than somebody dashing round filling your glass. But my colleagues were rather outraged, they thought it was an insult to their profession you see. So he got off on the wrong foot there by trying to be nice.'

The incident only served to exacerbate an already high degree of hostility towards Goldsmith.

Apart from the Marmite episode, many of the journalists were resentful of his heavy-handed approach to *Private Eye* and were suspicious of a businessman who had a reputation for strong views, strongly held. *The Observer* had long benefited from a liberal, hands-off approach by management and the great fear was that a new proprietor would tamper with its much-vaunted editorial independence. It was at this stage, according to Trelford, that the conversation became 'farcical'.

'He could tell that there was a good degree of hostility and fear of him and therefore he maintained that he wouldn't interfere at all,' he says. 'I remember we got down to one example where he said, "Well, let's say that the property correspondent was writing about an area of London that I knew a lot about and he was talking nonsense, I'd feel entitled to say something." I thought, "This is getting ridiculous." I mean, the reality, as we all know, is that people who own newspapers feel they are entitled, and probably are entitled, to express opinions about them. I thought he was being disingenuous to a ridiculous degree. He was tip-toeing around the subject, giving assurances that he couldn't possibly, and probably had no intention of, honouring. John Cole [Trelford's deputy, later to become the political editor of BBC Television News] and I left laughing about the whole thing and putting it down as a marvellous evening's experience. We didn't take it as a serious bid because I knew about Goodman's attitude. It was just a rather fun evening really.'

Not surprisingly, Goldsmith's own explanation of why he failed to get *The Observer* differs markedly. According to him, when he got round to examining the paper's balance sheet, it did not make encouraging reading. When Roy Thomson moved *The Times* from the offices it had shared with *The Observer* and where the papers had been printed on the same presses for years, *The Observer* made the mistake of taking on the printworks itself, saddling a once-a-week periodical with a seven-day-a-week wages bill. In the days of the print unions' stranglehold over national press production, this was not a cost that could easily be changed. Goldsmith's interest flickered and died.

Within a few months, however, he had transferred his attentions to another newspaper group. And Beaverbrook Newspapers was an altogether different proposition to the declining *Observer*. With the *Daily* and *Sunday Express* and the *Evening Standard* in its stable it was then one of the most profitable media outfits around. Goldsmith's interest dated back to a drink with Rupert Murdoch in New York. Murdoch, keen to raise cash for his North American operations, asked him whether he would be interested in buying his stake in Beaverbrook. This amounted to just under a third of the non-voting 'A' shares for nearly £1.6 million. On the face of it, the investment was not an attractive one. Owners of non-voting shares had no power in the boardroom and could only hope that the management of the groups would be sufficiently sound to ensure a steady income from dividend payouts and a potential profit from selling the shares at a premium – a particular possibility given the rumours that the Aitken family were ready to sell the group. In the short term, however, what the Beaverbrook shares did was offer access to the people who ran the country, or 'a seat at the top table' as Murdoch is fond of putting it. A more seemingly fanciful notion, but one nevertheless advanced by Geoffrey Wansell, is that it was part of his war with *Private Eye*. By buying Murdoch's shares he was keeping them out of the hands of Lord Rothermere, owner of the *Daily Mail* in which Goldsmith's private life was regularly scrutinised by Nigel Dempster's daily gossip column.

Whatever his motivation, he duly bought the shares and made a grand entrance at a lunch at the Beaverbrook-sponsored Boat Show, where the guests included Margaret Thatcher, then the leader of the Opposition.

Turning his investment into commercial clout was to prove an uphill struggle for Goldsmith, however. Lord Goodman, someone whom Goldsmith had identified as a man with a mission to foil him at every turn, re-emerged as a key player in the Beaverbrook saga. Goldsmith blamed him for turning Sir Max Aitken, son of the group's founder, Lord Beaverbrook, against him.

If Goldsmith was in any doubt as to the scale of the task ahead he was disabused by an ill-tempered meeting with Beaverbrook executives at his merchant bankers' company flat on Wilton Terrace. Jocelyn Stevens, Beaverbrook's managing director, opened the proceedings by saying that Beaverbrook regarded his shareholding as hostile and that if he thought that *Private Eye* had it in for him, he should wait and see what the *Express* titles were capable of. According to Ivan Fallon, Goldsmith reacted by announcing that 'at the first hint of any personal attack he would launch his bid'.

Goldsmith was on holiday when Goodman brokered a deal between Beaverbrook and Associated Newspapers whereby Associated would buy the *Standard* to help Beaverbrook meet its cash shortage. That deal was sabotaged within weeks by a fresh approach from Goldsmith and then Tiny Rowland, the head of Lonrho, pitched in with a proposal to buy the *Standard*.

The two men eventually got together to structure a bid through 'Cavrho', a joint venture between Cavenham and Lonrho. This level of co-operation was a remarkable illustration of both men's ability to let bygones be bygones. Relations between them had been strained to say the least since Goldsmith had lost a £5,000 bet to Rowland on the result of the October 1974 general election after backing a Heath victory. Rowland claims Goldsmith took his time in paying up and when he eventually did so it was in the form of a cheque from his St James's club. The ill-will that the transaction created was vividly displayed two years later when the mischievous Lonrho chief contributed an identical sum to *Private Eye*'s Goldenballs libel fund.

For weeks, the Cavrho offer remained the best bid on the table until Murdoch weighed in with a superior offer in June and Goldsmith bowed out. Rowland, however, recalls things differently. He said their deal foundered after a 10 a.m. phone call from Goldsmith on 26 June 1977. After agreeing to join Rowland in a £15 million bid to be launched the very next day, Goldsmith told him he was short of cash and asked if Rowland might lend him two, or two and a half million pounds. The Lonrho boss's contemporaneous account of the conversation records his response as: 'My dear Jimmy. If I lend you two million or two and a half million pounds, your word is good enough – pay me back when you can and, if it means in 12 or 18 months' time or whatever, that is good enough, as far as I am concerned.'

Rowland departed for the Sudan on a business trip the very next day but when he returned he found that Goldsmith had not made the agreed bid and the position was 'pretty well lost'. He was upset further to hear that Goldsmith was expressing some doubt over whether he would be sharing with 'his partner' the £1.8 million profit he had made on the sale of his shares to Trafalgar House, the group that emerged triumphant in the battle for Beaverbrook. Rowland took the view that Goldsmith's Beaverbrook shares should have been added to Lonrho's stake and, after allowing for costs and interest payments, the profit divided between the two parties on the basis that they were 50-50 partners.

'I was shattered,' he recorded in his notes, 'and, in the circumstances, accepted his suggestion that Jim Slater and John Tigrett should act as umpires.' Slater must never have felt a greater division of loyalties. Goldsmith may have been a close friend but just three years earlier Rowland had been the man to bail him out of his impending bankruptcy following the Slater Walker crash. On the other hand, Tigrett was very much a Goldsmith man. In the event, Rowland's view prevailed.

One of the most interesting sub-plots to arise out of Goldsmith's bids for *The Observer* and Beaverbrook, however, was his confrontation with Goodman. The product of an Eastern European Jewish upbringing, Goodman had risen to head one of the country's most respected law firms, Goodman Derrick. He became a close confidant to three prime ministers of different political hues and, when he and Goldsmith tangled in the late '70s, Goodman was master of University College, Oxford, as well as being chairman of the trust that funded Harold Wilson's office. Throughout his life – he died in 1996 – he retained a reputation as the consummate fixer, a man with a peerless range of contacts who wielded enormous informal power. It was power he used to foil Goldsmith at every turn. His most naked ploy came a week before the publication of Harold Wilson's resignation honours list in 1976. The Scrutiny Committee, which vets all candidates, had queried three nominees: the boxing promoter Jarvis Astaire, Joseph Kagan, the manufacturer of the Gannex raincoat, and James Goldsmith. Some inkling of its misgivings had reached Harry Evans, the editor of the *Sunday Times*. He duly approached Goodman as someone who might be able to firm up the story. Goodman, who was appalled at some of the names put forward – Goldsmith's in particular – duly leaked what he knew in a bid to build up a head of steam against Goldsmith's ennoblement. The *Sunday Times* story that subsequently appeared fell short of naming the individuals involved but the *Daily Express* obliged soon afterwards by splashing a rather different story across its front page with the headline, 'It's Lord Goldsmith'. In fact, it wasn't and never was to be. Joe Haines, Wilson's confidant and Press secretary, who saw the list two months before it was published, confirms that Goldsmith was, in fact, never up for a peerage. And when the official list appeared on 26 May, it emerged that Goldsmith was a mere knight.

Quite why Goodman bore such a grudge against Goldsmith – whom he does not dignify with a single mention in his memoirs despite their significant dealings – has never been made clear. They had their political differences but both were wealthy members of the Jewish establishment. One theory is that Goodman, a passionate Zionist, saw Goldsmith as a liability to the cause. Others trace Goodman's enmity to his close friendship with Max (Lord) Rayne, arguing that Rayne, through his marriage to Lady Annabel Goldsmith's sister Jane, had been turned against Goldsmith because of his philandering ways and had influenced Goodman accordingly. A third explanation is that

Goodman saw Goldsmith as a member of the 'Marfia'. This was the name given to the circle around Lady Marcia Falkender, Wilson's political and private secretary, who was seen as offering an alternative route to power and patronage. Goodman saw such people as the enemy within, whose ambitions were to be blocked at every opportunity. Indeed, Goodman told Haines at a dinner at his house in December 1995: 'But for that woman [Marcia] Harold would have gone down as a great prime minister.' Goodman's opposition would have infuriated Goldsmith, who, perhaps for the first time, had met his match. He responded in a way that can only be described as devious.

Bruce Page, a freelance journalist with a distinguished track record as head of the *Sunday Times* Insight team, was surprised to get a call from Goldsmith's PR man one day late in 1977. It was an invitation to lunch with the great man, an offer that Page could see no reason to refuse. He made his way to a duplex in the Barbican for what was obviously intended to be a discreet meeting. The meal passed pleasantly enough but it was not until his PR advisor had left that Goldsmith came to the point. 'What do you think about Arnold Goodman?' he asked. Page replied that he thought he was 'not as nice' as people thought he was and that he had little time for the routine process of law. He repeated a story he had recently been told about how Goodman had made it his business to ruin two young men who were suspected of introducing the son of one of his clients to drugs. This evidently struck a chord with Goldsmith who then asked whether Page would write a book about Goodman. Page, a little thrown by the question, pointed out that nobody had asked him to and asked what Goldsmith was proposing.

At this stage, Goldsmith obviously felt it wise to cover his back. 'I want to stress that I have nothing against Arnold at all,' he told Page. 'In fact, I rather admire him but I think his power is not properly understood in this country.' He went on to offer to cover all Page's research costs, to indemnify him against any legal action, and to pay him a fee if he would agree to go ahead and write the book. Page, uncomfortable about Goldsmith's unwillingness to specify what Goodman had done to him, refused the offer. 'He was charming and, in some respects, very intelligent, but clearly quite unscrupulous,' he recalls.

In the midst of his fruitless acquisition battles on one side of the Channel, Goldsmith pulled off a more painless coup on the other. And the prize was by no means insignificant. *L'Express* is the daily paper-turned-full-colour news weekly that changed the face of French publishing. Within a decade of its launch in the early '50s it had established itself as the authoritative voice of the liberal left. Circulation had peaked at 614,000 in 1973 but, according to Goldsmith, when he bought 45 per cent of Groupe Express for £3.6 million in 16 March 1977, circulation had declined to 490,000.

In many ways it was just the sort of magazine Goldsmith should have despised most of all. But it appears to have appealed to his sense of crusading zeal. After all, if he could tame this organ of the left and harness it to the conservative cause then he would be performing a service for the French people. That, at least, appears to have been his thinking at the time. 'I bought *L'Express* out of a consuming political passion but not a personal political passion [*sic*],' he said. 'I wasn't seeking office and high profile in France. I had that without seeking it. I realised that I could make a decent profit, but the reality is I ran it not as a business, I ran it to pay anything I could to get rid of the people I didn't agree with ideologically, to try and bring in the people we wanted.'

It cannot be denied that *L'Express* had its elements of loony leftery. On one occasion, executives were even sent to the former Yugoslavia to learn about 'newspaper management'!

But Goldsmith was not so driven by doctrine that he failed to see the importance of proceeding with caution. An overnight sea change in the magazine's political stance would have been disastrous in circulation terms. With this in mind, one of his first hirings as a columnist was Olivier Todd, a distinguished editor with the socialist *Nouvel Observateur*.

Despite their political differences, the two men formed a close working relationship. 'As far as I'm concerned, I think we lived with a permanent misunderstanding due to the fact that we both spoke French and English, which creates an artificial type of complicity,' says Todd, himself an Anglo-French graduate of both the Sorbonne and Cambridge and a former BBC presenter. 'Also, I didn't really mind telling him how I felt. I sense that he rather belongs to that category of very powerful people who want to have their way but who like to have one or two buffoons who tell them to go to hell, which I did.'

So why did Goldsmith want *L'Express*? 'He said he was tired of being a grocer and he was interested in news,' says Todd. 'My opinion is that he wanted power but he's a bit ambivalent about it. There is a question mark. Did he have political ambitions to become a minister? I think he got more interested in being able to apply pressure. It's obvious that if you own *L'Express*, you are much more powerful than a minister, junior or not.'

If Todd is philosophical about his time with Goldsmith, Jean-François Revel, a close friend of Todd and director of *L'Express* at the time of Todd's editorship, is less so. In his book of memoirs, *Le Voleur dans la Maison Vide* (*The Thief in the Empty House*), Revel portrays his former boss as a Jekyll and Hyde character, liable to fly into furies at any time but capable of sending the sweetest of billets doux when he sought to restore morale. He argues that while Goldsmith was clever – indeed, a 'lively, pleasant, spiritual' man – he had an attention span of five to six seconds and a ferocious temper. So frequent were the arguments and the arbitrary changes of mind that Revel used to imagine Goldsmith as a thoroughbred horse on which he would bet in vain. Its name? 'Mad Captain'.

'I think journalism is probably one of his very big disappointments,' says Todd. 'It's probably the only field in which he lost money.' That is certainly true of the disastrous launch of *Now!* Having failed in his attempts to acquire an established title in the UK, Goldsmith resolved to launch one of his own. Designed as an English version of *L'Express* but without the bleeding heart element, it was set up on the grand scale. The man he picked as editor was an assistant editor and columnist of *The Sun*, Anthony Shrimsley. It may sound an improbable choice but Goldsmith took his lead from Rupert Murdoch who had told him that if he had bought *The Observer* he would have made Shrimsley editor. Recruiting the other 73 journalists was not so easy. Many were sceptical about the prospects of a weekly news magazine in a market dominated by daily and Sunday newspapers and others were not prepared to work for the man who had dragged *Private Eye* through the courts.

His choice of managing director was unorthodox to say the least. Tony Fathers had been responsible for the dietary breads Slimcea and Procea until they were sold in 1975 and after that had worked for Bovril and on a marketing project for French cheese. But then Goldsmith refused to accept that there was anything unique about newspapers. He once told Bruce Page: 'Good God, do you think newspapers are difficult? You're talking to a man who's been in the grocery business. It's unbelievable. You buy all these commodities all over the bloody world, you make them up into Marmite, you stick them into stores then finally after about two years in the pipeline you get some money back. Newspapers seem pretty straightforward. You buy some paper, stick some marks on it and sell it the next day.'

He told Ivan Fallon that he bid for Beaverbrook 'out of anger' with newspapers. Anger not at criticisms of himself and his business practices but at those who had attacked his children and his family. This is never a sound premise for newspaper ownership, argues Page. 'I don't think Goldsmith is completely stupid but I don't think he could see that running a newspaper meant that you just had to put up with lots of these ghastly journalists writing all sorts of rubbish about you and your friends,' he says. 'You have to do that in order to get people to read it. And not only did you have to publish all this rubbish about you and your friends, but you weren't allowed to use it to write straightforward sterling stuff about people who were getting in the way of you and your friends.'

There was a vivid example of this syndrome when, at the beginning of 1981, *L'Express* published an article critical of Valery Giscard d'Estaing's chances in the forthcoming French presidential election. The article so infuriated Goldsmith, a close friend of the then president, that he ordered the entire issue to be pulped. Unfortunately, copies had already gone out to newsagents in the UK but he succeeded in preventing copies being sent to France or anywhere else in Europe.

Goldsmith maintained that he halted distribution on principle because he hated the sort of journalism that relied on unsubstantiated smears but it seems clear that he had a soft spot as far as Giscard was concerned. After all, it was a controversial *L'Express* cover portraying a clearly demoralised Giscard watching a television screen showing François Mitterrand in rumbustious form that incensed Goldsmith and led to the departure of managing editor Olivier Todd and the subsequent resignation of the magazine's director Jean-François Revel.

With the staff in a state of near revolt, Goldsmith went for the confrontational approach. 'You really fuck me off,' he told them, according to Revel. He informed them that he was now editor-in-chief and anyone who was not prepared to accept him should resign. He added that he was quite prepared to close the magazine if there was any trouble. In the event, 20 journalists went. 'For Jimmy to have been happy with his acquisition, *L'Express* would have had to be the faithful image of a world that did not exist, a world such as he wished for but which was not like that,' wrote Revel in his memoirs.

Now!'s first anniversary dinner on 14 September 1980 was one of the media events of the year. The prime minister, Margaret Thatcher, was the guest of honour and her speech was televised live. The magazine itself, however, did not live up to its publicity. Goldsmith had envisaged an agenda-setting weekly which would be required reading in the corridors of power but by the end of its first year it was clear that in these terms it was a failure. Nor was it a popular success. The first issue had been a sell out, with 400,000 copies sold but as time went on circulation dropped drastically and *Private Eye*, which had ridiculed the magazine from the outset, published damaging estimates of its true sales figures. *Now!*'s closure was finally announced on Monday, 27 April 1981 when its circulation stood at 119,000 copies. Eighty journalists were made redundant and total losses of the venture were eventually put at £10 million.

Meanwhile, Goldsmith's French holding company, Générale Occidentale, was in deep trouble. By 1978, shareholders who had resisted the temptation to bail out a few years earlier had finally had enough. The Prudential, which had succumbed to the charm of Madame Beaux at the time of the previous crisis in 1975, was determined to sell out this time, and disposed of 33,400 shares at a loss in April. By September, Renault was also determined to unload its 100,000 shares but agreed to hold off on condition Goldsmith undertook to buy them out by July 1980. There was more bad news in December when Hambros, which had long been a solid supporter of Goldsmith, reduced its nine per cent holding by selling 170,000 shares worth around £5.2 million.

By now, the only companies prepared to invest in Générale Occidentale were those companies controlled by Goldsmith himself. Prime among these was Argyle Securities, the British property company, which built up a 30 per cent stake. In April

1978, it had bought a Hong Kong investment company called General Oriental. When Argyle sold its property interests to Cavenham for £18.8 million in cash and raised a loan to acquire a further 17 per cent of Occidentale, it was clear that control of the group was heading inexorably from Paris to Hong Kong. The French authorities witnessed these developments with some alarm. While many governments consider a major car manufacturer a key measure of economic virility, the French, it appears, counted a competitor to the Swiss Nestlé and the American Unilever as an important symbol of strength. This would at least go some way towards explaining the dramatic events of 15 March 1979 when France's largest private electrical company, Compaignie Générale d'Electricité, announced an investment of £7 million in Occidentale. It was, to all intents and purposes, a rescue operation. As one business magazine observed: 'The industrial logic of a marriage between telephone exchanges and mustard is not obvious.' What it did do, however, as Goldsmith explained to a packed press conference of 60 journalists, was give Occidentale a firmer 'anchorage' in France.

One of Goldsmith's most remarkable characteristics was his ability not only to mastermind the most complex of deals but to flit from one industrial sector to another. He began in pharmaceuticals, switched to food and went on to run a huge financial services empire in Slater Walker. But perhaps his most impressive display of flexibility was his move into the oil business. It was the irrepressible Madame Beaux who first told him about an eccentric American oilman called John Park. He had discovered oil in a remote part of Guatemala and had set up Basic Resources International, a joint venture with the French oil giant Société Nationale Elf Acquitaine. Park held 75 per cent of the shares, Elf had 25 per cent but he was still touting for funds to build a pipeline to the coast, 125 miles away. The enterprise caught Goldsmith's imagination and, after flying to Central America with Park and his new mistress Laure Boulay de la Meurthe, he agreed to invest $5 million.

As the overheads rose, Goldsmith nevertheless retained his fascination in the project and he willingly injected a further $25 million. By now, Guatemala's military government had cottoned on to the fact that Park's find could be worth more than $3 billion and were determined to renegotiate their initial deal. The

American accepted that he had no alternative but to parley with the generals and after some hard bargaining it was agreed that the government would take 55 per cent of revenues and Elf would have 20 per cent of the joint venture and would become the operating company responsible for actually getting the oil out of the ground. Park was unhappy with the new deal but Goldsmith, who by now had become chairman of Basic, was content to be a passive investor.

All might have been well if Elf had not been greedy. Ivan Fallon, who had unprecedented access to Goldsmith and his papers, recounted an extrordinary tale of corporate malpractice. One of the clauses in its contract with Basic, Fallon explained, was that if Park and Goldsmith failed to come up with their 80 per cent share of the operating costs, they would be in default and Elf would inherit their revenues. With this in mind, the French company systematically set about sabotaging its drilling operation: tools would be dropped into wells, equipment would break down, even wells would be lost. At first, this strategy had the desired effect. In 1981, Goldsmith and Park were unable to fund the cost overrun caused by Elf's 'inefficient' drilling and were forced to give up 23 per cent of their equity. At this stage, Goldsmith refused to believe Park's allegation that Elf was sabotaging the operation but as more and more rumours reached him about Elf's motivation Goldsmith was forced to accept that he was being stitched up.

When Elf produced a second revised budget at the end of 1981, Park refused to accept it. This was just what the French giant wanted to hear. Now it was in a position to claim that Basic was in default and it should take on the entire concession. But Goldsmith, by now committed to the tune of $90 million, was not about to cave in. With the same energy he had brought to his legal battle with *Private Eye*, he set about fighting for damages of $294 million through the courts in both Guatemala and the US and through the International Chamber of Commerce in Berne.

When a judge in Houston ordered Elf to produce all relevant documentation, the company refused and attempted to destroy crucial papers by sending them to a refuse dump. Unfortunately for the French, Goldsmith's private detectives were tailing them and no sooner were the papers consigned to the pit than they were recovered by the opposition. It was at this stage that things turned really nasty and Goldsmith was told to remember the fate that befell a man called Mattei, the boss of an Italian oil company who was killed in a suspicious plane crash. In the presence of the bearer of the warning, Goldsmith promptly telephoned a friend who was a senator and told him the whole story.

By now, Elf had been totally out-manoeuvred and when Goldsmith's lawyers succeeded in serving subpoenas on senior executives as they checked in to the Meridian Hotel in Houston, Elf's chairman sued for peace. The resulting out-of-court settlement was a stunning victory for Goldsmith. He received what he reckoned to be the largest pay-out in French legal history, $130 million, and the promise of royalties of 80 cents on every barrel produced from the Guatemalan oil field for the next 20 years. Elf refuses to confirm or deny any of the above, taking refuge in a confidentiality agreement signed with Goldsmith at the time the case was settled.

Goldsmith consistently tried to present himself as an industrialist rather than a financier: someone who built businesses as opposed to a glorified asset-stripper who had little time for running companies once profits had been taken on the disposal of subsidiaries. There might have been a time during the '70s when Cavenham employed tens of thousands of people in food manufacturing when such a self-image would have been justified. But, in 1979, Goldsmith turned native, broke up Cavenham in a matter of months and emigrated to the US with the proceeds to become one of the most feared corporate raiders of the '80s.

The dismantling of Cavenham must count as one of the speediest corporate break-ups in business history. First to go was Bovril. Beecham paid £42 million in cash for the company for which Goldsmith had paid £7 million after selling off the parts he did not want. French, Swedish, Austrian, Spanish and Belgian interests soon followed suit and by March 1980, Goldsmith was sitting on a £100 million fortune. Goldsmith's defence of this abrupt deconglomeration was that he was only doing what any predatory raider would have done.

The growth of Grand Union in the US had helped turn Cavenham into the third largest retailer in the world behind Safeway and Kroger with sales of £3 billion and conventional wisdom dictated that there was no synergy between distribution and manufacturing. In the modern high street, it was best to shop around for stock. Manufacturing had also become a relatively trivial element of his business. In 1980, retailing accounted for 93 per cent of his sales and 80 per cent of his profit, while manufacturing was responsible for just 7 per cent of turnover and a measly 1 per cent of profit.

The centrepiece of his business was now Grand Union, the company in which he had bought a controlling share for $62 million in 1973. Then it was the tenth largest supermarket chain in the US with sales of £1.5 billion from 600 shops but it was in decline. Over the years he added hundreds more stores in the US. In 1978, he paid $133 million for the 359-strong Colonial chain of supermarkets and a little over a year later he added the 100 stores of the Texan Weingarten group.

At this stage the group was a mess. Grand Union itself had no unifying culture. While its more successful competitors concentrated on developing a brand image which was consistent nationwide, Grand Union outlets ranged from hypermarkets to convenience stores, expensive stores selling high-quality lines such as chemical-free vegetables to discount shops competing at the lower end of the market. The way Goldsmith and his associates turned Grand Union into an innovative and upmarket chain of supermarkets has gone down in corporate history as one of the most impressive examples of enhanced competitiveness on record. Milton Glaser, the man who invented the much-copied 'I love New York' slogan which used a red heart symbol in place of the word 'love', was drafted in to redesign the chain's house labels and packaging. But he was soon involved in a much wider-ranging restructuring. After a successful trial in New York, Goldsmith resolved to concentrate on what he called 'real food': organic produce along the lines of free-range eggs and beef from a ranch that used no hormones. In-store piazzas broke up the rows of shelving and helped create a light and airy atmosphere. Delicatessens offered a fresh alternative to the pre-packaged goods available in the rest of the shop. Spice centres based on the souks Goldsmith had seen on holidays with Annabel in north Africa were introduced and aquaria with exotic live fish were installed to amuse children. The company started off hiring trained bakers to prepare fresh-baked bread but soon discovered that they tended to be prima donnas about their craft and decided to train clerks to do the job instead. A rewards system distributed gold, silver and bronze crowns to the most diligent employees, with the worker of the month being treated to a dinner with his or her spouse.

This was a concept, however, that would only work on a relatively limited scale and so Goldsmith authorised a dramatic downsizing of the chain from 800 to 300 stores. Between 1981 and 1983 sales plunged from £4 billion to £3.5 billion and losses rose to $10 million a month. Salvation came in the form of Floyd Hall, a hardbitten retailing professional of 45. After leaving school at 15 he had worked his way up the hard road to become chief executive of Target Stores. Goldsmith offered him $1 million a year and a slice of the profits, promising him he would make $30 million in five years. In the event, he made $60 million in three after reducing Grand Union's complement of stores to 379 by 1985 and raising profits to $60 million as sales dropped to £2.6 billion.

With this crisis averted, Goldsmith embarked on a series of takeovers in the US which would dwarf the acquisitions he had made in Europe. Goldsmith's first takeover target was the relatively unglamorous Diamond Corporation, the company that had introduced the safety match to America a century before. In the decades since it had diversified into paper plates for the fast food industry, playing cards and speciality papers. This had helped it grow to the point where its sales stood at $1.2billion but profits were low. Its great attraction for Goldsmith lurked unnoticed in the balance sheet. The 1.6 million acres of forest that provided the raw material for many of the company's products had not been revalued since 1900 and were listed as being worth $27 million when their real value was much, much higher. Four years later they were to be valued at $723 million. In 1979, Goldsmith began buying stock in earnest.

It was his aggressive approach and the furious reaction of Diamond's chairman William Koslo that made the battle something of a *cause célèbre*. Both sides took out law suits against the other, Koslo hired private detectives to delve into Goldsmith's antecedents, and the *Wall Street Journal* discovered to its surprise just how wealthy the predatory limey really was. It noted that he held a 30 per cent share in Trocadero Participations, the company that controlled Générale Occidentale, a private French group with revenues of $6 billion a year.

Despite his assets, however, Goldsmith was becoming overstretched. Grand Union's restructuring was costing him $120 million a year, and his Guatemalan adventure was haemorrhaging cash. Goldsmith needed a friendly bank. While he had seen the potential in Diamond's undervalued forest holdings, no bank would accept them as collateral for a loan without gaining some assurance as to their real value. What Goldsmith needed was a company which would guarantee to buy the forests for a certain fee should his bid succeed. While it would not oblige him to sell at that price it would reassure the bank. In the event, the Travellers Insurance company, for a fee of $12.5 million, agreed to pay $250 million and Citibank agreed to lend him the cash required.

In all, Goldsmith had to borrow $660 million at a time when interest rates were running at between 16 and 18 per cent. With his interest bill running at around $2.5 million a week, he could not afford to hang around. But it was not until December 1982, that Goldsmith finally gained the shareholder acceptances he needed and he could begin the sell-offs that would enable him to repay his huge loans. The delay was damaging from the point of view of his interest bill but it benefited him to the extent that it allowed the stock market rally he had predicted to gather pace. Within months he had raised $334 million from the sale of six divisions and by the end of 1983 another three had gone for $353 million. He was to hold on to the 1.6 million acres of forest for some years but the valuation of $723 million put on them in the summer of 1983 established that he had made a paper profit of $500 million. The deal confirmed Goldsmith as one of the names to be reckoned with in the American takeover game.

The Diamond deal had also turned Goldsmith into a logger and he was now aware that if he could increase his timber holdings to ten million acres he could become one of the leading players in a raw material sector which still had a vital role to play in the national economy. In the circumstances, the St Regis Corporation was a natural target. It had no less than 3.2 million acres of timberland and, like Diamond, this was grossly undervalued in its books at $223 million. After the white-knuckle ride of the Diamond deal, however, Goldsmith decided to adopt a more cautious approach to fund-raising. Instead of calling on the banks with their high interest rates, he formed a partnership with Jacob

Rothschild, Kerry Packer, the Australian media magnate, and Gianni Agnelli, whose family owns Fiat. Between them they bought more than three million St Regis shares, nearly nine per cent of the total, in February 1984.

After abortive talks both sides offered to buy out the other, with Goldsmith going so far as to organise financing for a $1.8 billion deal which rated the company at $52 a share. St Regis chairman William R. Haselton called his bluff, offered $52 a share in return, and Goldsmith and his millionaires' club accepted. They may not have got the company but for a month's work they collected a profit of $51 million.

In Wall Street parlance, this was 'greenmail'. The Diamond deal had made Goldsmith a man to be reckoned with in corporate America. No company chairman could afford not to take his calls and if he did decide to start buying stock, he could not be ignored. He was now in a game where fortune favoured the brave. If a bid failed, the probability was that the share price had been inflated in the heat of battle and the predator could dispose of his shares for a handsome profit. If the management came up with an offer he couldn't refuse – greenmail – he could console himself with the thought that while he hadn't gained his prize he had earned a fat fee.

Goldsmith vigorously denied the charge of greenmail in relation to his bid for St Regis but when he gave his own definition of a greenmailer in a court deposition a few years later, it bore a striking resemblance to his behaviour on that occasion: 'If a company or an individual buys shares of a company with the specific purpose of frightening management so as to put management into using corporate funds to protect their position by buying back that block at unusually favourable terms, then I would call that person a greenmailer.' Goldsmith would presumably have claimed that it had not been his 'specific purpose' to frighten the management.

Three months after the St Regis settlement Goldsmith and his 'fan club' were back in the ring. The company in their sights was the $5 billion-a-year turnover Continental Group. Its core activities were can-making and packaging but it had diversified into insurance, oil and gas. Naturally, it also had 1.4 million acres of undervalued timberland.

This time there were no half measures. On 5 June 1984, the

syndicate made a bid of $50 a share, valuing the company at $2.12 billion. Unlike St Regis's Haselton, Continental's chief executive S. Bruce Smart – later to become President Reagan's undersecretary at the department of commerce – immediately went in search of a white knight to rescue it from its challenger. He effectively put his company up for auction.

Goldsmith and his partners raised their bid first to $55 a share and then to $58 but when a rival bidder offered just 50 cents a share more they pulled out of the race. It was an uncharacteristic loss of nerve on Goldsmith's part. The successful team, Peter Kiewit, a mining and construction company, and David Murdock, a financier, went on to do exactly what Goldsmith had proposed. (This is not surprising as Kiewit had initially been a partner in Goldsmith's bid.) After selling off what Goldsmith would describe as 'inappropriate diversifications' – interests in insurance and paper products, a gas pipeline, petroleum reserves and other non-core activities – Kiewit was left with the core can and packaging company and the undervalued forests for a net outlay of $200 million. Goldsmith's return of $35 million was small beer by comparison.

By now Goldsmith's detractors were beginning to see him as a greenmail specialist. This view was reinforced later in 1984 when he took a five per cent stake in Colgate-Palmolive only to pull out with a profit of $30 million after another very public struggle.

His next bid was to be more successful but it also turned out to be the most acrimonious. In Goldsmith's eyes, Crown Zellerbach was yet another company which had turned itself into an unwieldy conglomerate through a series of unsound acquisitions. And there was the usual tranche of undervalued timberland.

Like Diamond, Crown Zellerbach had a long pedigree stretching back 115 years. When Goldsmith announced his intention to buy up to 20 per cent of the company's shares in December 1984, Crown Zellerbach's chairman William T. Creson made it clear the bid was not welcome. Although the company had reported a $100 million loss in 1982, the year he took over, Creson felt he had made good progress in turning the company round to the extent that it was back in the black by the time Goldsmith announced his bid.

For a time it looked as if Goldsmith's bid might end in the same way as his offer for Continental. The Mead Corporation announced a friendly merger with Crown which valued the company at $50 a share. This would have meant a healthy profit not only for Goldsmith but for Ivan Boesky, the notorious arbitrageur who was later jailed, who had his own 7.4 per cent shareholding in Crown. With the shares trading in the market at $33.25, however, the Mead board rejected the deal as overpriced. Goldsmith resumed his share buying and by May had 19.6 per cent of Crown's shares.

By now he was a whisker away from triggering Crown Zellerbach's 'poison pill' defence mechanism. This was a complex financial instrument designed to deter predators. Once a bidder breached the 20 per cent share ownership barrier, the poison pill was activated and if the bidder went on to bid for 100 per cent of the shares, the company could issue new shares and charge the interloper double. The snag was that this condition applied to white knights too and when Goldsmith made it clear that he would take his holding over 20 per cent Creson had no alternative but to negotiate. After a series of ill-tempered negotiations between Goldsmith and the Crown board, and Creson in particular, Goldsmith got what he wanted: 1.9 million acres for less than $100 an acre, $90 million in cash and $330 million in other assets. Wall Street later estimated that he made a paper profit of between $340 million and $440 million.

The executive brought in to merge Crown and Diamond's forestry interests was Al Dunlap, a man Goldsmith was to call 'my Rambo in pinstripes'. The former executive officer of a nuclear missile base had made a small fortune by reviving the fortunes of Lily-Tulip, a paper cup business languishing on the edge of bankruptcy. He performed similar miracles with Crown Zellerbach. It had made a profit of $25 million in 1985 but within five years this had risen to $130 million.

By now, Goldsmith was seriously rich.

After four years in which he had made more money than he had made in all his years in England and France, Goldsmith geared himself for his most ambitious bid to date. The Goodyear Tire and Rubber Company was the 35th biggest company in the US with a turnover of $10 billion. Active in 28 countries, it employed no fewer than 133,000 workers.

Goldsmith made his move on 25 September 1986, when

Merrill Lynch, the merchant bank, bought 1.7 million shares on his behalf at $33 apiece. It was not until a month later that Goldsmith was unmasked as the mystery buyer and the share price spiralled to $48 in anticipation of a hard-fought takeover when Goodyear chairman Robert Mercer made it clear that he did not welcome his new shareholder.

After exploratory talks between Goldsmith and Goodyear executives, Mercer agreed to meet Goldsmith for lunch at his brownstone on 80th Street in New York. He later described it as 'the most expensive lunch I've ever had'. By 31 October Goldsmith had acquired 11.5 per cent of Goodyear's shares at a cost of $530 million. This time round he had recruited two of the biggest names in British business as his co-conspirators, James Hanson and Gordon White of Hanson (both later made peers). Within a week he was in a position to tell Mercer that he would be making an offer for the remaining 88.5 per cent of Goodyear stock for $49 a share, a bid that valued the company at $4.7 billion.

Mercer's first ploy was to pull the rug from under his opponent by adopting just the sort of policy that Goldsmith was advocating. The board agreed to sell off its Celeron oil and gas company, and dispose of its aerospace division, manufacturer of the famous Goodyear airships. Both men accepted that this would push the share price above Goldsmith's offer price of $49. At this stage, Goldsmith agreed to a two-week stand-off. It was to prove a fatal mistake. Mercer used the breathing space to put in place one of the most effective public relations campaigns of its type ever staged. Everyone from senators to schoolchildren was mobilised in an attempt to present Goldsmith as an unscrupulous raider who would turn Akron, Ohio, Goodyear's company town, into a ghost town. 'Within days, we had an astonishing whip-up of hatred and emotion,' Goldsmith once said. 'We had Ohio schoolchildren chanting anti-Goldsmith songs and making anti-Goldsmith masks and sending me hate mail.'

There were dramatic scenes in Washington when Goldsmith arrived to give evidence at a meeting of a sub-committee of the House of Representatives on 18 November 1986. Outside Goodyear workers jeered as he got out of his car and his attempts to debate with members of the crowd were drowned out by hecklers. Inside, the atmosphere was no less tense. He came under sustained assault from a series of speakers who argued that his activities were detrimental to the US and a number, including Goodyear's Robert Mercer, called for stricter regulation of takeover bids. When Congressman John Seiberling, a grandson of Goodyear's founder, questioned his motives, Goldsmith snapped: 'Check your facts before jumping to yet another prejudiced conclusion.'

He made a detailed attack on Goodyear's management and its policies and accused his detractors of undermining the American dream. 'I come from Europe and I have seen European freedom and prosperity destroyed by the triangular alliance of big business, big unions and big governments which have throttled entrepreneurs,' he said. 'If you are going to follow Europe's example and catch the same disease and all this nonsense which I have heard this morning is believed by your citizens then you have already got the European disease good and proper.'

But in many ways Goldsmith appears to have misjudged the tenor of the event. When Seiberling asked: 'Who the hell are you?', he prompted wild applause from the Goodyear supporters. Goldsmith responded with a ten-minute monologue about his financial expertise, repeatedly stressing: 'I'll put our cash flow, our capital spending up against anybody.' It was hardly the sort of fare guaranteed to win over the man on the production line. He may have been perfectly correct in his criticisms of the Goodyear strategy but it wasn't what the people crowding the committee-room were there to hear and, as time went on, he probably realised it himself.

Nor did his forceful responses during the televised proceedings make Goldsmith many friends among the public at large but he was determined to go ahead with his bid. He even paid a $22 million fee to his bank on the Tuesday morning to keep his credit line open. That day he lunched with Mercer and warned him to expect a tender offer the very next day. Mercer countered with an offer to buy Goldsmith's shares for $620 million, a price that would leave him with a gross profit of $93 million. Goldsmith turned it down but as the day progressed his mood changed. After watching a video of his performance during the Congressional hearing in his hotel room he declared himself horrified at how unpleasant he appeared. 'I can't believe how nasty I look on this thing,' he said. 'I look like a monster. It's incredible.'

He took a break from the Goodyear saga that evening to host a dinner for a Washington-based think-tank at which President Reagan was the guest of honour. There were yet more Goodyear negotiations after the function and they proceeded to stretch on through the night. At dawn, there was just time to shower and shave before heading for a TV studio to participate in a debate on NATO.

It was a weary Goldsmith who returned to his suite at the Hay Adams hotel later that morning. He decided to accept the Goodyear offer.

The tide was turning against the raiders. The week before, Ivan Boesky, the ultimate insider trader, who couriered briefcases packed with $100 bills to his sources in Manhattan's investment banking community, had been arrested. That fact was shocking enough but the news that rocked Wall Street was that he had spent the past six weeks recording all his business dealings to the extent of going into meetings wired for sound. These tapes were now in the hands of the police. Boesky's arrest was followed by others and there began a powerful backlash against takeover culture.

The Goodyear affair at an end, Goldsmith's American period was almost over. There was one last brief flirtation – with PanAm, the ailing international airline – but that ended as soon as Goldsmith's team had examined the books and discovered the scale of its problems.

By now innoculated against acquisition fever, Goldsmith was in a position to sit back and contemplate the future. And he did not like what he saw. Stock markets around the world were riding high but Goldsmith divined the root causes of a slump in the offing. The US trade deficit was deteriorating as US companies became less competitive on the world market. As the deficit rose, so did the national debt and the dollar became less attractive to international investors. Interest rates were set to rise in a bid to attract investors and strengthen the dollar but this would have a deflationary effect on share and bond prices.

Goldsmith, 'fantastically counter cyclical' in the words of one acquaintance, resolved to liquidate all his shareholdings.

Time, which devoted its cover story to the tale of the most inspired hunch in stock market history, described Goldsmith as 'The Lucky Gambler' and compared him to Joe Kennedy, the father of President John F. Kennedy. 'Kennedy liked to tell the story of how he saved his fortune just before the Wall Street Crash of 1929,' recorded *Time*. 'He was having shoes polished one day when the shoeshine boy told him about how he was picking stocks. Kennedy then and there decided that a market in which shoeshine boys were giving market tips was no place to invest. He promptly pulled his money out of the market, thereby saving millions of dollars.'

The scale of Goldsmith's liquidation left Kennedy in the shade. It was like a giant closing down sale: everything had to go. Not just the corporate shareholdings but his stake in Aspinall's London casino, and even the home in New York on which he and Laure had lavished so much time and attention. In July he sold all but five per cent of his holding in Générale Occidentale for $500 million and stashed the cash in Lichtenstein. According to *Time*, the money was placed in the Brunneria Foundation, a family-owned holding company that controlled another two companies in Panama. These, in turn, owned 90 per cent of General Oriental, which was registered in the Cayman Islands. In 1987, *Time* listed General Oriental's holdings as '$500 million in securities ($200 million in debt), all of Diamond Land and 54 per cent of US-based Cavenham Forest Industries, which manages Crown Zellerbach'. The forestry interests were later sold for $1.6 billion and made Goldsmith a sterling billionaire.

The depth of Goldsmith's vision and the confidence with which he backed it are all the more impressive considering how many of the world's shrewdest stock market players were caught cold on 19 October 1987: the day that has been immortalised as Black Monday. Rupert Murdoch and Robert Holmes à Court, then two of the brightest stars in the financial firmament, suffered almost catastrophic losses. Murdoch's family company, Cruden Investments, lost £700 million in paper profits. His fellow Australian fared almost as badly when shares in his Bell Group lost $500 million of their value in less than half an hour.

It was an understandably contented Goldsmith who spoke to *Time* in November 1987. 'I am now fully invested in short-term securities of the highest quality, such as Treasury bills and notes in a basket of currencies,' he explained. 'I would not go back in except in a very special situation. If I went into anything, it would be more in the role of a catalyst than a market-oriented operation. But like the scorpion in La Fontaine's fable, I may be tempted to sting, even if it's not in my best interests, just because I like to sting.'

Chapter Six

Jimmy in wonderland

HAVING made his fortune, Goldsmith set about creating a network of dream homes around the globe. His project was complicated by the need to maintain his wife, ex-wife and mistress in the grand style to which they had all become accustomed. Annabel was already well catered for with her comfortable mansion on Richmond Common and a Spanish estate for summer breaks. Laure shared Goldsmith's home in Paris with his second wife, Ginette, but her magnificent New York house had gone, a victim of Goldsmith's remorseless financial logic, and something else would be required. As it turned out she came into two remarkable properties in Mexico and France.

Goldsmith's choice of Mexico as the location for one of the most remarkable private estates ever conceived stemmed partly from his desire to create his own paradise on Earth far from the threat of the nuclear holocaust he feared might turn western Europe into a radioactive wilderness and partly from his links with his first father-in-law, Antenor Patino. In the mid to late '80s, a fear of nuclear devastation was not quite the paranoid position it would be seen as today. After all, the Cold War was very much a reality and then, as now, Switzerland demanded that all new homes be built with a nuclear shelter. Mexico was not only appropriately distant from the European theatre but it was also a country that Goldsmith had got to know thanks to a thaw in his relations with the man who had made such efforts to block his marriage to his first wife. Antenor Patino was the first member of Goldsmith's extended family circle to spot the potential of the Central American state. As far back as 1968, he was investing heavily in Las Hadas, a beachside development on the outskirts of the bustling port of Manzanillo on Mexico's Pacific coast, confident that a tourist boom stoked by Americans in search of winter sun would yield a handsome return. Such was his confidence that he also bought the Hacienda San Antonio in 1979. Renowned as one of the most beautiful houses in Mexico, his plan was that San Antonio would become an exclusive inland retreat, with guests shuttling between the hacienda and Las Hadas by helicopter. When he died in 1982, however, his dream was largely unrealised. Las Hadas became briefly fashionable among the jetset and reached its apotheosis as an international destination when it served as the backdrop for the sex comedy, *10*, starring Dudley Moore and Bo Derek. But following his death, Patino's family sold Las Hadas to the Alfa Group. It has changed hands three times since and is now run by the hotel chain Camino Real.

Goldsmith's own love affair with Mexico began in the '70s when he rented a house in Careyes, two and a half hours' drive north of Manzanillo. But it was not until the mid-'80s that he bought his first property there. His daughter Isabel and two of her aunts had each inherited a third share in the ranch of El Jabali and the nearby San Antonio on Patino's death but none of them was keen to take on the responsibilities associated with running what was a working cattle ranch as well as a beautiful, if inaccessible, retreat. So when Goldsmith offered to buy them out in 1986, all three willingly agreed.

At one time, the Hacienda San Antonio was something of a local attraction. Visitors were permitted to tour the house and its grounds but since Goldsmith took it over a beige-uniformed guard wearing a smart brimmed hat has kept out the general public. The only window of opportunity for the curious comes at two in the afternoon on Sundays when Father José Villaseñor drives up from Colima to say mass in the tiny church that butts on to the end of the *casco*, or main building. Father Villaseñor commands a congregation of up to 300 estate workers and villagers, according to the gateman, and nobody is going to be churlish enough to bar the odd pious tourist. For them there is a treat in store, a six-foot high, nineteenth century *retablo*, or carved wooden screen, stands behind the altar. The air of tranquility is highlighted by the sound of spring water from the surrounding hills passing through an aqueduct that stretches more than 100 metres from the gate past the side of the church. At its end, the water cascades from a height of around 15 feet on to piles of coffee beans below, breaking their shells and washing away the waste. An estimated 100 locals are employed on the estate's coffee plantation.

In the house itself, all the doors are hand-made from local woods such as *caoba* and *cedro* and the overall style – the work of Goldsmith's daughter Alix – is described as 'Mexican but luxurious'. The hacienda is built around a courtyard which boasts a fine stone fountain dating back more than a hundred years. Alongside the hacienda, a 30-room hotel has been built at a cost of several million pounds and the rear block of the main house contains the services for it, including the front desk and the dining-room. No one seems to know when it will open for business but it is said to be ready for guests and Goldsmith used it to entertain his friends. The attraction San Antonio held for Goldsmith is easy to see. Apart from the charm of the house itself, its setting is magnificent. It stands in the shadow of the Volcan de Fuego, or Fire Volcano, which has erupted regularly since 1585 and, perhaps worryingly, has already done so four times this century between 1902 and 1913. It renewed its discharges of smoke and red-hot igneous rocks in 1957 and these have intensified since 1975.

None of this deterred Goldsmith, however, and it was at a party at the hacienda in the '80s that he resolved to buy his own stretch of coast and build the estate which came to be known as his very own San Simeon, the ambitious folly built by William Randolph Hearst in California. It was always going to be a heavy investment in both money and time for Goldsmith and he wanted to be absolutely sure that he was making the right decision. His epiphany came in the form of two enthusiastic *mariarchi* singers, a celebrated Mexican bullfighter called Capetillo and a former tax collector from Manzanillo called Memin. They serenaded him relentlessly all evening, cheekily calling him 'Schmidt de Oro' and pursuing him wherever he went. Goldsmith far from being irritated by this persecution was charmed. 'That night I think he decided he liked this country and that he would invest in Mexico,' says one who was there.

Goldsmith found his Shangri-La on the Pacific coast at Cuixmala, 200 miles north of Acapulco. It was 18,000 acres of almost virgin jungle when he began buying it from the hundreds of smallholders who each had title to a part of his private wilderness. On reconnaissance visits with Laure, he saw swampland, where pelicans, herons and other seabirds nested; a mature coconut plantation; and distant hills which were home to pumas, jaguars and ocelots. But most beautiful of all was the beach of fine white sand, which stretched for miles in either direction.

This, then, was to be the site of Goldsmith's Central American fiefdom. His palace was to be built on a hill overlooking the ocean, from which giant turtles crawled to lay their eggs on the beach. And there would be individually designed villas dotted around the estate to house members of his family and a steady stream of visitors.

Laure chose as the designer Robert Couturier, the young Frenchman who had renovated their New York townhouse five years earlier. This was to be the biggest project he had ever undertaken. His vision was of a white-walled Moorish castle, with a Y-shaped floor area of 60,000 square feet, capped by a magnificent dome in blue and yellow ceramic tiles. Mindful of the ever-present threat of earthquakes, the steel-reinforced concrete walls were built several feet thick to withstand all but the most violent tremors. There is a vivid reminder of this potential for disaster in nearby Cihuatlán where the hands on the clock on the tower of the derelict church are frozen at 9.40, the time when an earthquake struck the area in 1995.

The main house, officially called Casa La Loma but known locally as El Castillo, has only two bedrooms, Goldsmith's highly effective way of ensuring his own privacy. 'Visitors are all very well,' observes one local ex-pat, 'but they are like fish. After a few days they start to smell.' Guests are lodged in villas dotted around the grounds, where service matches that of any five-star hotel. One visitor, the author Laline Paull, recalled her surprise on returning to her 'perfectly appointed' villa: 'I was startled to find that my hairbrush had been meticulously cleaned, my make-up bag zipped closed, my clothes hung up and the fruit basket, from which I'd taken a few grapes before leaving, entirely replenished. This happened every time.'

No amount of luxury could compensate for the almost tangible air of tension that hung over the estate and its inhabitants whenever the master was at home, however. This was something that Ginette Lery felt particularly keenly, according to Paull. During her stay, Goldsmith's second wife invited the writer to escape the overpowering grandeur of Cuixmala for a brief foray into everyday life at a nearby seafront village. 'Sitting at the sandy, basic beachfront café, with the local people splashing and playing in the sea, boisterous and natural, I realised how much tension there was in the air everywhere around Jimmy,' said Paull. 'How everything seemed to be balanced on his pleasure and approval.'

More than two thousand local workers were employed on the construction of Cuixmala, a project on the scale of an Egyptian pyramid. They arrived each morning by the truckload from the local villages of Franceso Villa and Emiliana Zapata and from further afield. Hundreds toiled for months digging foundations for the main house, guest villas, and the support village. Others worked on the 4,000-foot airstrip. Yet more workers were employed to build the road that led from the main road to the house, which, at four miles, must be one of the longest driveways in the world. At intervals along its route are a succession of sleeping policemen to slow down the traffic.

The construction of all this had to be carried out at breakneck speed, however. Couturier says: 'The thing that comes to mind the most are the furies that he went through because things never went as fast as he thought they should go. He was always a little upset about that. He always had a sense of urgency about him. Things needed to be done fast.'

Once his Xanadu was finally completed, Goldsmith decided he needed a private army to keep it secure in a land where kidnapping and murder are commonplace. To this end he beefed up the local police force, providing them with cars and radios. No one quite knows how many armed guards he had but estimates range from 50, Ivan Fallon's figure, to 1,200, the estimate of Robin Leach, who visited the area for his television series, *Lifestyles of the Rich and Famous*. Every entrance to Goldsmith's estate is guarded round the clock by police provided by the governor of the state of Jalisco. This obsession with security is seen as a little extreme but Goldsmith, as a rich man surrounded by poor and sometimes desperate people, did have something to fear. In the early '70s, *bandidos* arrived on horseback at the nearby Club Med and toured the resort, holding out their sombreros, requiring the tourists to deposit their watches and jewellery inside. Thinking it was all part of the fun of a theme holiday, the holidaymakers laughed and cheered their muggers as they obliged. It was not until the bandits rode off with their haul that they realised they had been robbed. The security situation worsened in the early '90s when the United States' Drug Enforcement Administration launched a purge which drove out the drug barons and denied a living to their henchmen on the ground. Many of them turned to mugging and burglary. Since then owners of large properties have taken stringent precautions to protect their homes.

There are natural hazards too. At Cuixmala, the ancient Aztec canals have been reconstituted and now teem with hundreds of crocodiles, many more than 12 feet long. A more day-to-day threat are the scorpions that infest the area. Each entrance to every house is protected by a scorpion trap, a tiled trench from which careless scorpions find it impossible to escape, and in the evenings staff tour the perimeter of each building, ultra-violet light in hand, on scorpion patrol. None of this was enough to prevent a scare when Jethro, Goldsmith's youngest child by Laure, then 18 months old, was stung after standing on a scorpion by the swimming pool. Fortunately, Laure was well-drilled in the emergency procedure. She immediately immersed her baby son's foot in ice and the resident medic came running with the appropriate antidote.

Goldsmith found that it was not only the suburban middle class who have problems with their neighbours. On the adjoining stretch of coast to the north of his property is the holiday resort of Careyes, an idyllic development of *casitas* – or chalets – which slopes down to a beach lined by picture postcard palm trees. Each *casita* is painted in bright pastel shades of orange, pink and blue, and they are surrounded by palms and colourful orchids. In addition to the *casitas*, there is the Club Med and three hotels, the Playa Blanca, the Playa Rosa and the Bel Air. When Goldsmith first sat on the terrace of his sumptuous home he was lord of all he surveyed. There were no buildings to ruin his sightlines or close neighbours to invade his privacy. Then Gianfranco

Brignoni, the wealthy Italian banker who developed much of Careyes, began work on Tigre del Mar, a house with a large blue tower, which took its inspiration from two local lighthouses. While the site was three miles distant, Goldsmith quickly realised that it would enable the occupants of the house to see into his property. It was time for action.

Relations between the Goldsmiths and the Brignonis had fluctuated between outright antagonism and grudging warmth for years. There is a blood link between the two families by marriage. Goldsmith's first wife was a Patino and his business manager in Mexico, Luis de Rivera, is a relative of Gianfranco Brignoni's wife thanks to his marriage to one of the Patino clan. These connections had failed to prevent a bitter spat over Brignoni's plans to develop an area of wetland, however. Disputes over the boundary between the two estates had been simmering for some time, but things came to a head when Brignoni decided he wanted to drain what Goldsmith considered an ecologically important site to which many species of bird migrated each year. Goldsmith led local protest against his neighbour's plan to build on the land and won.

In the case of the house with the tower, however, he suffered a rare defeat. So important was it to Goldsmith that aides were even sending him pictures of the house under construction when he was in London orchestrating a takeover bid for BAT. 'Oh yes, that was a big fight,' says one member of the Goldsmith family. 'It was war.'

This is not the only example of Goldsmith's obsession with privacy. When he bought El Jabali, his 2,500-hectare ranch near the village of Chamela, he was irritated by the fact that the residents of the community of La Baranca passed close by his house on their way to and from work. His response, according to locals, was to offer all 100 families the choice between 35,000 pesos – approximately £3,500 – or a new home at La Becerera, a hamlet further from his residence.

And this was not the only conflict that arose out of his acquisition of El Jabali. He had bought the land from the Buenrostro family in the early '80s but Francisco Buenrostro Caballos, who had inherited the lagoon of Calabozo from his father, Napoleon, held on to it when the surrounding land was sold. But it soon became clear that Goldsmith was intent on

The *Sunday Times Magazine* cover from June 1975, which so enraged Goldsmith. It shows his mistress, the then Lady Annabel Birley, with Lord Lucan the year before he disappeared following the murder of his children's nanny (courtesy Vintage Magazines)

Las Alamandas, Isabel Goldsmith's
luxury retreat for millionaires near
her late father's vast estate

Right: Cuixmala, Goldsmith's
Moorish-style palace on the
Mexican coast

Jemima and Annabel Goldsmith arriving for a party at the Café Royal
in London (© Richard Young/Rex)

Jemima Goldsmith and Imran Khan on the town (© Rex)

Conservative MP David Mellor (left) is heckled by Goldsmith as he makes a speech after losing his Putney seat at the general election of 1997 (© Press Association)

Opposite: Sir James Goldsmith on the hustings just a few months before his death (© Rex)

Isabel Goldsmith at her Chelsea home

acquiring the lagoon too. To this end he targeted the 20-strong co-operative, which had fished the Calabozo for years. By the time Goldsmith bought El Jabali they had well-established sidelines in cattle rustling and deer hunting. Apart from this, Goldsmith resented the fact that they crossed his land to reach the lagoon and so he decided to block their path. First he erected a barrier of wire and rocks, guarded by sentries, then he put up a more permanent chain-link cyclone fence.

In the circumstances, Francisco had little option but to sell and the members of the co-operative, who were not locals but workers from a sugar plant at Quesera, responded by staging a demonstration on the streets of the state capital Colima. Carrying placards with the words 'Gringo go home' and 'Yankee go home' they marched the streets. Again, it was money that resolved the problem. Each fisherman was paid compensation of around $3,000.

Land rights are a sensitive issue in Mexico, a country which spent almost three centuries under the colonial yoke following the Spanish invasion under Hernan Cortes in the sixteenth century. It lost almost half its territory to the United States after the war of 1846. Following the revolution of 1910, fought on the slogan 'Land and freedom', against the dictatorship of Porfirio Díaz, a new constitution was drawn up which, among other things, revised the rules surrounding land ownership. To this day, no alien is entitled to own land within 50km of the coast or within 100km of the frontier. Foreign residents like Goldsmith, with beach-side properties, got round this rule by appointing a *presta nombre*, a Mexican citizen who would nominally hold the land. It was obviously vitally important that such an individual was totally trustworthy as, in theory, there was nothing to prevent the *presta nombre* occupying the land himself. There were also cases where the son of the original nominee refused to honour the deal agreed with his father. In a bid to encourage tourism, the law was changed in the '70s so that foreigners could become trustees of land for a set period of years and this arrangement remains in force today.

In addition to his 18,000 acres on the coast side of the road, Goldsmith bought another 50,000 acres of mountainous forest on the other side and set up an ecological reserve staffed by five scientists from the National University of Mexico. A sign by the side of the track that leads to the biological station boasts that the site is 'one of the most important such stations in the entire country', with 1,000 plant species, 20 amphibians, 69 reptiles, 270 birds, 75 mammals and no fewer than 2,000 insect species. Many of these species cannot be found outside Mexico and academics from American universities visit the reserve to carry out field work.

For the locals there was a downside to Goldsmith's obsession with ecology. The meat from wild deer has always been an important part of the local diet but after Goldsmith established his ecological zone, hunting was forbidden. Fishing was hit too. Seafood has always been a key part of local subsistence but when local fishermen attempt to dive for octopus and lobster close to the beaches that surround Cuixmala these days the police, who have been provided with a bungalow of their own on the sand, warn them off with loudhailers. Strictly speaking, the locals do have the right to access the coastline but Goldsmith's heirs have the forces of law and order on their side.

The most dramatic conflict between Goldsmith and the local population came to light late in 1996. 'We've been deprived of our lands,' ran a headline in *El Correo de Manzanillo* on 18 November. It proceeded to tell the story of a bitter feud between Goldsmith's men and members of an *ejido* – or agricultural commune – near his estate over a stretch of beach known locally as Piratas or Pirate's Beach.

The dispute ended in a bloody confrontation. Manuel Ornelas Novoa, his wife and children and others were fired upon by a group of armed men. One of the women supporting Ornelas was shot in the back and Ornelas's own van was riddled with bullet holes. He claims that when he reported the incident to the local police, far from taking action against his attackers, he was arrested and thrown into jail on the grounds that he was trying to hold on to land that was not his.

Ornelas's version of events ran to more than 1,500 words in *El Correo* and it provoked a furious rejoinder from a lawyer representing 'Golsmit'. Four days after the article appeared, a long rebuttal was published in the form of a full-page advertisement taken out by Salvador Barragan Ochoa, the solicitor for the Emiliana Zapata *ejido*, at a cost of 1,500 pesos (£150). It told a rather different story, pointing out that

Goldsmith had brought public utilities to the area and members of the *ejido* that held the original claim to Piratas held him in high regard.

It is certainly true that resentment against the foreign invader was not the only sentiment around. In the villages of Emiliana Zapata and Francesco Villa – both named after patriotic heroes – he acquired a reputation as a benefactor. The majority of the 3,700 villagers are landless peasants who must accept whatever work they can find and Goldsmith's arrival meant hundreds of new jobs. Even with the building programme at Cuixmala long completed, up to 500 people were employed when the master was at home, with men working in the garden and on maintenance, while women found jobs in the kitchen and as cleaners. And Goldsmith had a reputation as a good payer. At a time when the average wage was around 180 pesos (£18) a week, he was paying 420 pesos (£42). 'He's the best thing that ever happened to this village,' says Leopoldo Sahagun Michel, the *commisario ejidal* or leader of the local farmers' association. 'Yes, without a doubt. A lot of people got a start because of him. They could finish their house or whatever. Maybe one in a hundred would talk badly of him because they don't like foreigners.'

Many sceptics were won over by acts of philanthropy which included the funding of a drinking water project and an extension to the local school. Mindful of the pulling power of Catholicism, Goldsmith even paid for the renovation of the church of Our Lady of Perpetual Succour in Zapata and the construction of an entirely new one, the church of San Francisco, in Villa. Fifteen community leaders were invited to his home to discuss the projects over soft drinks and he visited the village with Manes to inspect the work in progress.

Even the fishing in the river that divides the villages from the Goldsmith land has improved, says Sahagun Michel. Goldsmith stocked his lake with fish and when the rains come and the sluices are opened, many fish escape with the water and the villagers are assured of a bumper catch.

Goldsmith's efforts to win over the people of Mexico extended to the state capital of Jalisco, Guadalajara, when he funded a poetry prize, known as the Cuixmala Award, at the annual festival, Fiestas de Octobre.

The biggest beneficiaries of Goldsmith's largesse were not the villagers, however, but that select band of plutocrats, bankers and academics who were members of one of the most exclusive clubs in the world, the Friends of Jimmy. They would fly in to the international airport at Manzanillo; the wealthiest arriving in their private jets, while the relatively impoverished slummed it on scheduled services. But the luckiest guests of all travelled in Goldsmith's Boeing 757. Designed to carry 233 passengers in commercial service, his Boeing had been converted into a palace in the air for the privileged few. The only external clue to the luxury within lay in the plane's call sign, VRC-AU. While VRC was nothing more than its Cayman Islands registration code, AU was chosen by Goldsmith as it is the chemical notation for gold.

Passengers entered by what is called Door Two, just forward of the port side wing. Inside, the cavernous airliner was split into three luxurious compartments behind the galley – a lounge, a bedroom with a king-sized bed and en suite bathroom and a combined meeting-room and office. The kitchen area was at the front of the plane and, while Goldsmith often transported delicacies from Laurent, his Paris restaurant, in the hold, he insisted that no hot food was ever prepared on board: he hated the smell of cooking.

The large lounge area was decorated in burgundy and cream and fitted out with sofas and seating for up to 30 people. The crew would include at least two stewardesses, more if there was a full complement of passengers on board. There were always at least two pilots, with a third enrolled for longer trips when the plane made use of its long-range fuel tanks located in the belly of the aircraft. The Boeing was fitted out in Dallas to what is known as an 'executive configuration' and the mainly American crew operated from a base on Long Island, New York State.

Few private individuals can afford to run 757s, which are chartered for up to £6,000 an hour. The Greek billionaire John Latsis, a friend and patron of the Prince of Wales, owns one and there are not many who could afford to top him and Goldsmith in the jet-owning stakes. Only the Sultan of Brunei and a handful of Middle Eastern heads of state operate 747 jumbo jets like Air Force One, which carries the president of the United States. Goldsmith certainly outdid the British prime minister who is not entitled to a personal aircraft but travels by chartered jet.

Not that the Boeing was Goldsmith's only aircraft. He also had a Gulfstream II G2V, which he acquired when he bought Diamond International, the forest products company, in 1981. Laure was a frequent traveller in the Gulfstream which had luxurious white leather seats. 'Jimmy always sat in the first seat on the right as you got on the plane, which was facing backwards,' says one who flew in it as his guest. 'He loved to sit there because he could put his feet up on a sort of armchair. It had one of those satellite maps, which showed where you were and what speed you were doing, or you could watch videos. It had a proper bathroom with a shower and hanging rails at the back of the plane.'

His fleet was completed by a twin-engined Otter which he used to travel from Manzanillo to Cuixmala, the steward draping a strip of red carpet over the wooden steps used to climb into the plane each time. Goldsmith was not permitted to fly direct to his estate because of the need to clear immigration and he had to change planes anyway because his huge Boeing could not land on the grass airstrip at his estate. Even in the Otter, take off and landing at Cuixmala could be a hair-raising experience, as Australian media tycoon Kerry Packer can testify. He was one of Goldsmith's earliest visitors and he was not amused when the plane clipped trees at the end of the runway, which is less than a mile long. These natural hazards were swiftly removed.

One effect of the remoteness of Goldsmith's retreat was that his guests were very much in his power once they touched down on Mexican soil. A good example of this was the occasion that Richard Branson came to stay. A group of businessmen and environmentalists had been flown in for an ecological talking shop. The first afternoon went off well enough, with the guests' children playing noisily by the pool and pushing each other in as children do.

That evening, the grown-ups gathered for a superb dinner by the pool. It was a warm Mexican night and the atmosphere was relaxed. Open-necked shirts were the order of the day rather than dinner suits. And there were no complaints as Goldsmith moved from table to table to greet his 60 guests and satisfy himself that they were settling in well. The Virgin boss, whose party trick was to approach a woman at a function, sweep her up in his arms and turn her upside down waited patiently for his host to reach his table. As he did so, the entrepreneur sprang out of his chair and shoved Goldsmith, immaculately dressed as always, headlong into the pool. He must have realised almost immediately the enormity of his mistake. The buzz of conversation ceased abruptly to be replaced by the sort of eerie silence that, in that part of the world, precedes a hurricane. The storm came in the form of Goldsmith's Mexican bodyguard who was incandescent with rage. Not only had Branson assaulted his charge but in doing so had offended his honour. Even as Goldsmith was being helped out of the pool, the bodyguard was in the midst of a furious confrontation with Branson. For some moments it looked as though things might turn really nasty. Indeed, without the intervention of Goldsmith, water still dripping from his clothes, at least one guest reckons Branson could have been shot where he stood. The following morning a chastened Branson received a note from his host saying 'due to a clash of cultures' it would probably be best if the entire Branson family left that day.

For those who stayed the course, however, a sojourn at Goldsmith's Mexican idyll could be a delight. The company was likely to be invigorating for a start. Guests have included Henry Kissinger, the former US secretary of state, Robert Redford, Conrad Black, the owner of the *Daily Telegraph*, Jocelyn Stephens, the chairman of English Heritage, and the academic Hugh (Lord) Thomas, whose works include a doorstop history of Mexico.

The food was tasty and varied. There were no fewer than three cooks: one Italian, one Indian and one Mexican. They prepared meals using the finest ingredients: ranging from delicacies flown in from Goldsmith's restaurant on the Champs Elysées to entire carcasses brought in by light aircraft from El Jabali. Meals were often served on the terrace overlooking the Pacific where visitors could choose from a selection of dishes laid out on a carousel.

Horse-riding facilities were available and there were floodlit tennis courts. Guests taking advantage of the latter did well to be aware of their host's rubber phobia, however. Goldsmith himself refused to take to the court in anything other than rope-soled espadrilles. So acute was his aversion to rubber that none of his children were permitted to have Wellington boots and, while he was said to have become more tolerant of trainers towards the end, any doubles partner would make him feel more comfortable if he turned out in espadrilles. Musical entertainment was likely to be provided by an indigenous *mariachi* troupe or one of Goldsmith's favourite jazz bands flown in from the US or Brazil for a three-month stint.

A highlight of anyone's stay was a bonfire party on the beach, when everyone sat on cushions and watched the sparks fly both literally and metaphorically. According to one guest, preferment at these gatherings was based primarily on sex or sexiness. Seated closest to the camp fire, as it were, were the grizzly older males of the tribe. Goldsmith might have tolerated shapely young second wives in this inner circle but the older and dowdier females were banished to the outer ring with the younger men who had yet to prove themselves.

It is deep in another dark forest half way around the globe that Goldsmith's European Xanadu can be found. Like Cuixmala, the seventeenth-century chateau of Montjeu is set like a fortress on a hilltop. Life being what it is in the Burgundian village of Autun in the depths of rural France, there would appear to be little need for the levels of security that persist in Central America, but Goldsmith is said to have transported Mexican gun culture to chateau-ridden Burgundy. According to an article in London's *Evening Standard*, armed sentries patrol the 11-kilometre perimeter and the ten-foot-high walls that enclose 700 hectares of woodland that teem with deer and wild boar. The curious are further discouraged by the barbed wire wrapped around telegraph poles that overlook the grounds. And security cameras at the gate ensure that no one enters uninvited. When a group of water board officials had the temerity to let themselves in to inspect a lake that provides water for the local village they found themselves surrounded by gun-toting guards. 'There's a whole army in there,' they told the *Standard* reporter.

This image of Montjeu as a fortified castle, bristling with armoury, is hotly disputed by Teddy Goldsmith, however. 'There is just one security man there and he doubles as an electrician and chauffeur,' he says. 'Now Mexico, of course, is a different story . . .'

The villagers of Autun knew when their local *grand fromage* was heading home by the noise of a helicopter in the skies overhead. But while Goldsmith's helicopter may have flown over their houses, they were forbidden from flying over his: members of the local aero club were banned from passing over Montjeu.

The house itself has historic connections. Built by one Pierre Jeannin, the son of an Autun tanner made good, it went on to house some of the most famous names in French history: the Talleyrands, the Le Pellettiers and the Dukes of Valois among them. By the time Goldsmith bought it in 1990, however, it had fallen into disrepair. The Great Gallery in the north wing had been damaged by fire in 1963 and the rest of the house and the grounds were run down. Given its historical and architectural significance – the gardens were designed by Andre Le Notre, who later planned the gardens at Versailles for Louis XIV – local heritage officials offered advice and grants for Montjeu's renovation. Goldsmith turned down both and obstinately refused to allow any subsequent inspection of his work. We do know, however, that the gardens have been restored to their former splendour. Today vistas envisaged centuries ago have been opened up anew and fountains that had grown clogged with weed play once more.

On the downside, Goldsmith's takeover ended centuries of local access to the grounds. He immediately ended the tradition that the annual gymkhana be held on his parkland and even schoolfriends of Goldsmith and Laure's children, Charlotte and Jethro, had to be left by their parents at the entrance of the estate.

'Once,' a parent told the *Standard*'s Alex Renton, 'they invited all their friends to come and play at the chateau. What was extraordinary, though, was that we were not allowed to take them there. We had to leave our children at the main gate and the guards came and picked them up.' On another occasion, a mother expecting her young daughter home from school received a telephone call from the girl who announced that she was ringing from the Goldsmith helicopter. She and her friend Charlotte were being taken for a spin.

The security arrangements are not the only aspects of the Montjeu operation that mirrored what went on in Mexico. As at Cuixmala, Goldsmith employed a number of local people at a handsome premium on the going rate for the job. His paternalism even extended to sending one of the gardeners to the United States for heart surgery. But other local people were not so enamoured of their new squire. Some asked what motivated Goldsmith to buy such a grand home in such a remote location.

The answer may lie in the response given by Montjeu's first tenant, Jeannin, to a similar question almost 400 years ago: 'So I'll always be far enough from those who'd do me harm, and so my friends will always know where to find me.'

Goldsmith's Mexican retreat may sound like a lavish holiday home but business was rarely far from his mind. It was over breakfast taken under the palapa-lined roof of his seafront terrace one day in early 1989 that Jacob Rothschild first raised the subject of British American Tobacco. Goldsmith had given up on the American takeover scene on the basis that he and his partners could not compete with hired guns working for huge fees employed by pension funds and insurance companies with tens of billions of dollars at their disposal. The British scene, however, was different.

Goldsmith was already familiar with Rothschild's proposed target. In 1973, he had run the rule over the company with a view to making a bid but had been persuaded by the then prime minister, Edward Heath, that anything other than an agreed takeover could be damaging to his re-election chances. When BAT's then chairman Sir Richard Dobson made it clear that his advances were unwelcome, Goldsmith let it drop.

Now it was ripe for the picking. Like all Goldsmith's targets, BAT had undertaken what he saw as a series of unsound diversifications. The company had long been a conglomerate with a wide array of interests beyond its core tobacco interests but since the '70s it had expanded these to include companies such as Saks Fifth Avenue and Marshall Fields. Earlier in 1989 it had even completed the $5.2 billion acquisition of an American motor insurance specialist, the Farmers Group. But perhaps the most challenging aspect of all was that the takeover battle would be the biggest ever waged in Britain as, to have a realistic chance of success, any bid would have to exceed £13 billion. The principals were to be Goldsmith, Rothschild and Kerry Packer, who also flew to Mexico to discuss the deal. They were each to put up £250 million but no less than £12 billion of the offer capital was to be borrowed.

The stock market had been primed for an announcement in March when Goldsmith had bought a 37.4 per cent stake in Anglo Leasing from Jacob Rothschild. In itself, the move was hardly earth-shattering but it was the wording of the accompanying press release that gave it added significance. Anglo was defined as a vehicle 'for identifying and acquiring one or more publicly quoted UK companies whose business can benefit from greater focus and improvement in operating efficiency'. Goldsmith was back.

The market's reaction was a measure of its respect and fear for the man who was known as one of the most ruthless takeover merchants in the business. Share prices rose and a chill ran through many a boardroom.

As preparations were made for the BAT bid, Goldsmith saw another opportunity. Bakery group Rank Hovis McDougall was vulnerable following a takeover bid for the Australian food company Goodman Fielder Wattie which had gone hideously wrong. The market had reacted so badly to the news of the bid that RHM shares plunged from 465p to 341p. Goldsmith's takeover team duly picked up 29.9 per cent of RHM's stock from Goodman Fielder, which had earlier failed in its own bid for RHM and had then been turned on by its quarry.

In the short term it was an extremely shrewd move. The share price rocketed on news of the bid, leaving the Goldsmith team with a paper profit of £94 million within 24 hours. Goldsmith then acted uncharacteristically. He pulled back and decided to let RHM's chief executive take his advice free from the threat of takeover. It proved financially disastrous. By the time he, Rothschild and Packer sold their holdings each man had lost £33 million.

Meanwhile, preparations for the BAT bid continued. Given the poor reputation enjoyed by corporate raiders thanks to the fall-out from Boesky's arrest less than three years earlier and the subsequent well-publicised round-up of other crooked Wall Street figures, Goldsmith and his team were keen to come up with a more attractive term than 'demerging' or 'breaking up' to describe their plans to overhaul BAT. Both expressions were thought to have destructive connotations and it was Goldsmith himself who invented the word 'unbundling' to convey what they had in mind.

Their strategy in place, Goldsmith, Rothschild and Packer duly announced a £13 billion bid for BAT through Hoylake, a Bermuda-registered company, on the 11 July. Within three hours, BAT's market value had increased by £3.7 billion. The battle that ensued was to prove every bit as bitter and arduous as any Goldsmith had been through before. BAT hired the private detective agency Kroll to look into Goldsmith's past and mounted a highly effective public relations campaign. In September, there was more bad news for the bidders when its target announced a big rise in profits to £2 billion and an enhanced dividend. Soon afterwards it went some way to spiking Goldsmith's guns by carrying out a limited unbundling of its own with the creation of two slimmed down divisions, tobacco and financial services.

But the issue that confounded Hoylake's bid was not so much BAT's improved profitability or its restructuring as the complexity of the regulations governing insurance companies in the United States. Gilberte Beaux had lined up the French insurance group Axa-Midi to take over Farmers in the event of the bid going through. And it was Axa-Midi's chief executive Claude Bebear who had the most thankless task of all the participants in the bid: winning over the American insurance regulators state by state. Naturally, BAT did everything it could to stir up opposition among the state authorities and, as the bidders contemplated a seemingly endless series of hearings complicated by legal actions and delaying tactics, they began to lose the initiative. BAT's chairman Patrick Sheehy was bounding ahead with his enforced rationalisation, Saks and Marshall Fields were all in the process of being sold and other interests were being floated off. But the death knell for the bid came when California's insurance regulator ruled that Axa-Midi was not an acceptable alternative to the existing management. Bebear was willing to fight on in the hope that California's insurance commissioner could be persuaded to change her mind but, with his partners losing their stomach for the battle, he too was eventually convinced that the situation was hopeless. The Hoylake team withdrew their bid in April, 1990, with Goldsmith, Rothschild and Packer each taking another hit in the tens of millions. As BAT's Patrick Sheehy might have said: 'Close, but no cigars.'

Chapter Seven

Lone wolf

A SIMPLE white marble headstone marks the last resting place of Isabel Goldsmith in the cemetery of Père Lachaise in Paris. There is no personal inscription, merely the words Isabel Patino Goldsmith followed by the years of her birth and death, 1935-1954. 'The cold facts,' as her mother, the Duchess of Durcal, puts it. Visitors to her graveside are few and far between these days. Isabel's plot is some distance from the graveyard entrance and only those with a special pass may drive their cars into the cemetery. As a resident of Paris, the duchess has a pass. Her grand-daughter, Isabel, is not entitled to one. She goes often, Isabel less so. And yet it was the death of her mother within hours of her birth that condemned Isabel to a life of emotional isolation. By her late twenties she had inherited as much material wealth as any woman could want; enough to travel the world at will and maintain properties on three continents. But there has never been a house she could truly call home.

Few people have had an upbringing as turbulent as Isabel Goldsmith's. Delivered by caesarian section from the womb of an unconscious mother, she spent her formative years being used as a pawn in a conflict between two strong-minded patriarchs. Her childhood was spent in a series of homes where she was welcomed but never fully accepted and at a school where her exotic looks and background cast her as an outsider.

As a baby she was left in the care of a strict English nanny, Deborah Cockbill, while her grief-stricken father worked round the clock to make a success of his first business and to support the sizeable retinue imposed on him by the custody judgement.

Perhaps as a result of the furore that surrounded her premature entry into the world and the custody battle that followed, Isabel was seen as a delicate child. She was given sleeping pills and a regular series of brain scans and tests for trauma. Nanny Cockbill lasted four and a half years until Goldsmith, impatient with what he saw as her mollycoddling, dismissed her, and stopped all his daughter's medication. Far from going into a decline, she thrived.

By now her father's lover, Ginette Lery, was pregnant with Manes and, when he was born, Isabel felt sidelined. As she grew up she spent many holidays with her Patino cousins and was to say later that there were times when she felt more of a Patino than a Goldsmith. The simmering feud between Goldsmith and his late wife's family continued to make life difficult for her, however. Goldsmith had always been a devout atheist, while the Patinos, and the Duchess of Durcal in particular, were unreconstructed Catholics. He resented their attempts to turn his daughter into a believer and was scornful of their gifts of holy pictures and a prayer book.

Things came to a head when Isabel, then aged 11, went to spend Christmas with her aunt Christina and her cousins Mini and Diana de Beauveau-Craon in the Austrian skiing resort of Lech. Isabel, who knew her father did not want her to have a prayer book, neglected to pack it. Her grandmother would never have learned of this oversight had her cousins' nanny, an Englishwoman called Nina Baker, not taken it upon herself to inform her. When Isabel returned from her holiday, she found herself being interrogated by the duchess on her piety during the Christmas holiday. Asked if she had been to mass on Christmas Eve, she replied truthfully that she had. But when she claimed that she had taken her prayer book, her grandmother knew that she was lying. Outraged at her grand-daughter's dishonesty, the duchess ordered her to write out one thousand times: 'I am a liar'. Not for the first time, Isabel was the victim of a dispute between two warring families who put her in a no-win situation.

But if relations with her maternal grandmother were strained, she did get on well with her other three grandparents. Easter was spent with her father's parents at Cannes, where she would meet up with her young cousins, Teddy Goldsmith's daughters, Dido and Clio, and spend time with Frank's wife Marcelle, the grandmother she knew as Mimi.

Meanwhile, Antenor Patino, who had married Countess Beatriz di Rovasenda in the teeth of heated opposition from his first wife, continued his efforts to make Isabel one of the Patino family. Every summer from the age of six, she was invited to spend the holidays with her cousins at Quinta Patino, his house near Estoril in Portugal. These were exciting times for an impressionable young girl. On one occasion, when she was 14, Patino organised a ball and his wife had an up-and-coming young Italian designer make dresses for herself, Isabel and her two cousins. He wasn't anybody much then but today the world knows him as Valentino.

Like his son-in-law, Patino loved to be surrounded by women and, while he didn't really know what to say to young children, by the time Isabel turned 16 the pair were quite close. She made regular visits to his flat in Paris for lunch, to be greeted with his trademark kiss first on the cheek and then on the forehead. His death, when Isabel was 28, hurt her badly. 'He was a fixture in my life,' she says. 'He was the one stabilising factor, so suddenly the whole foundation of my life had vanished.'

Isabel's school-life began in Miss Ironside's school in Elveston Street, Westminster. From there she was moved to a Swiss convent school in Fribourg but the switch was not a success. Isabel vividly recalls her mounting confusion as wars which had once been taught as victories were now taught as defeats. Unsurprisingly, perhaps, she lasted just one term. By the time she was old enough to go to secondary school, Goldsmith's business interests had taken him to London and he had begun his affair with Lady Annabel Vane Tempest Stewart. As a result, he decided to send Isabel to Annabel's alma mater, Southover Manor in Sussex. For a girl brought up in the world of the international jet-set it was a singularly unsuitable choice. Most of the pupils were what Isabel calls 'nice county girls' and she found it difficult to make friends. 'I looked extremely strange and exotic and odd and bizarre and very much the outsider,' she says. She completed her education in France, where she studied for her A-levels in French and art at the British School in Paris.

She looked forward to the holidays when she could rely on her favourite grandmother to lay on a more varied and interesting itinerary. Apart from broadening her horizons with trips to unexpected places – Mimi took her on a tour of Amsterdam's red-light district when she was 16 – she cultivated Isabel's burgeoning interest in art. Their visits to galleries in Florence and elsewhere fired an ambition to go to art college. She could not have come up with a more inflammatory proposal in her father's eyes, however. He viewed art colleges and universities as hotbeds of anarchists and was determined that no daughter of his would ever attend one. He was no more sympathetic to the suggestion that she should go to London and find a job with Christie's or Sotheby's on the grounds that such work was for dilettantes and her interest in art was merely a passing phase.

Her adult life began, appropriately enough, with a party. And what a swell party it was. Even the Ritz had never seen anything quite like it. The hotel's own decorations were removed from the mirrored basement to be replaced by a riotous display of orchids and palms. Five jazz bands were flown in from New Orleans. And the guest list read like a *Who's Who* of London society. Apart from half the Cabinet, many of the leading figures in banking, journalism and industry turned out. And, although Annabel was Goldsmith's hostess for the party that was at least partly in celebration of his upcoming 40th birthday, it was Isabel, looking young and delicate in white, who stood beside him in the receiving line. This enabled Goldsmith to pass off the extravagant event to a censorious press as an 18th birthday party for his eldest daughter but the sad truth was that Isabel's name was not on the invitation and she had not invited any of the guests. Twenty-four years later, she has still not forgiven the oversight. 'My father's not very good on presents,' she says, 'not very regular. He doesn't mark events. He doesn't appreciate the importance of traditional occasions. So my 18th, 21st, marriage: all of those were ignored present-wise.'

In the circumstances, it was left to her maternal grandfather to mark the occasion. And it was at the ball he threw in Paris that Isabel met the man she was to marry. The event, held at the Cercle Interallie club on the Rue de Faubourg St Honore, was a joint party for Isabel and her two Patino cousins. It was a grand affair with a pink theme and Isabel wore an off-the-shoulder dress of silk organza from Courage Couture chosen for her by her grandfather.

The official photographer for the event was Baron Arnaud de Rosnay, 26, who had achieved a certain notoriety for his nude photographs of the model and actress Marisa Berenson, a former girlfriend. Isabel admits to finding him 'cute' at the time but soon after the ball she flew to Portugal on holiday and enjoyed a romantic interlude with Thierry Roussel, the French playboy who went on to marry Christina Onassis. The couple even got 'informally' engaged. 'I was sort of flattered and amused by the whole thing,' she recalls. 'I can't say it was a great love thing. I don't know how it came about really. It got suggested and I thought, Oh, what a good idea! I've never been engaged before, why not?

'Thierry was very good-looking but the problem was I had absolutely nothing to say to him. I would always have to have a third or fourth person there at dinner. But at the time, because I was very young I wouldn't dare admit to myself that he was very boring, I just thought I was being very shy and incompetent.'

It was over dinner back in Paris that she was reintroduced to Rosnay, Roussel's best friend. Rosnay came from an aristocratic French family which had owned sugar plantations in Mauritius since the French Revolution. He was also strikingly good-looking and his conquests included some of the wealthiest and most beautiful women of the day, including Brigitte Bardot and, like Roussel, Christina Onassis. Isabel was smitten and soon Roussel was history and the couple were engaged within weeks. 'He was nice looking and he wasn't gay,' she explains. 'Everybody else I knew or I was in love with was gay. He had ambitions to work which also made a change from everybody else I knew who just wanted to go partying. So he seemed fairly responsible. Basically, I could introduce him to my father.'

Rosnay's undoubted charm was not the only factor behind Isabel's desire for marriage, however. Even in the '70s it was not usual for a girl of her class to marry quite so young. What was equally significant was the fact that the spectre of her mother had never left her.

'I thought my mother got married at 18 and so it was the thing to do,' she says. 'It was a sort of target, I thought maybe I'd die also at 19. I thought history would repeat itself. So I was a little worried about that and I wanted to leave home.'

Goldsmith was not overly impressed with his daughter's catch, however. 'My father's reaction was that he didn't think he was good husband material,' she says. Even Isabel, herself, was not wholly convinced that Rosnay would stay the course. 'To tell the truth, I didn't think this was going to be the love of my life,' she says, 'I just thought it would last five years and it was a convenient thing.'

But while Goldsmith did not wholeheartedly approve of the match he stopped short of attempting to block it, perhaps recalling his own experience just 20 years earlier. He duly arranged an engagement party for 200 people at Laurent, the restaurant off the Champs Elysées, in April 1973. It was a glittering affair with members of the Goldsmith, Patino and Rosnay families brought together for the first time. Annabel, John Aspinall and Dominic Elwes had made the trip from London; Isabel's beloved grandfather, Antenor Patino, was there; as were Rosnay's parents. Isabel's fiancé gave her an engagement ring featuring a Salvador Dali miniature of a swan on a lake set in diamonds. It was as impressive a gift as any young woman could ask for and his plans for her wedding present were even more extravagant: a 2,400-acre island in the Mozambique Channel off the coast of east Africa.

But it was a memorable night for more reasons than one. Despite all the diversions, Goldsmith found time to do a little business. He had spent the evening admiring his surroundings and even took himself on a tour of the small rooms, each with its own private terrace, on the first floor. By midnight he had decided he liked the restaurant so much he wanted to buy it. When he approached the manager, he was initially taken for a customer who had had one too many. But after succeeding in persuading the young man he was serious, he arranged a meeting the next day and, within a month, the restaurant was his.

Two months later, his daughter was married at the Church of San Clothilde, close to Goldsmith's Paris home on the Rue Monsieur. As a confirmed atheist, Goldsmith was happy to leave most of the arrangements for the occasion to Isabel's maternal grandfather. It was he who helped her choose her wedding gown, compile the wedding list and sort out the invitations.

Organised down to the finest detail, Isabel's wedding day went off without a hitch and the couple enjoyed a honeymoon which took them to Juan de Nova, the island west of Madagascar that Rosnay had promised her as a wedding present. There was no electric light when the generator was turned off but in every other way their surroundings were idyllic and Isabel has fond recollections of the trip. But, like many things that Rosnay promised, it was never delivered. The family failed to gain the necessary option to develop it and so Isabel not only lost her island but the house her father had promised to build for her on it.

The honeymoon over, her family rallied round to find her new husband a career. First Rosnay went off to work for Antenor Patino at his Las Hadas resort in Mexico but, after deciding the hotel business was not for him, he funnelled all his energies and his limited funds into a board game called Petropolis, a sort of Monopoly with oil wells. Unfortunately for him, the project was a flop.

It wasn't long before fault lines began to appear in his marriage too. At first, the couple masked their growing private troubles with a united front in public. But Rosnay, an inveterate philanderer before marriage, began to return to his old ways. At parties he would flirt outrageously with the prettiest girl in the room and within a year he had embarked on the first of a series of extra-marital affairs. Isabel found it a heartbreaking and humiliating experience.

Just how bad things had become was made clear the night the couple attended a black-tie dinner party at Regine's, the Paris night club. They arrived late but, despite this, Rosnay insisted they leave just as coffee was being served. When Isabel protested that it would not be polite to depart so promptly given how late they had turned up, Rosnay revealed a vicious streak. Oblivious to the stares of the other guests, he marched angrily up to his wife. 'He grabbed my hair at the back and just lifted me off the chair by pulling my hair,' Isabel recalls. 'I had fallen and he was literally holding me up and dragging me along by my hair, caveman-style.' Perhaps frozen in shock, none of the other guests at the event moved to intervene.

The marriage limped on for another year after this episode but, as Rosnay's infidelity grew more marked, he became, in Isabel's words, no more than 'an unpleasant flatmate' and she began to look forward to his absences. He had bullied Isabel into believing that any social success she enjoyed was due to him. But as she began to socialise alone more and more, she discovered a social identity of her own and recovered her self-esteem. The marriage might have drifted on, following this pattern, for some time had it not been for a chance meeting between Isabel and Marisa Berenson in the ladies loo at a dinner party. When Berenson asked Isabel if she was happy, she broke down and said: 'No, he's horrible to me'. To Berenson, who had had a long relationship with Rosnay before his marriage, it was a familiar story. 'The only way he feels confident is by making you insecure,' Isabel says Berenson told her. 'Leave him'.

Isabel duly demanded a divorce after two years of marriage and six months later her one brief flirtation with married life was over. Rosnay obviously felt that his short trip on the Goldsmith gravy train would continue in a more restrained way. He was staying at Goldsmith's apartment in the Carlyle Hotel in New York when he took a call from the gossip columnist Nigel Dempster: 'I will be keeping on our house in Paris,' he declared confidently, when quizzed about the break-up in October 1975. Blood, however, is thicker than water. When the divorce went through, Goldsmith, who had been paying the rent on the couple's apartment in Paris, cancelled the lease.

Acquisitive to the last, Rosnay made sure he got his pound of flesh. He and his mother toured the flat on the Place Vaubon in a fashionable quarter of Paris packing up half of everything. 'If there had been a dozen plates, I found myself with six, and I thought, Hang on, these came from various members of my family,' recalls Isabel. 'The silverware, everything, was packed up by him and his mother.'

Rosnay went on to marry a statuesque American windsurfing champion, Jenna Severson, and became an accomplished windsurfer in his own right. As part of his research for a book about the world's most significant straits, he began a tour of international waterways. He had already made hazardous crossings of the English Channel, the Straits of Gibraltar, the Bering Straits between Alaska and Siberia and the Soya Straits between Japan and the Russian island of Sakhalin when his luck finally ran out. It was on an attempt to windsurf the Taiwan Strait between the nationalist island and mainland China that he went missing presumed dead in November 1984.

Isabel, meanwhile, was struggling to come to terms with life as an heiress-in-waiting. Following her divorce she moved to a tiny flat above a restaurant at 41 Rue St Andre des Arts in the 6th *arrondissement.* Today it is pedestrianised and fast food shops have replaced the craftsmen's workshops that once dotted the street. But in the mid-'70s it was a charming place to live. Left with an allowance of just £400 a month from her father, money was tight. Her grandfather, for once, saw no reason to help out as she had a 'perfectly wealthy father'.

No fan of convenience food as a rule, she did become partial to the cut-price frankfurters in baguettes served by a local shop. At F3.50, they made a filling repast when times were hard. On the worst days they did for both lunch and dinner. But she had another advantage over people in similar straits, a ready supply of dinner invitations. These would be accepted with alacrity as her allowance dried up towards the end of each month. Nor were party frocks ever a problem. As an attractive twentysomething from the right background, she could always rely on top designers to lend her their most glamorous creations. Despite this, she felt obliged to hawk some of the jewellery left to her by her mother. She didn't miss the '50s-style jewellery at the time but now they have become fashionable again she regrets that they had to go to cover the bills at a difficult time.

Eventually, she decided she had had enough of life on the baguette line and moved back into her father's house on the Rue Monsieur. 'I realised that financially things were very difficult for me and nobody else ever had to think about any bills, and I just found the pressure unfair so I moved back,' she says. 'I thought, Why am I having to worry about everything? Other members of the family just haven't got a clue. It's good to have a touch of reality but this is very extreme.'

Life back under her father's roof was not as uncomplicated as she might have anticipated, however. The distance between herself and Ginette had only been accentuated by her brief marriage and the domestic trench warfare that accompanied her return was almost comical in its pettiness. Isabel would find that three steaks would be ordered for Ginette and her two children but nothing for her. In a bid to counteract this, Isabel took to ordering food in the name of another member of the family or eating leftovers from one of her father's dinner parties. When the rest of the household went on holiday, she would be left in the empty house with only the doors to her bedroom and the laundry left unlocked. She found herself similarly isolated at Ormeley

Lodge. There the Christmas spirit deserted her on Boxing Day when she would wake up to discover that Annabel and her children were leaving for Barbados that very day. She may have been an heiress and the daughter of a multimillionaire but, with no provision having been made for her holiday, she had no alternative but to stay where she was or return to Paris.

It was in these relatively impoverished circumstances, in January 1982, that Isabel decided it was time she visited her sick grandfather in New York. By the time she arrived, he had been taken into hospital with flu and bronchitis and she was banned from visiting him on the grounds she might bring in germs. So she resolved to sit it out. Initially she stayed with her step-grandmother and her aunt Christina in Patino's apartment on Fifth Avenue. There she shared a room with her chain-smoking aunt. This proved something of an ordeal for the health-conscious Isabel and after two weeks it was decided that it would be better for everyone if she moved to a hotel. On a budget of £400-a-month this was always going to be a financial strain but Goldsmith children are not used to slumming it. Daddy's favourite had always been the Carlyle, New York's most exclusive hotel, so that was where Isabel headed. 'I might have been broke but I wasn't going to lower my standards,' recalls Isabel. 'It never actually occurred to me that one could stay anywhere else, I must admit.'

With her funds running low, Isabel made an anguished call to Dr Isadore Rosenfeld, a cardiologist who doubled as her grandfather's personal physician. He confirmed that Patino's condition was serious and that he would have to remain in hospital for some time. Unable to visit him, she returned to France – flying economy – on the advice of her relatives. No sooner was she back in Paris, however, than the news came through that her grandfather had died. It transpired that he had been in a coma all along. It came as a bitter blow to Isabel who had lost the one man who, after her father, had offered her the unconditional love and affection that had been denied to her as a child.

Whatever her grief at his passing, she would also have been aware that her grandfather's death would make her extremely rich. Just how wealthy she became is a matter of conjecture. The most quoted figure given for her legacy is £50 million but this is an estimate she strenuously disputes. 'It was seriously inaccurate, it would need to be supplemented by the lottery to reach that figure,' she says. 'I'm not very rich. Quite wealthy is the way I describe myself. It's not an astronomical figure but it's enough to pay for all my needs and to be able to live very well and not be dependent on anyone. That's the luxury.'

Whatever the scale of her new-found riches, when she received the first instalment, Isabel did what most women would have done in her position. She went shopping. Her first stop was at Fitch in New York, where she treated herself to a fur coat. It was very much a self-indulgence for, in the West, a vociferous animal rights movement made it virtually impossible to wear such coats in public and the weather in Mexico, where she began to spend more and more of her time, was never cold enough to justify it.

The lure of Mexico was a 1,500-acre plot of land on the Pacific coast which Antenor Patino had left jointly to his wife, his daughter Christina and to Isabel. The three women could not agree on what should be done with it, however, and, in the end, Isabel, intent on realising her grandfather's dream of establishing a resort there, bought out the other two and began developing a retreat for millionaires, Las Alamandas. She could not have chosen a more stunning location. Clear blue waters pounded on to no fewer than four beaches while, inland, the site was a riot of exotic trees, palms, flowers and wild birds. The setting has already made it a favourite with picture editors. *Playboy* has photographed centrefolds there and *Le Figaro* has used the resort for fashion shoots.

Isabel's vision was of a small collection of villas, with all the facilities of a luxury resort, dotted around a 70-acre site surrounded by tropical vegetation. The project was eventually completed in 1990 and it soon became a favourite of some of the biggest names in showbusiness. Robert de Niro, who persuaded her to build a gym, has an option to visit every Christmas. The French tennis player, Yannick Noah, endeared himself to the staff by turning out for the Las Alamandas football team. Rod Stewart has been there twice with his wife, Rachel Hunter. Other guests have included Richard Gere and Cindy Crawford; Tim Jeffries, one of the heirs to the Green Shield stamps fortune, and Elle 'The Body' McPherson; and Simon Le Bon, the former lead singer with Duran Duran and his wife, the model Yasmin Le Bon.

It's not hard to see why. In addition to the well-equipped gym, Las Alamandas offers a seafront swimming pool and a floodlit tennis court. Guests, who pay between £230 and £630 a room per night, may also go horse-riding, fishing, and hiking. For the more adventurous there are even trips in the resort's very own hot-air balloon. With an average of 20 days of rainfall per year, the weather in Mexico could not be more conducive to tourism. When it does rain, however, the consequences can be devastating. When Hurricane Hernan hit the coast in October 1996, the paved road between Manzanillo and Las Alamandas was closed briefly by flood water. The rutted track that leads to Isabel Goldsmith's retreat would not have stood a chance. The entrance to the resort itself is surrounded by a bed of the yellow flower that gives the resort its name and, more sinisterly, guarded by two armed men in uniform.

Isabel rarely spends more than four months in Mexico to see out the British winter. At the end of April she returns to her London home in Tregunter Road, Chelsea, where her wealthy neighbours include Oliver Hoare, once a close friend of the Princess of Wales. The house is a shrine to her passion for collecting, an obsession which stretches from old magazines to pre-Raphaelite paintings. Apart from the paintings that line the walls and the art nouveau figurines and *objets d'art* that stand on columns and shelves, she has stacks of catalogues and magazines marked with Post-It notes to remind her why she kept them.

This squirreling instinct extends to the bathroom where there are boxes of lipsticks, packets of soap, jars of bath oil and numerous pots of skin cream. According to Nigel Dempster, Annabel Goldsmith complains that Isabel 'totally denudes the house' when she leaves Ormeley Lodge, carrying with her a black dustbin liner full of loo rolls, washing up liquid, soap and anything else she can find. Isabel claims this is an unfair generalisation based on an isolated incident when she was living in a small flat in Queen's Gate, without staff, and didn't want to face supermarket queues. Defending her position, Isabel points out Annabel has never had to pay for anything.

Isabel consulted an expert in Feng Shui when she called in the builders. He persuaded her to move a mirror from a 'bad position' and to put I-Ching coins in the foundations of her new extension along with eight pennies from her own purse. 'There are all these magnetic fields under the earth and this (*Feng Shui*) is the study of the flow of these fields and their energy and how to use them to your advantage and to protect yourself from negative fields,' she explains. 'There are certain places that make you feel better than others and there are certain places that seem to be bad luck. In Mexico, I put some crystals in the foundations, I thought that would be rather good.'

In addition to her homes in London and Mexico, Isabel also has what she calls a 'tiny flat' in Los Angeles. When in Europe, she uses her London home as a base but makes frequent weekend visits to Paris. She is also a regular visitor to New York and Delhi. New Year was usually spent at her father's house in Mexico, where the annual party became something of an institution.

Of all the Goldsmith children, no one would have had greater justification for resenting their father than Isabel. She may be wealthy and independent now but in the years when she was a dependent child there was no mother protector to look after her interests on the all too frequent occasions when her father was away empire-building. Manes and Alix, Jemima, Zak and Benjamin, even Charlotte and Jethro may have felt the aftershocks of the waxing and waning of Goldsmith's ardour for their mothers but each woman has remained on the payroll and, more to the point, alive. Isabel, however, had no buffer between herself and the outside world. She described the experience of growing up without a mother as 'going through life as if I had been skinned alive'. She was the perpetual cuckoo in the nest, called upon to mind her ps and qs by stepmothers who tolerated her at best and, at worst, made her feel unwanted. Her defence mechanism was to develop an iron-clad, indeed excessive, regard for etiquette as a measure of respect. The slightest perceived infringement of the high standards passed down to her by her grandfather – 'He was always impeccable, I mean totally immaculate as a person. I never saw him with a hair out of place' – would excite her anger. And as she grew up, she developed a reputation for being difficult. During an interview with one journalist at the Berkeley Hotel in London, she broke off to harangue a waiter about the sound of workmen hammering nearby. 'I am Isabel Goldsmith, can you stop this!' she upbraided. On returning to her seat, still agitated, she complained: 'He said he couldn't do anything and I said, "Yes you can. It's called ringing the manager and getting him to stop it." This wouldn't happen in my hotel, it is bad manners.'

It is almost as if she is visiting on those around her the same pressures that have been applied to her by a string of powerful and demanding relatives. Whatever the truth of the matter, men seem to find her difficult. 'The thing about Isabel,' said one, 'is that not even the most dedicated fortune hunter would be able to stay the course.' The flip-side of her cold-eyed fury, however, is a warm, congenitally Goldsmith charm and this, coupled with her wealth and undoubted beauty, makes her unusually eligible. At 43, she remains single nevertheless. Not that an impressive list of admirers hasn't come and gone. There was Spyros Niarchos, the wealthy son of a Greek shipping magnate; ballet dancer Wayne Eagling; Guy Greville, heir to the Earl of Warwick; and Lord Mancroft, the fox-hunting baronet, who works for drug-rehabilitation charities.

Her relationship with the one man for whom she appeared to have unqualified love and admiration, 'Daddy', was not what it might have been. As a father to three other sets of children, Goldsmith never devoted to her the time she would obviously have desired and he instilled in her a curiously unfilial sense of reverence. She admired him most for what one of his political groupies might have admired him – his grasp of global economics, his valiant fight against the yoke of Brussels – instead of some touching act during her childhood. 'You know there are certain people you sit up for?' she asks. 'Being the eldest, I have known him when he was not as powerful as he became but he was always the same person. For me, now, it's quite amusing to look back and to realise that at a particular time he had no money at all, because he was always the dominant person within his circle. He was always the one who dominated conversations, he was just a natural leader. I never saw the table not revolving around him at any meal.'

But one thing even Sir James Goldsmith could not do was to replace her mother. As one interviewer wrote: 'Yes, Isabel Goldsmith has a lot of things but what she has never had is a mother. This fact lies at the epicentre of her being.'

Chapter Eight

The next generation

THE circumstances of Isabel's upbringing are in sharp contrast to the close family atmosphere cultivated by Annabel in the village of Petersham close to Ormeley Lodge. Her three children by Goldsmith may have been born into fabulous wealth but she was determined that they would grow up unspoiled by it. Child-rearing in a Goldsmith context was always something of a challenge. It was a world of nannies and exclusive schools; generous allowances and trips by private jet; magnificent homes and select holiday resorts. It takes an unusually scrupulous parent to turn out well-adjusted children in such circumstances. If anyone was equipped to do it, it was Annabel. Goldsmith had been impressed by the children she had by Mark Birley. They were good looking and bright and he admired the way she insisted they took holiday jobs. But Birley's wealth was negligible compared with his own. Annabel's solution was to send her young Goldsmiths to a local nursery where the fees were low – £12 a term in 1962 – and the children of the squirearchy mixed with those of the local taxi driver. Mrs Margaret Luddington's Sudbrook kindergarten in Petersham insisted on uniforms and taught the old-fashioned virtues. Engraved in stone above the main door of the village hall where classes were held were the words: 'Till thy kingdom come' – a phrase which may have had metaphysical significance for many but took on a more temporal meaning as far as the Goldsmiths were concerned.

For her part, Annabel would personally ferry her children to and from school – rather than leave the job to a nanny or chauffeur – oversee their homework and even ration their intake of chocolate biscuits. 'She may live in the grandest house in the village but she has a down-to-earth quality to her,' says one neighbour. She would insist that her jetsetting husband adjust his priorities to the extent that he attended landmark events in the school year, even if he did sometimes turn up at the last minute. On one occasion he was unable to make a donation at the Christmas concert because he had no English money on him.

After leaving Sudbrook School at the age of five, Jemima went first to The Vineyard infant school and then on to the Old Vicarage, a local prep school for girls, on Richmond Hill, while Zak was sent to nearby King's House School. Like Mrs Luddington's kindergarten, King's House – though private – was a relatively egalitarian institution, though occasionally there were signs of latent class war. Annabel's brother Alexander, Lord Londonderry, once found himself in an altercation with the formidable Ron Sharp, landlord of the Shaftsbury Arms, after their sons had a dispute at the school gates. Sharp junior had shoved Londonderry's heir, Viscount Cowdray, and when Londonderry warded him off the other boy's father weighed in. It was only the intervention of the school's headmaster, David Dearle, that prevented the incident escalating. Typically, it was Annabel who subsequently went to see Dearle to calm matters.

Goldsmith's acquisition of the news magazine *L'Express* in France in the late '70s had entirely unexpected ramifications for his children. Death threats to Jemima were phoned through to the Old Vicarage and then the King's House junior school matron, Beryl Meier, began receiving similar threats aimed at Zak. In what Mrs Meier calls a 'cloak and dagger' operation, the police provided the school with a tape recorder to attach to the phone and Zak and Annabel were assigned a police escort to accompany them to school each day.

While the Old Vicarage took the decision not to inform other parents of the calls, Dearle felt it was his duty to tell them. Most parents accepted his assurances about the school's security after a meeting of the governors had concluded that no pressure should be put on the Goldsmiths to remove their son, but one notoriously troublesome parent complained: 'Why should this boy stay here, there are schools for people like that.' It took more diplomacy from Annabel to bring her on side. 'She talked to that parent over the phone and allayed her fears,' says Dearle. 'I mean, obviously the worry was that there were going to be gunmen coming into the junior school'.

The threats were taken particularly seriously because there had been recent news reports of a pupil being kidnapped from the playground of another school. 'It was very frightening at the time,' says Maureen Zisserman, head of the junior school. She herself was offered police protection at night as she slept at the school during the week and staff were instructed to search their classrooms each morning before lessons began. The affair did have its elements of farce, however. When one call came through just as the junior boys were heading for lunch, a harassed Mrs Meier agitatedly told the would-be assassin to call back later. And while one female member of staff did refuse to come in for two days when the threats were first made and others looked nervously under their cars for bombs, Zak's class teacher took a rather more phlegmatic view of the whole thing. 'Zak was very fair-haired,' recalls Dearle, 'and she said, I'm not worried, Mr Dearle, because there are three or four boys with fair hair in my classroom, suggesting that when somebody came to do the deed, he might get the wrong boy.'

Meanwhile, Goldsmith called in security experts to protect Ormeley Lodge and his chauffeur was sent on a driving course to learn techniques in evading would-be kidnappers and hitmen. When Zak was eventually moved to the Mall in Twickenham it was for another reason entirely. Some of the boys in Zak's class were being moved up a year in the middle of term as was customary practice with the brightest pupils. Fired with ambition for her son, Annabel felt that Zak should be among them. Unfortunately, his teacher and the junior school head, Maureen Zisserman, thought differently and Dearle backed their judgement. Zak was removed from the school shortly afterwards.

Like his father he spent his secondary school years at Eton. And, again like his father, he left abruptly at 17. With no pressing need to earn a living, he embarked on a marathon backpacking tour of Pakistan and Nepal. His travels took him to Ladakh, in the foothills of the Himalayas, where he spent months examining a society which has become a model for ecologists studying the lessons that industrialised nations can draw from traditional cultures. Living conditions in this remote part of Kashmir are testing, to say the least, with temperatures falling as low as minus

50 degrees centigrade. This experience, coupled with ecological studies in the United States, made Zak a natural candidate to work for the Bristol-based International Society of Ecology and Culture, a group set up by Helena Norberg-Hodge, a close friend of his uncle Teddy. Norberg-Hodge is the author of *Ancient Futures, Learning from Ladakh*, the fruit of her 17 years' work in the area. The Society's rather pious entry in the Directory of the Environment states it 'educates people around the world about the root causes of the environmental, social and psychological breakdown which now threaten the very future of this planet. Work is based on insights gained from experiences in Ladakh, which brought into focus the principles on which industrialisation is based and a belief that traditional cultures like Ladakh provide a baseline from which to examine the most modern parts of the world and the concept of progress.'

Not surprisingly, Zak is considered the most academically minded of the younger generation of Goldsmiths. Largely self-taught – unlike Teddy, he never went to university – he has, nevertheless, mastered his subject and is described as a *'Trap-addict'*, a fervent believer in the views laid out in his father's bestselling personal manifesto on politics and the environment, *The Trap*.

Life is not all lentils and sandals, however. With an annual allowance well into six figures, Zak is in a position to paint the town red on a regular basis. While not a noted womaniser, he appears to share his late father's enthusiasm for gambling and was once often to be seen at Bristol's Stakis Regency Casino. In London, he settled down to a steady relationship with hat designer Caroline Hickman, the great niece of Cardinal Hume, the leader of England's Catholics. She is an old flame of Piers Adam, the owner of Fulham restaurant Kartouche, where Zak's sister Jemima was once a regular.

Much was expected of Zak. He comes across as sensitive and self-effacing and while Goldsmith may have been pleased at Zak's concern for the environment there can be little doubt that he is not the type of son he had in mind when he first heard Annabel was pregnant with his fifth child. Goldsmith confided to his first biographer, Geoffrey Wansell, that he was anxious that the child be a boy. 'Perhaps another son might be more interested in the prospect of ensuring that the family's revived reputation would continue to prosper,' wrote Wansell. As it turns out, Zak appears to have little interest in the world of finance. He has a reputation inside the family for having an independent streak but lacks the drive and ambition that characterised his father at a similar age and few see him taking on his mantle.

The child who is showing the most signs of having inherited his father's business acumen is, surprisingly enough, 16-year-old Benjamin. Once a collector of tobacco pipes, he now takes a keen interest in the fluctuations of the stock market. 'Benjamin is very warm, very good-looking, very sweet and very bright,' says one member of the family, 'but for years he's been very business-minded. He loves money. Nothing could make him happier than a cheque at Christmas.' He takes after Goldsmith in another way too. At Eton, the conservation-conscious Benjamin and Prince William, the son of his mother's friend, the late Princess of Wales, argue fiercely about the heir to the throne's penchant for shooting 'anything that moves'.

For her part, Jemima proved a model pupil. At the Old Vicarage, one of her earliest compositions made the 1981 issue of the school magazine. *Windy Nights*, by Jemima Goldsmith (aged seven), betrays a sense of the dramatic: 'The wind howls and blows/I shiver and shake/The trees wave their beautiful branches around/The wind blows through every crack/Oh, how it blows away.'

After leaving the Old Vicarage for Godolphin Latimer, she moved on to Francis Holland in Pimlico. There she exhibited an early public-spiritedness by persuading her classmates to accompany her on morale-boosting visits to old ladies on the local council estate. Outside school her great passion was horse riding, a hobby her father was well-placed to indulge. He kept her supplied with a string of ponies and horses and, after she qualified for the Horse of the Year Show at the age of 12, he even bought a £75,000 showjumper. In her early teens she was a regular competitor at gymkhanas around the country. With Annabel supporting her at ring-side, she participated in shows as far afield as Harrogate, competing for prizes as low as £22. She won 12 county shows and five championships in all, including the Tower McCall Classic, the FA Cup of the sector.

As Jemima grew older, she began to devote more time to her studies and was rewarded with a string of A-levels and a place at

Bristol University to study English. There, while most of her fellow-students rented grotty rooms in run-down houses, Jemima lived in a house bought for her by her father in the fashionable district of Clifton. Her parties tended to be rather grand too. For her 20th birthday, Goldsmith flew 100 of her 'best friends' to Paris and put them up at the Ritz. Jemima wore a white Bruce Oldfield dress for the party at Laurent, her father's restaurant near the Place de la Concorde, and the music was provided by a jazz band flown in from New Orleans. While many of her fellow students contented themselves with takeaway curries and canned beer back in Bristol, those lucky enough to have befriended Jemima were served smoked salmon, caviar and vintage champagne. As the event jointly celebrated her father's 60th birthday, guests included Henry Kissinger, the former American secretary of state, and Prince and Princess Michael of Kent.

Trust fund babe she may have been, but Jemima was no wild child. Indeed, Annabel told one of Jemima's friends that she had never given her a day's trouble. Just as she had worked conscientiously at school, she partied sedately, her only vice the odd gin and tonic. Her dress sense was stylish without being flashy. She may have favoured jumpers and jeans but they would have to come from chi-chi boutiques like Joseph and Jigsaw. And when she drove her green limited edition Peugeot convertible, she ignored the entreaties of friends to put the roof down on the grounds it would attract too much attention.

Her romantic life was conducted with equal discretion. There was never any shortage of admirers for the heiress who combined looks with brains, but she sifted applications carefully. Her only serious boyfriend before Imran Khan was Joel Cadbury, whom she went out with from the age of 17 until her second year at Bristol. One incident during their courtship illustrates a businesslike streak. It was reported that he gave her an expensive diamond ring in return for the gift of a Labrador puppy and, when she ended the relationship, the ring stayed on her finger.

She was in her final year at Bristol when she met the man who was to become her husband. The origins of the romance can be traced back across the globe to a dinner party in Bombay in 1994. There her half-sister India Jane Birley got talking to Imran Khan, the former Pakistan cricket captain and one of the greatest all-rounders in the modern game. He had become a national hero in his native land by leading Pakistan to a famous victory over England in the World Cup of 1992, an event which capped a distinguished career in English county cricket where he spent 11 years playing for Sussex. Off the pitch, his Oxford background and rugged good looks won him a following among high society women and he earned a reputation as a jet-setting playboy.

But, by the time he sat down to dinner that evening in Bombay, he had grown weary of life as a single man and his conversation with India Jane soon turned to his romantic aspirations. At 42, he said, he had had enough of bachelorhood and was looking for the right woman with whom to settle down. His family was already searching for a suitable Pakistani girl but had so far failed to turn up anyone who appealed. In India Jane, however, he had struck upon the matchmaker of his dreams. When she suggested he consider Jemima, he was initially sceptical, on the grounds that, at 21, she was too young for him. But India Jane stuck to her task, persuading him that Jemima was mature for her age with a serious-minded attitude to life.

An equally enthusiastic Imran supporter was Jemima's mother Annabel and it was she who eventually introduced them. At first sight, they made an unlikely pairing. Apart from the age difference, the contrast between their backgrounds could not have been more marked. She was the pampered daughter of a half-Jewish billionaire who had turned philandering into an art form. Imran, on the other hand, was a born-again Muslim of modest means who had views on a woman's role which conflicted sharply with liberal Western thinking. In many ways, however, the Islamic attitude to women was not as alien to Jemima as it would have been to many of her contemporaries. Her father was a man who preferred his women to be home-loving mothers. If Jemima had missed her father as a child, she may have seen in Imran's recipe for a happy marriage the possibility of gaining the sort of love and security that she had lost out on, despite her mother's best efforts.

This is certainly the view of Moya Tong, who spent some time living on Goldsmith's Mexican estate when her fiancé worked for him. 'Rather than being shocked by the way Islamic women are treated, I suspect she will find it somewhat familiar,' she wrote in a letter to the *Daily Mail* in May 1995. 'Sir James can be a fascinating man for women but he likes them to stay in the background. He has no truck with working women and tends to dismiss them with a charming smile. Jemima's mother has provided much love and security but the frequently absent father, the ever-growing step family and the element of difference and distance in her life with Sir James may be why Jemima has turned to Imran, his religion and country.'

Whatever her rationale, it soon became clear that she was besotted. She began jogging up to five miles a day and working out in the student gym in an effort to meet her new boyfriend's athletic expectations.

One of the reasons that Goldsmith wanted children by Annabel was because he found his first son, Manes, wanting. He loved the boy but realised early on that he was not a suitable heir. When Manes began falling behind at school, his mother, Goldsmith's second wife, Ginette Lery, took him to see an expert who diagnosed him as severely dyslexic. As a result, he was removed from his school near Brighton and transferred to Millfield, where Goldsmith had begun his own education in England and where he had met one of the few teachers for whom he had any respect, R.J.O. 'Boss' Meyer. He had been a pioneer in the teaching of children with learning difficulties and, under his supervision, Millfield had become a haven for dyslexics. And there the matter might have rested. Unfortunately for Goldsmith, Manes grew into a feckless, if charming, young man.

His first job after he left Millfield was on the toy counter at Harrods, where he earned £43 a week. Eighteen months later, his father set him up with a tobacconist's in Twickenham called Mayfair. But even the valuable custom of Goldsmith's friends, including the cigar-chomping John Aspinall, failed to avert financial trouble and Manes's first foray into business ended in closure. By this time, he had become a fanatical Chelsea supporter and was one of the guests at a stag night for the team's veteran defender Ron 'Chopper' Harris in 1980. He proved an enthusiastic bidder at the auction for the tracksuit top that Harris had worn at the 1970 FA Cup final when Chelsea beat Leeds United. The bids came thick and fast, with Manes repeatedly topping previous offers until it was finally knocked down to him for an impressive £900. But when Harris attempted to get Manes to pay up, the millionaire's son reportedly refused to hand over a penny more than £150, claiming he had been 'artificially bid up' at the auction. Harris even complained to the then chairman of Chelsea, Brian Mears, when Manes continued to avoid him, although the debt was eventually settled.

It is not hard to see why Harris was so upset. Only the previous week he would have read that Manes's father had sold the Bovril part of his food empire for a cool £42 million. And it was his father's wrath that the 20-year-old feared most. 'His rage will be enormous if he hears this,' said Manes at the time. 'He'll go up the wall when he finds out.'

Manes could not have been more right. We will never know exactly what passed between them when the incident reached his father's attention but, according to *Private Eye*, Goldsmith fired off a letter to Fleet Street editors as a result. This was not the first time Manes had got into trouble over money. While he was at Millfield he stayed with Annabel at Ormeley Lodge. According to his step-sister Isabel, during his stay with Annabel he disposed of the Londonderry family silver. 'He sold it by weight and it was melted down,' says Isabel.

Goldsmith began to grow more and more irritated at his son's antics. One journalist who got to know Manes well at this time was the gossip columnist Christopher Wilson. The black sheep of the family told Wilson of his father's 'rages' over his conduct. While Manes revelled in the novelty of seeing his name in print, as a high-profile businessman his father saw things differently. 'I once had lunch with him at Drones and he arrived with a car and driver,' recalls Wilson. 'It was quite clear that the driver was actually his minder, there to look after him and to make sure that he didn't do anything naughty or irresponsible or whatever.' There was other evidence that Manes lived comfortably despite his father's disapproval. Wilson notes that he arrived at Drones wearing an ankle-length cashmere coat 'which would probably have maintained a small family for quite some time'.

It was soon after this that Goldsmith obviously reached the end of his tether. The next call Wilson received from Manes came not from Ham but from Auckland, New Zealand, almost 12,000 miles away. He told the writer that he had been sent there by his father against his own wishes. 'The call I got from him was very anguished,' recalls Wilson. 'I think he was frightened and he hadn't got any friends.'

It was in a bar in Australia that the football-mad Manes ran into the Mexican squad who were touring the country. One thing he does have in common with his late father is a capacity to charm and by the time the team returned home he had become such a part of the furniture that he went with them. Once there, he succeeded in joining the hierarchy of the Mexican football association, becoming manager of the national amateur squad, public relations assistant to the president of the 1986 World Cup operation and then manager of the junior team.

Goldsmith built him a house on his Cuixmala estate but Manes spent much of his time in Colima, the capital of the state of the same name, staying first at his father's house nearby, the Hacienda San Antonio, before moving into a hotel in town, the Costeno. He later moved to an apartment in the upmarket district of Lomas Vistahermosa and it was there that his behaviour again earned him press coverage. The local paper, *El Mundo desde Colima*, reported discontent among his neighbours about the amount of noise he and his friends were making and Manes responded in a way that was reminiscent of his father at his bellicose best. The portly 38-year-old stormed into the office of the editor and publisher, Manuel Sanchez de la Madrid, a cousin of the former president of the same name, and made his views known with much shouting and arm-waving.

Manes was still preoccupied by football and Goldsmith even bought the local second division team, Los Jaguares. Manchester United it was not and Goldsmith was obviously not prepared to play sugar daddy. Fixtures were played at the San Jorge stadium in front of crowds which rarely exceeded 5,000 and there were no star names to set the pulses racing. But it was just what Manes needed to keep himself occupied and he became a familiar presence at training sessions. The team was later sold and Manes, a fluent Spanish speaker, unlike his father who used Luis de Rivera as his interpreter, went to live in Buenos Aires, Argentina. He later returned to Mexico where he lives to this day.

His sister Alix divides her time between Mexico, where she also has a house on the Cuixmala estate, and Europe. An enthusiastic collector of ethnic Mexican art, she was also responsible for the interior design of the Hacienda San Antonio, a project which took two years and which is considered a great success. She spends much of her time in Europe, flitting between

England – where Stanhope Administration rents her a house in west London – France and Switzerland organising exhibitions.

She was born in January 1964 and named after her father's cousin and then business partner Baron Alexis de Gunzburg. Her marriage to Giofreddo Marcaccini, who is half Italian and half Greek, took place at Montjeu, Goldsmith's chateau in Burgundy in 1991. The couple have two children and Marcaccini now works at Cuixmala.

Chapter Nine

From privilege to purdah

MOONLIGHT bathed the Shaukat Khanum Memorial Cancer Hospital in Lahore as the tall European stood alone, lost in thought, on its manicured front lawn. He gazed at the oriental red-brick building for almost a quarter of an hour, oblivious to the curious stares of the sentries at the gatehouse behind him. A few yards away, Mohammed Osman waited patiently at the wheel of his battered yellow taxi. By now it had dawned on him that the well-dressed stranger was more than a tourist with a passing interest in the monument built by Lahore's most famous son in memory of his mother. Throughout the 20-minute journey in Osman's ageing Daewoo, this most unusual of fares had pumped him for his opinions on Imran Khan, the Pakistani cricketing hero behind the £10 million medical showpiece that was their destination. 'When I picked him up outside the Pearl Continental hotel I asked him his name as I do with all my passengers,' says Osman. 'He said Michael. Then he started asking me all sorts of questions about Imran Khan. Did I think he was a good man? An honest man? Did I reckon he would ever be prime minister? Would I vote for him?'

By the time his passenger had broken off his reverie and eased himself back into the cramped saloon with its torn plastic seats, Osman realised why his imposing fare had seemed so familiar. He had seen his blurred black and white picture in a recent edition of the local paper. 'I don't think your name is Michael,' said the streetwise cabbie, 'I think you are Sir James Goldsmith.'

'He just laughed,' says Osman, recalling the incident a year after Goldsmith's visit in October, 1995. He had good reason to remember the night that he chauffeured a billionaire. For a trip that would normally have earned him just 500 rupees – less than £10 – he was rewarded with £100 sterling in crisp £20 notes, easily the biggest tip he had ever received.

For Goldsmith too, it was a night to remember. It was his first visit to his daughter's adopted city and the first chance he had had to examine his new son-in-law's achievements and experience Imran's cult status in his homeland.

The announcement of Jemima's engagement five months earlier had surprised the European jetset. Her suitor was, after all, a Pakistani Muslim, twice her age, with a colourful love life to his credit. Their marriage would entail Jemima converting to Islam and moving nearly 4,000 miles to Lahore where she would be obliged to live with her in-laws. On the plus side, Imran undoubtedly had sex appeal. His good looks and his pedigree as an international sporting hero ensured that he was never short of admirers. Nor can Jemima fail to have been impressed by his tireless fundraising efforts in support of the cancer hospital.

But perhaps most significantly of all, her marriage to Imran rocketed Jemima to superstar status. As the daughter of a man once billed by the *Sunday Times* as one of the richest people in Britain, she had always had a place in the gossip columns. But, apart from occasional snippets on her love life or brief reports of her horse-riding activities, the young student was largely ignored. When she abandoned her English studies at Bristol University, many blamed her romance with Imran but Jemima denies this. 'It was nothing to do with the marriage or anything like that,' she said. 'I was ill in the second last term of my third year, which is a very crucial time. I had a kidney infection and ended up in hospital so I missed the whole term and there was no way I could complete my finals.'

Following the announcement of her engagement, overnight she became the darling of a press hungry for an alternative society lovely to supplement the Princess of Wales, then riding high in the public's affections. Jemima's taste for gowns with plunging necklines may have been replaced by one for more modest *shalwar kameez*, a form of traditional Pakistani dress more in keeping with Muslim sensibilities, but she was soon a fixture in the minds of tabloid picture editors. Nor did the couple resent the exposure as they hosted grand parties to raise cash to rebuild Imran's hospital in the wake of the bomb blast that tore through it in April 1996. They even prevailed upon the gossip columnist Nigel Dempster, whose wife is close to Jemima's mother, Annabel, to print their office telephone number at the foot of an item in his column.

If Goldsmith had any reservations about the match, he soon overcame them in the face of strong support for the couple from his wife, Annabel, and in May a Muslim ceremony was held at his home in Paris. A month later, he played the proud father at a reception in the grounds of Ormeley Lodge.

Confronting the reality of his daughter's new life in Pakistan must have given rise to some misgivings, however. While the upper echelons of Lahore society lead lifestyles as comfortable as their equivalents in the West, he would have discovered that Imran did not number among the city's pampered elite. Until Zulfikar Ali Bhutto, the father of Benazir Bhutto, took power in 1971 and nationalised much of the country's private wealth, 22 key families dominated Pakistan's business and social scene. They suffered further under his successor, General Zia ul-Haq, when a new breed of self-made men consolidated their position. Since then many of the ancient families have recovered their status and today they comprise the nation's elite along with the new industrial barons and bureaucrats who have grown fat on graft.

The Khans, however, fell into none of these categories. Imran has his mother, Shaukat, to thank for the family home in Zaman Park, a pleasant enough district of Lahore. Her family, the Burkis, came from Jullundur in the eastern Punjab, which stayed with India after partition in 1947. It was her brother, Lieutenant-General Burki, who obtained the land, which had been made vacant by a mass exodus of Hindus to India, when he was made a member of Mohammed Ayoub's martial law cabinet in the late '50s. Imran's father, who had a modest career as an engineer comes from less influential stock. 'There's nothing aristocratic at all about his [Imran's] background,' says Salmaan Taseer, a wealthy investment banker and a former candidate for the then ruling Pakistan People's Party or PPP. 'They were never part of the society here. They were never part of the rich feudal families.'

In contemporary Pakistan there is a more meritocratic sentiment abroad. Imran's achievements on the cricket field made him a national hero and his tireless fundraising for the cancer hospital served to cement his growing public profile. Today he is welcome at the dining tables of the grandest families in the land. But he does not consider his own home good enough to return the compliment. At number two Zaman Park, he and Jemima occupy a self-contained upstairs flat in the six-bedroom house they share with his father, Ikramullah Niazi. When Jemima moved in, two of Imran's sisters and their families were already in residence while their houses were being completed across the nearby canal, and chickens and a goat stalked the garden.

If Imran wants to entertain, he uses the homes of his wealthier friends. So when Mick Jagger hit town with his daughter Jade after a trip to India to watch the cricket World Cup in 1996, Imran turned to Youssef Salahuddin to provide a venue fit for a millionaire rock star. Salahuddin's home is one of the most remarkable houses in Lahore. The Barood Khana, as it is called, is a sprawling, antique-filled affair built around two courtyards in the Old City. Once past the armed guard at the gate, guests are greeted by a tiny monkey, chained in an alcove, which nods at visitors as they stroll past.

Intriguingly, Youssef is an active member of the Pakistan People's Party, or PPP, the party of Imran's sworn enemy, the former Prime Minister Benazir Bhutto. Despite this, Youssef is widely regarded as Imran's best friend in the city and, as a result, Jemima became close to his now ex-wife, Embesat.

Embesat is one of only a very limited circle of friends that Jemima cultivated after her marriage. As Imran's wife, she has been obliged to adhere to a stricter code of conduct than many other women in her stratum of Pakistani society because her actions are circumscribed by his right-wing political position and the need to placate his conservative supporters. According to former ITN journalist Cathy Saigol, who married a prominent Pakistani industrialist and lived in Lahore for more than 20 years, the Punjabi capital is no stranger to alcohol, drugs and promiscuity. 'It's like being in downtown New York or LA,' she said. 'What Imran has done is to keep Jemima away from that section of society.'

But while Jemima is young, at 23, she is nobody's fool. And the few people she is exposed to are not home-bound *naifs*. Jemima could not have chosen a more fascinating companion than Embesat, for example. The Barood Khana is situated in the heart of Lahore's red light district and Embesat – who has since got divorced from her husband and is no longer in touch with Jemima – became a formidable ally of the local prostitutes in their battles with abusive clients and bullying policemen. If any of the euphemistically named 'dancers' had a problem they knew they only had to call Embesat to be assured of a sympathetic hearing.

Apart from this freelance charity work, Embesat also had a formal role as an adviser to the Ministry of Human Rights but she nevertheless found time to act as a sounding board for her friend. She learned to stock the freezer with *kulfa*, the Pakistani ice cream made with nuts to which Jemima says she became addicted, in advance of her visits. 'I like her a lot,' she said. 'She's a lot of fun but she's also a good polite person. She seems to be a very balanced woman, not a crazy fun-loving little doll. She's a sensible woman, a little aggressive for her rights and she knows life. She is the daughter of a very well-known man, a very rich one also, but she doesn't even let you feel that she belongs to that family.' She adds, tellingly: 'Not that she's here that much anyway.'

This is certainly true. Much has been made of Jemima's successful integration into the Pakistani way of life. Press coverage concentrated on her arrival in Lahore to a hero's welcome – thousands of people had gathered at the airport to greet them and hundreds more congregated at Imran's home – and the mornings spent learning Urdu and reading the Koran with Imran's sisters. But the truth is that following the midsummer ball thrown by her father in celebration of her marriage in June, 1995, Jemima spent much of her time out of the country. First there was the honeymoon at her parents' estate in southern Spain, when she and Imran were caught *in flagrante delicto* by the prying lens of a paparazzo on the hill opposite as they made love on a balcony. That December, it was back to London to spend Christmas with her family. She was in London again for Easter and at the beginning of July she and Imran hosted the Mughal Evening, a fundraising dinner, at the Dorchester Hotel in Park Lane in the presence of the Princess of Wales. Then she settled down at Ormeley Lodge to see out the remaining four months of her pregnancy. But this was not all. In between these long sojourns in England she accompanied her husband on a gruelling round of fundraising trips around the globe, taking in Japan, India, America, the Gulf States and Saudi Arabia. She even found time to visit her half-sister, India Jane Birley, in Bombay. This globe-trotting apart, her acclimatisation was not helped by a severe dose of amoebic dysentery. As Salmaan Taseer puts it: 'She's been on the can since she came here.'

With Jemima in England for much of the second half of 1996, her husband concentrated on building support for what he persisted in calling a political movement rather than a party.

Imran Khan is the people's saviour from Central Casting. Dressed from head to foot in brilliant white, during the election campaign of 1997 he toured the most deprived areas of the country like a latter day messiah, attracting vast crowds of disciples. His *shalwar kameez* was buttoned to the neck so that the top resembled a clerical dog collar and the messianic look was completed by the garlands of flowers and tinsel that his admirers draped over him wherever he went. He looked every inch what he professed to be: a man with a mission to clean up one of the most corrupt nations on Earth.

Pakistan is certainly a country in need of a redeemer. Less than 20 per cent of its population of 130 million is literate. Unemployment stands at 60 per cent in rural areas where two thirds of the people live. While the majority of the population live in abject poverty, a charmed circle of politicians and bureaucrats have grown rich by looting the national coffers. A handful of the country's most senior bureaucrats are said to be worth more than $2.5 billion each thanks to a culture of corruption that bleeds ten per cent of the country's $70 billion gross national product. As an almost inevitable result, just one per cent of the population controls 70 per cent of the wealth. In the circumstances, it is no surprise to find that in 1997 all the political parties campaigned on anti-corruption platforms. Imran was no different. As a celebrity who had not been tainted by office, however, there were early signs that people were more inclined to take his message at face value. Indeed, he went so far as to advocate the death penalty for those found guilty of corruption.

Imran on the stump was certainly something to behold.

Enthusiastic crowds thronged his Toyota Land Cruiser and showered it with rose petals as he passed through villages on the campaign trail. On one visit to the town of Gujranwala, in Imran's native Punjab, in October 1996, his convoy was joined by a fleet of Suzuki vans crammed with supporters and young men on motorcycles waving flags. The procession grew as Jemima's husband and his entourage made their way to Sheranwala Bagh, a large park, colourfully lit and festooned with flags and bunting. There as everywhere, thousands had turned out to hear him speak, cheering references to the man he alleged to be the country's biggest *bimari* or disease, Benazir Bhutto's husband, Asif Zadari. Then known as the First Man, as opposed to the First Lady, Zadari was also a member of his wife's Cabinet. Once imprisoned for two years on charges of murder and extortion, he had become a figure of hate among the public at large. 'With these looters, this country has no future,' Imran told the heaving rally. He never missed an opportunity to emphasise that corruption was public enemy number one. Indeed, the name of his party, Tehreek-I-Insaaf, was designed to ram this message home. It means the Justice Movement. But personal ambition obviously played no small part in Imran's decision to involve himself in politics. Embesat Salahuddin recalls his euphoria on his return from one particular rally: 'Imran came to my house, sat here and said to me, "You know what happened today?" – and his eyes were bright and shining. 'The people were chanting, "Prime Minister Imran Khan." '

As one supporter, the taxi-driver Mohammed Osman, says he told Goldsmith: 'We like Imran Khan very much. He's honest. Even the party name means honesty. One day he will be our prime minister.'

Not everyone shared Osman's ardour, however. Imran's opponents were scathing about his electoral prospects, arguing that he would be lucky to win any seats at all in the 217-seat National Assembly, which has been dominated for years by the Pakistan People's Party and the Pakistani Muslim League, or PML.

Salmaan Taseer claimed that Imran drew the bulk of his support from the urban areas, where his cricketing reputation stood him in good stead. In the rural areas, he argued, it would be a different story. There political support depends on local

171

loyalties. 'People have built up generations of connections,' he said. 'They have spent years attending marriages, getting people out of police stations and fighting their battles. It's a system of relationships, what we call *biradari*. The word means brotherliness, it means you are from the same caste.'

Breaking up these age-old allegiances was the greatest challenge Imran faced. But he had other problems too. As late as the end of 1996 he had conspicuously failed to persuade a single politician of any note to defect to his Tehreek-e-Insaaf. Taseer is also scathing about Imran's claim to be a Pathan, a descendent of the romantic warrior tribe that originated on the north-west frontier. It may sell well around Belgravia coffee tables but is it true? 'Calling him a Pathan is ridiculous,' says Taseer. 'It's like calling me French because perhaps 300 years ago my great great grandmother may have been French, for example. The first thing a Pathan has to do is to speak *pushto* and he can't. He presents himself as a Pathan because they have a tall and warlike image that appeals to the British. But his father is a Punjabi from Mianwali and in Pakistan you take your tribal identity from your father. If you asked the real aristocratic Pathan families of the frontier: "Is Imran a Pathan?" – they'd laugh.'

Imran was more seriously compromised by the adoption of a political philosophy that clearly conflicted with his womanising reputation. He may have successfully reinvented himself as an orthodox Muslim and faithful husband but his new guise as a champion of traditional morality and female subservience smacked of political opportunism in a land where the forces of Islamic fundamentalism were on the march. These views represent a remarkable transition from hedonistic bachelor to devout family man. His time in London was marked by an epic series of conquests. Apart from his well-documented relationships with the likes of actresses Goldie Hawn and Stephanie Beacham, portrait painter Emma Sergeant, models Jerry Hall and Marie Helvin, Viscount Linley's ex-girlfriend Susannah Constantine and former MTV presenter Kristiane Backer, he fathered an illegitimate child by Sita White, daughter of his father-in-law's late friend and fellow tycoon, Lord White. This was to have far-reaching ramifications for his political career in Pakistan. Although Imran's supporters claimed that Muslim League agents had prevailed on White to launch a paternity suit in the hopes of damaging his campaign she was adamant that this was not so. White had begun her affair with Imran in 1986, shortly after he had finished with Emma Sergeant. Their relationship ended after two years when he wrote her a note saying, 'I cannot love you as Emma will always be the love of my life'. But White became pregnant when they slept together for one last time in 1991 and she gave birth to a daughter, Tyrian.

Lord White disapproved of the mixed race relationship, however. 'Dad wasn't into Imran because of his publicity as a womaniser,' Sita said. 'He said I was making a fool of myself but, if I wanted the child, I should be a single mother. After Tyrian was born, Dad's first words were, "You know that this is not a white child." This completely devastated me. I'm not racist at all and the only reason I did not put Imran's surname on the birth certificate is because Dad asked me not to.'

It was always assumed that Imran's new-found Islamic fervour precluded a match with a non-Muslim and so it came as something of a surprise to Pakistani as well as London society when he announced his engagement to the daughter of a man who personified Western decadence. No one was more surprised than Kristiane Backer. She claimed that she had been dumped unceremoniously just a month before his engagement to Jemima was made public, on the grounds he was to marry a docile Indian girl in a ceremony arranged by one of his sisters. When the true identity of his mystery fiancée was revealed, the focus of the debate immediately switched to what effect this would have on his burgeoning political fortunes at home. After all, Jemima was hardly the modest handmaiden calculated to endear him to the masses.

Not only was she not a Muslim but she was part Jewish. The figure-hugging gowns she wore to London parties were a far cry from the all-concealing robes that Imran himself advocated as the appropriate garb of an Islamic wife. Her strong personality also appeared to make her temperamentally unsuited to her new role as the wife of a man who never lost an opportunity to stress that a woman's place was in the home. One ex-boyfriend, Joel Cadbury, who found himself stranded on the M25, dumped along with his luggage after one particularly spectacular row, pronounced her 'the least docile person I know'. And yet she has shown an unexpected willingness to conform to the traditions of her adopted country.

What is not in doubt is the key role Jemima's transformation into an Islamic housewife had in reassuring her husband's supporters. As Pakistani journalist Rao Amjad Ali says: 'Not only did it make her acceptable but I think Imran gained some mileage from the fact that here was a partially Jewish lady of acceptable wealth. In goes our hero from the land of the prophet, converts her into a Muslim and marries her. So there is one less Jewish person. I think that sort of argument has prevailed.'

Imran had no doubt that his beautiful young bride, through a combination of modest piety and good works, would win the hearts of his people. In fact, his ambition has always been for her to become a Pakistani icon. In a revealing interview published in *Country Life* in January 1996, he said: 'I'd like to think that Jemima will become even more popular in Pakistan than the Princess of Wales is in Britain. The Princess of Wales is popular because she's seen by people as someone who does something for others. Whenever celebrities do something for others, they get love and popularity.'

Imran quickly realised this was a soundbite too far. In an unguarded moment he had betrayed a degree of calculation which sat badly with his insistence that his motive for setting up the cancer hospital was a purely altruistic one. His words made clear that he was fully aware of the power of good works in promoting a personality cult having watched and learned from the actions of Diana. Aware of this and the possible offence his comparison of Jemima with the Princess might cause, he proceeded to act in an extraordinary way. Despite the fact that the interview had been conducted by a friend, Sophie Swire, and that his every word had been recorded on film for a television documentary, he resolved to prevent his unfortunate statements being repeated. He immediately fired off a complaint to the Press Complaints Commission arguing that, while he had agreed to be filmed by Transworld Sport, he had not consented to an interview with *Country Life*. This naturally caused some consternation in the offices of a magazine whose idea of a controversy would be a heated debate in the letters column over who had spotted the first cuckoo of spring. Sandy Mitchell, its deputy editor, was mortally offended. '*Country Life* is not the sort of magazine, as you can imagine, that would, for a moment, think of doing an unauthorised interview, particularly with somebody like that,' he says. Plans to syndicate the article around the world were dropped and a few months later, its purpose achieved, Imran's complaint was quietly allowed to lapse.

If Diana had taken offence at the article, she didn't show it. Five weeks after it was published she was still prepared to do Imran a valuable favour. With his hospital up and running, a royal visit was just what he needed to reinvigorate his fundraising campaign. Maintaining a high-tech medical facility with 560 employees, some recruited from abroad, was proving an onerous financial burden. The Princess of Wales, who had become something of a professional hospital visitor on home turf, took little persuading to make a high-profile visit to one run by such dear friends on the other side of the world.

Imran's determination to ensure that it was he, not the government, who took the credit for the royal visit turned the affair into something of a public relations disaster, however. The arrangements for her trip were made in conditions of unprecedented secrecy. In London, the first Pakistan's High Commissioner knew about it was when a request for a visa arrived at 5.15 p.m. on Friday, 16 February 1996, just two days before she was due to travel.

In the absence of the High Commissioner, his secretary called the Consul-General and, within the 15 minutes left before the office closed, the most unexpected VIP visa the Commission had ever been asked to provide had been processed in the name of Her Royal Highness, the Princess of Wales, and the £40 fee was waived.

If the Pakistanis were shocked, the British were no less taken aback. When the High Commissioner met the marshal of the British diplomatic corps at a cocktail party that evening, the marshal paled visibly when he was told that the woman the Royal Family regarded as its loosest cannon was making a freelance trip to one of the most politically sensitive nations in Asia.

Meanwhile, in Lahore, the rumours had been building for days. Jemima's best friend Embesat Salahuddin first heard about Diana's planned trip from a source in Islamabad ten days before her eventual arrival. 'I called Imran and asked, "Is Princess Di coming?"' she recalls. 'And he said, "No, no, no, no". Then he came and spent an evening with me and Youssef and he whispered, "Shhh, don't tell it to anyone but yes she is coming." Jemima wanted to give her a *shalwar kameez* when she arrived, so we arranged that together but it was a big secret that Princess Diana was coming.'

One man who was in on Operation Diana from an early stage was Imran's father-in-law, Goldsmith. After all, it was he who was expected to provide transportation worthy of a princess. He duly laid on his private plane to ferry Diana, his wife Annabel and her niece, Lady Cosima Somerset, to the sub-continent in spacious splendour. 'None of us slept during the trip,' recalled Annabel, 'which she [Diana] put down to my non-stop chatter. I put it down to her: she made me laugh until my sides ached.'

While they relaxed in the air, how ever, confusion reigned on the ground. The Pakistani government, snubbed by the royal visitor, was nevertheless obliged to make security arrangements. The only problem was, no one seemed quite sure where her plane was due to land. In the belief she was flying in to the capital Islamabad, the Pakistanis had prepared a top level welcome there. Dignitaries were waiting at Arrivals to receive her and armed police were stationed at intervals of 100 yards on the airport road. Then came word that the royal guest was heading for Lahore and hurried security arrangements were made there. The most chaotic royal visit of modern times had got off to an inauspicious start.

'The British ambassador was really pissed off because they never informed him of her arrival and the government of Pakistan was very angry because they thought it was sheer insolence,' says Salmaan Taseer. 'They felt they should have been informed because security is the responsibility of the government. We have a system here of four provinces and law and order is a provincial subject so the government of Punjab was responsible for security. But nobody had the decency to inform them. They heard about it from a news bulletin.

'They rang up Imran Khan to ask him about it and he started acting as if somebody was trying to muscle in on his act. He refused to tell anyone and the British ambassador was telephoned. He had not heard anything about it. So he called London to ask, "What the hell's happening? Is she coming or not? Because people here are getting really annoyed."'

The rebellious Princess's first stop was the home of the Munnoos, a wealthy Lahore family which built its fortune in the textile industry and the importation of Toyota cars. If Imran had had his way she would have stayed in much grander surroundings. The Munnoos' house is large and modern, with its own swimming pool, but it does not bear comparison with the palatial home of Mrs Akhtar Ehsan, head of one of the 22 families who once controlled much of the country. Her mansion, Ashiana, is a step back into the grandeur of the Raj. Mango trees line the drive that sweeps through extensive grounds before ending at a huge oaken front door flanked by stained glass windows. Inside, there are wood-panelled rooms full of antiques, an enormous tapestry lines the main staircase and crystal chandeliers hang from almost every ceiling. In the cloistered central courtyard, hand-painted marble columns surround a tiled pool and sunlight dances on the water spouting from its fountains. It even has its own private mosque. As one local society figure put it: 'The Munnoos' house is very nice but it is very much the Holiday Inn to Mrs Ehsan's Claridge's.'

Annabel certainly did not find the accommodation up to her standards, especially when the electricity failed and the water supply proved erratic. 'I found myself somewhat disgruntled, having to shower under a trickle of water, with the aid of a torch,' she said. 'Diana fared somewhat better in her attempts to bathe, with the exception of several interruptions from the houseboy who kept appearing in her room with a copy of the Koran in one hand (a present for her) and a notepad and pen in the other. He wanted her autograph.'

The reason the superior attractions of Mrs Ehsan's house were denied to the visitors was because Imran had called upon her goodwill once too often. He had not spoken to her since borrowing Ashiana a few months earlier and Mrs Ehsan, feeling her generosity was being abused, was not about to do him another favour. Indeed, such is her status that if Diana had wanted to meet her, she would have had to call on her rather than the other way round.

As the diplomatic ramifications of her visit rumbled on, Diana embarked on her itinerary seemingly unperturbed by the fuss. One of her first appointments was at the home of Youssef and

Embesat Salahuddin. Imran led Diana up a flight of stairs so that she could get a good view of the city, says Embesat. Unable to attend Imran's reception at the hospital the next day because of their political differences, Embesat and her husband then joined Diana, Imran, Jemima, Lady Annabel and a select group of other local notables for dinner that night at The Village, Lahore's most exclusive restaurant. It was there that the media finally caught up with 'Lady Di'. Photographers sprang from behind cars in the car park to take the only impromptu pictures of the Princess they were to get during her entire visit. A sympathetic management offered the party the use of a private room but Diana was only too happy to eat among the regular diners and queue up with the men at the buffet counters where cooks in brown robes and white chef's hats dispensed an appetising array of meat, fish and vegetable dishes. The Karachi magazine, *Men's Club*, later reported that the Princess was 'a very flirtatious woman'.

The next day, the Princess visited the hospital for a series of engagements. First Imran, Jemima and Imran's first cousin, the hospital's chief executive Dr Nausherwan Burki, escorted Diana, Jemima and Lady Annabel on a tour of the Shaukat Khanum's facilities. This was followed by what is known as an *Eid Milan* party, where the guests watched a variety show performed by children who owed their recovery from cancer to the hospital's treatment.

But the highlight of the day was a fundraising dinner. Imran's hospital newsletter (editor, one Jemima Khan) reported it as a glittering success under the charmingly inaccurate title 'Lady Diana and the Hospital'. 'Present among the invitees were a number of national and international celebrities and the major donors of the hospital who have continuously provided their support throughout the years,' it said. 'This exclusive dinner helped in raising a considerable amount of approximately four million rupees [about £70,000].'

The newsletter report also illustrates how alert the Khans have become to using social contacts. The Duke of Hamilton is listed as one of the guests, despite the fact that he was only in the hospital by chance because the son of his partner, Kay, works there as a radiographer. 'I didn't meet the Princess of Wales,' he told the authors. 'It was a complete coincidence. We were actually invited to the banquet at the last moment. We certainly weren't there because the Princess of Wales was there. But we weren't hauled along for social reasons at all, I don't think. It was nothing to do with my title, I don't think they knew who I was. I rather suspect they found out later.'

There is no doubting Imran's commitment to the hospital's fortunes, however. It was the death of his beloved mother in 1985 that turned the playboy into a samaritan. Imran had always been closer to his mother than his father and the suffering she endured in her last days affected him deeply. She died in agonising pain following the late diagnosis of colonic cancer. In his authorised biography of Imran, Ivo Tennant explained that, in Pakistan, cancer is known as 'a rich man's disease'. Despite the fact that 200,000 new cases are diagnosed each year, most government-run hospitals are too poorly equipped to treat it effectively and the family flew Shaukat to London's Cromwell Hospital for an operation in 1984. By then, however, the cancer had taken an ultimately fatal hold. Imran saw his mother's case as a damning indictment of healthcare in Pakistan: 'My mother died because the hospital facilities in Pakistan were so dirty, overcrowded and very primitive. By the time she realised it was something very serious and got a second opinion, it was too late.' He has since maintained that he dreamt about her every night for a year before resolving to build a cancer hospital in her memory.

It was, from the outset, a hugely ambitious undertaking that would require the collection of millions of pounds from a poverty-stricken population who were ill-prepared to give. While the Punjabi provincial government handed over 20 acres of wasteland at Jauher Town on the outskirts of Lahore, it soon became clear that funding the initial phase alone would cost £5 million. This total was to spiral as the project developed, with a fortune in bribes having to be built into the cost.

It was clear that collecting such a huge sum from the population of a country whose average annual income was just £260 would be well-nigh impossible and that an international effort was required. Fundraising offices were set up in London and New York and Imran proceeded to call upon the contacts he had made during two decades of extensive socialising. His friend Lulu Blacker, a former flatmate of the Duchess of York, succeeded in persuading the notorious Fergie to attend one reception at the Victoria and Albert Museum. More welcome

179

publicity was generated when Imran's old flames Jerry Hall and Marie Helvin accompanied Mick Jagger to fundraising dinners. In South Africa, where apartheid had prevented him ever playing cricket, President F.W. de Klerk, Nelson Mandela and Dr Christiaan Barnard, the heart transplant pioneer, lent their names to the cause. And, in the Muslim Middle East, during a tour of Abu Dhabi, Dubai, Kuwait and Sharjah, Imran was fêted to the extent that some women were even moved to hand over their gold bangles.

But with the opening running drastically behind schedule, a dramatic final push was required. To meet his target, Imran embarked on a marathon fundraising campaign in his native Pakistan in 1994, when he undertook a tour of 32 cities in six weeks and raised a massive £2.5 million. The sums donated often came in denominations as small as ten-rupee (20p) notes.

Imran's tactics were not universally appreciated, however. Following Pakistan's victory under his captaincy in the 1992 cricket world cup, some players were upset at what they saw as his hijacking of the team's success. Salmaan Taseer explains: 'They said that if people were giving money it should have been divided among the team and they got furious because this was a big chance in a lifetime for them, frankly. Now you can say that they should have been very noble and given it all to the hospital. Why? For why? Why should they?'

The hospital finally opened its doors more than four years after the prime minister, Nawaz Sharif, laid the foundation stone in 1991. Years of frenetic fundraising, setbacks and rows paid off on 28 December 1994, when the first patients arrived. By October 1996, the hospital claimed to have treated 26,000 patients, 90 per cent of them without charge.

The controversy did not end there, however. Imran's opponents remained convinced that his ultimate aim was political power and saw the hospital, in part, as a huge public relations exercise designed to consolidate his popularity. No one puts this point of view more bluntly than Salmaan Taseer. 'What's the point in helping cancer patients when most cancer patients are terminally ill by the time they find out they've got it anyway?' he asks. 'For the same money you could save hundreds of thousands more lives. Secondly, you are replicating what is already happening. For example, hospitals have got cancer wards, some of them have got these CAT scan machines that cost a million dollars which are 20 per cent utilised. When you get cancer you get other problems, like a stomach problem, and you need a general hospital behind it. Even in America you don't find this. There are about three cancer institutes in America. So in a country like Pakistan, cancer wards are part of a hospital. It goes together. It's ridiculous to have a cancer hospital in the back of beyond where it costs 200 rupees to get there – and we're talking about poor people. If a rich man gets cancer he's not going to hang around for Imran Khan's hospital, he'll go straight to Sloane Kettering Hospital in New York or somewhere else. As a concept, it is ridiculous. It's losing money, it will always lose money and now he's saying the government should foot the bill.'

The hospital is certainly a huge drain on Imran's resources. As Ivo Tennant observed in his biography: 'When eventually the construction was complete and the equipment installed, the running costs would be such that Imran would be shackled to the project for the rest of his life.' This is something that Jemima has had to come to terms with since moving to Lahore in 1995. 'People talked endlessly about the culture shock that awaited me,' she wrote in *Vogue* in December that year. 'But it's not the country or the culture or the people; it's the franticness of Imran's life that's the real shock. I've never known anyone dedicate themselves to charity as wholeheartedly as Imran does to the cancer hospital. Beyond his basic requirements, all his cricket earnings, every bit of money he makes and every bit of time he has, go to the hospital. He goes there every day and he's constantly rallying support. We went on a fundraising trip to Japan and by the end of ten days I was literally unable to smile any more I had such jaw ache.'

Ever since he gave up his post as ambassador for tourism under Benazir Bhutto, the government had feared that Imran might one day exploit his huge popular following for political ends. But, for years, Imran denied that he had any desire to climb the greasy pole. As late as January, 1996, he was trotting out what had become a familiar line. 'They are scared that I will be able to convert the popularity I have from the cancer hospital into political support,' he told Sophie Swire. 'Despite my denials, there has been speculation that I'm about to enter politics. But democracy, which is a joke in this country, is falling apart. The system is completely corrupt. To get elected you either need a lot of money or you need strong-arm tactics. I have neither, so the best thing for me is to speak out against the injustices.'

Within months, however, he had had an abrupt change of heart. The event that precipitated this was a bomb attack on the hospital that left eight dead, including two children, and 37 injured. When the remote-controlled device ripped through an out-patient department on 14 April 1996, at 12.23 p.m., Imran was due to have been showing a wealthy Pakistani businessman around the hospital. Fortunately for him, the appointment had been cancelled at the last minute. 'It could have been meant for me,' he said later, 'but I think it was more likely to have been a warning. They wanted to show what they were capable of.' A fortnight later, Imran held a press conference to launch his Justice Movement at the Holiday Inn in Lahore. The budding politician had broken cover for the first time.

If anything was calculated to heighten Goldsmith's fears for his daughter's safety, it was just such a move. There are few careers more perilous than that of the Pakistani politician. Former prime minister Zulfikar Ali Bhutto, the father of Benazir, was hanged after losing power to General Zia ul-Haq. He, in turn, was killed in a suspicious plane crash. More recently, Benazir's estranged brother, Murtaza, who had formed a breakaway faction of the Pakistan People's Party, was shot along with seven of his friends and bodyguards. If Goldsmith needed a reason to fund his son-in-law's election bid, then this was it. But at a campaign rally Jemima denied accusations from her husband's opponents that her father was funding him as part of an international Zionist conspiracy. 'Imran is an honest man and my father is not helping either Imran or his party,' she said. 'Please don't believe the lies in the newspapers about Imran.'

The man largely responsible for the formation of Imran's early political incarnation was Lieutenant-General Hamid Gul, the retired spymaster of Pakistan's military intelligence. This former intimate of General Zia ul-Haq is the man seen by many as the architect of the Soviet Union's defeat in Afghanistan. But even with this wily old soldier at his side Imran's political naivety was often evident. On one occasion, when asked about the sensitive issue of independence for Kashmir, he blundered by saying he saw no reason not to allow autonomy if that was the wish of the majority of the people of the region. Given that a UN resolution dating back to 1948 only goes as far as saying that the Kashmiris should be offered a choice between being part of India or Pakistan, this was seen as a rash answer. If both countries were to relent on independence for Kashmir, the argument runs, there would be a domino effect among the other princely states. His detractors point out that, while he studied PPE – politics, philosophy and economics – at Keble College, Oxford, he gained a disappointing degree after devoting much of his time to cricket. And one irreverent local paper has gone so far as to dub him 'Im the Dim'.

Meanwhile, Jemima was pregnant and, after having had a miserable time of it for weeks with a bad bout of amoebic dysentery, she had returned to Ormeley Lodge to see out her term in more salubrious surroundings. There she found plenty to divert her. In July she was joined by Imran, in London to defend himself against a libel suit taken out by the former England cricketers, Ian Botham and Allan Lamb. They claimed he had called them racists and said they were uneducated and lacked class or upbringing in an interview with the magazine *India Today* in 1994. The High Court hearing provided pages of knockabout fun for the newspapers as they recorded the testimonies of some of cricket's most colourful characters from the witness box. But no one received more coverage than Jemima, who accompanied Imran to court each day, as did her mother Annabel. Every step of their short walk from car to court entrance was picked over by the fashion pundits and amateur psychologists among the media. Jemima, they noted, walked not three deferential steps behind her husband but clung to his arm, the picture of wifely devotion. Inside the courtroom, however, sharp-eyed commentators discerned signs of tension. Writing in the *Daily Telegraph*, Caroline Davies observed: 'On several occasions, as she removed the plastic butterfly clip that pulled her long hair from her face and fiddled with it in her lap, Imran grew irritated and snatched it away from her . . . If she bent over to whisper in his ear, he would hiss sharply at her to be silent.'

The jury found in Imran's favour and Botham and Lamb were left with a bill for his legal costs, as well as their own, of an estimated total of £500,000. The case was not only distinguished by the celebrity of the participants. It was also marked by a last-minute intervention from an unidentified businessman who offered to pay both parties' costs if they agreed to halt the action. Botham and Lamb refused the offer.

There were rumours that the mystery benefactor was none other than Goldsmith himself, possibly acting through an intermediary. If it was, it wouldn't be the first time he had involved himself in his son-in-law's affairs. When he had visited Lahore nine months earlier he had made it his business to charm Imran's most bitter foe. He and his French mistress Laure Boulay de la Meurthe went to the prime minister's house in Islamabad for what is described as 'a cosy meal' with Benazir and her husband. The pair were said to be excited about the prospect of meeting the billionaire, particularly Zadari, who is known as something of a power groupie. What passed between them has never been made public but Salmaan Taseer asked Benazir about it afterwards: 'She just laughed and said, "We chatted about this and that, Oxford and so on." Then she said, "I'll tell you what we didn't discuss: Imran Khan."'

Imran soon had other matters on his mind than Benazir's scorn for his ambitions. He was lifted by the birth of a son, Sulaiman, on 17 November 1996, but, come election day on 3 February 1997, Imran's party failed to win a single seat. The Pakistan Muslim League under Nawaz Sharif recorded a landslide victory, winning 136 of the National Assembly's 217 seats, reducing Bhutto's PPP to a rump of just 17 seats. As a result of his disastrous showing, Imran is now seen as a spent force in the country at large.

Chapter Ten

How green is my valley?

THE atmosphere in the dining-room was decidedly uncomfortable. There was nothing wrong with the service or the fare. The waiters in white jackets were as attentive as they could be and each course was immaculately presented. Nor was the host at fault. Goldsmith beamed expansively and chatted animatedly to those around him, making sure that no one felt left out. The problem was the guests. Rarely had a group looked less at ease in jacket and tie. They ran their fingers around the inside of shirt collars that had not been buttoned to the top since the day they were bought. Many were more used to the sort of bean and pasta bakes offered by cafés with names like Food For Thought. And as the wine was poured they pined inwardly for jugs of real ale.

This was the scene when the forces of green radicalism met those of transnational capitalism.

The power dinner had been an integral part of Goldsmith's approach to his dealings with the environmental movement since his brother Teddy first shook him with his apocalyptic rhetoric in the late '60s. Over the years, Goldsmith hosted such events in a variety of locations. Apart from Ormeley Lodge, the cream of green society has been entertained in Sir Jacob Rothschild's magnificent dining-room overlooking St James's Park, the private room at Wilton's restaurant in Belgravia, and Teddy Goldsmith's Victorian semi in Richmond.

But perhaps the first of these money-meets-muesli events occurred at the beginning of the '70s when Walt Paterson, then an activist with Friends of the Earth, was invited to Goldsmith's home near Regent's Park along with a group of other environmentalists. The head of Cavenham Foods had grown alarmed by his brother Teddy's warnings of catastrophic consequences if the world's industrialists were not brought to heel by a global commitment to environmental reform. He wanted to know from a cross-section of other green thinkers whether this view was widely shared. 'The upshot of the discussion around the table as I recall it was that we broadly indicated that none of us had this transcendental despair that Teddy was wallowing in,' says Paterson. 'We considered the situation pretty dire but reckoned that if we got seriously to grips with it we could do something about it.'

In those days, at least, Teddy refused to accept that anything other than wholesale reform would solve the problem and argued that any tinkering would only make matters worse. Success in reducing pollution would only prolong the chase for economic growth, he argued. This approach would hit the buffers when natural resources were exhausted. And if, by some miracle, both the problems of pollution and declining levels of raw materials could be solved then population growth would lead to food shortages which would, in turn, lead to a panic-stricken rejection of pollution regulation and result in 'frightful' social and health problems. It was a wonderfully circular argument. 'My ecological message is depressing,' he once admitted. 'If you tell people we are destroying the planet it doesn't make it easy for them to fit into this world. I'm not helping them to get a job, so I'm worrying: is it to their advantage to know this? My wife warns me: "Be careful who you take under your wing, they could end up killing themselves."'

Certainly, by the time Paterson and his colleagues arrived for dinner, it was clear that Teddy's forebodings had got to his brother who had become seriously concerned about what effect his brother's prognosis might have on his commercial interests. 'I came away with the feeling that we lifted Jimmy's spirits somewhat,' says Paterson. 'Teddy had cast such a pall of gloom over the future that we sounded as though we were actually seriously trying to do something about it and there was actually something that could be done if enough people took it seriously.'

Whatever their differences, Jimmy and Teddy came across as prophets of doom. 'I had ecology forced down my throat at every one of his [Teddy's] Sunday lunches,' Goldsmith's daughter

Isabel once said. 'You came out of there feeling suicidal. My father and uncle always talked about Doomsday, they just disagreed on the timing of it.'

Following that initial meeting at the house on Regent's Park, Goldsmith went on to become a figure of some note in environmentalist circles, his profile helped, naturally enough, by a willingness to award generous donations to causes that caught his imagination. One of these was Friends of the Earth's contribution to the Windscale Inquiry in 1977. The Windscale plant was designed to reprocess nuclear waste – principally from Japan – and has gone down as a *cause célèbre* in the history of the nuclear industry in Britain because it appeared to be an example of a developed country needlessly laying itself open to long-term pollution in the interests of short-term profit. In Teddy's words, Britain had joined 'the ranks of the banana republics whose political leaders are prepared to do dangerous, biologically destructive and socially destructive things for other, richer countries in order to earn quick money'.

Goldsmith provided £25,000 towards the £100,000 cost of Friends of the Earth's case against the plant. He has since described nuclear power as 'Satan's energy' and an example of man's 'hubris' but Tom Burke, the Friends of the Earth organiser who dealt with Goldsmith over the telephone at the time, picked up a different motive. 'He vaguely had the view that Britain was a great country and that we shouldn't be taking in other people's washing,' he says. 'I got the impression that his principal preoccupation was that we were being subservient to the Japs.'

Like his brother, as a young man, the tall and handsome young Teddy had an eye for a comely young heiress. He had just completed his degree when he wooed the Honourable Sarah Rothschild, daughter of Victor, the third Lord Rothschild, and sister of Jacob, one of Jimmy Goldsmith's business partners. The story of their relationship offers a fascinating insight into a man who is often seen as the Professor Branestawm of the Goldsmith family. Sarah was just 16 when the pair met in Lausanne where she was attending Brillantmont, one of the smartest Swiss finishing schools. She had been sent there by her anxious Jewish parents after confessing that her stint at St Juliana's Convent near Oxford had persuaded her that she wanted to become a Catholic. Teddy, by now 22, was at the local hotel school. The moment he heard there was a Rothschild in town, he decided he must meet her. It would be a liaison, he knew, of which his father could not possibly disapprove. So he called Sarah at Brillantmont, informed her that they were cousins and suggested dinner. To the teenage Sarah this was a romantic proposition. The girls were not allowed to go out on dates but if the man in question was a relative that made all the difference. They duly arranged to meet. Sarah, now 62, takes up the story. 'I said, "How am I going to recognise you?,"' she recalls. 'He said – he's always been quite sophisticated has Teddy – "I'll wear a carnation in my buttonhole." Then he said, "But how am I going to recognise you?" So I said, "I'll wear a carnation too." Then we both had the same thought that we might find the other hideously unattractive so both of us decided independently that we wouldn't wear carnations. We'd go there and see the person with the carnation and decide whether we liked them or not. So both of us arrived at this hotel in Lausanne without carnations and spent ages desperately looking round for someone with a carnation but, of course, there was no such person, so we both went home.'

The two did subsequently meet for dinner and, while Sarah was feeling self-conscious about her bright red face after a day in the sun on the ski slopes, it proved a great success and they decided to meet again. Opportunities for trysts were strictly limited in Lausanne, however, and it was not until Sarah returned to England that their budding romance really took off. In keeping with the mores of the times, their relationship was chaste by modern standards. When Sarah sifted through some letters following the death of her mother in 1989 she came across a rather sweet one from Teddy to her mother. 'I'm afraid I missed the last bus back to Oxford and so I had to sleep on your sofa. I'm so sorry. Everything's all right,' he wrote.

He proposed soon afterwards and Sarah accepted. To mark their engagement, Teddy – already showing signs of the eccentricity which was to become his trademark – produced not a ring but a black umbrella with gold spots. 'I came waltzing home to my mother at the weekend and said, "Mummy, I'm engaged to Teddy Goldsmith,"' she recalls. 'And she said, "Oh don't be ridiculous, darling." And I said, "Look what he's given me as an engagement present", and I produced this black umbrella with gold spots and she said, "Don't be ridiculous, no one could be serious if they gave you a black umbrella with gold spots on it. Of course, it's just a joke." '

Cajoled by her mother into ending their relationship, Sarah told Teddy that his present showed that he was not serious about her and so she was breaking off the engagement. 'He was awfully upset,' she says. 'He told me later that he had, in fact, bought me an engagement ring in Paris, with a pearl shaped like a tear.'

The jilted Teddy tried to woo her back using John Aspinall as a go-between. He would visit Sarah in the small Oxfordshire town of Woodstock, where she lived with her mother, to press Teddy's case. The two sat by the lake in the grounds of Blenheim Palace, Aspers nervously throwing pennies into the water as he told her how much Teddy loved her, but it was all to no avail.

By this time, Teddy was working in Paris and it was there that he met his first wife, an English model for Christian Dior called Gill Pretty. They married in 1953. Things cannot have been easy for Gill. Her husband, while a courtly and charming man, was, if anything, more shiftless than the young Jimmy. While Teddy's younger brother built up thousands of pounds of gambling debts as a young man, he had largely grown out of such excess by the time he went into business at the age of 20. Teddy, on the other hand, was a 30-year-old married man with two daughters when his mother bailed him out of his debts by selling her apartment in Chantilly. Gill, in a revealingly terse reference to their married life in *Vogue* in 1996, said: 'The children were raised in straitened circumstances in a little village outside Paris. It would be too unflattering for my ex-husband to go into details.' The couple separated and Gill is now the Comtesse de Montpezat, wife of the French wine producer Jean Baptiste de Montpezat, whose brother, Prince Henri, is the husband of Queen Margarethe of Denmark.

It was not until 1981 that Teddy eventually married his long-term lover, the 29-year-old New Zealand ecologist, Katherine James, eight months after the birth of their first son, Benedict.

They have since had a second son, Zeno.

Teddy has never made any secret of his lack of business acumen, once observing that 'my father only employed me in the company for philanthropic reasons'. But, for years, he plugged away, at one time securing the French franchises for hi-fi manufacturers Bang and Olufsen and Akai. It was only when his father died in 1967, leaving him a handsome legacy, that things got easier. His new-found private income meant that he could finally afford to indulge the intellectual passions that had gripped him since childhood. For Teddy Goldsmith was environmentally aware long before anyone had heard of the Greenhouse Effect.

His long haul to educate himself began in 1952, soon after he had left Oxford with a modest degree in Politics, Philosophy and Economics (PPE). It was while he was working in Paris that he embarked on a work which was to consume much of his spare time for years but was never published, *The Theory of Unified Science*. In his struggle to make other scientists understand him he even invented 200 words to explain concepts he felt could not be described with the vocabulary at his disposal. His commercial activities over for the day, he would work late into the night. When he decided that he needed a secretary to sit with him while he dictated summaries of the books he was reading as part of his research, he placed an ad in the *International Herald Tribune*. The unworldly Teddy's wording was a little unfortunate, however. After asking for a secretary to provide 'nocturnal services', he was inundated with replies from women who were offering an altogether different kind of activity. One friend was so impressed with his response that he placed the same ad and ended up marrying one of the respondents.

By the late '60s, under Jimmy's stewardship, his father's legacy had multiplied to the extent that Teddy could afford to return to England and put his green beliefs into practice. This meant leaving London for a rural fastness where it would be possible to live a largely self-sufficient existence. To this end, Teddy bought a small farm near Wadebridge in Cornwall and moved in with a group of other enthusiasts. All forms of technology were avoided, including the television. Even human waste was recycled as manure for the fields which grew the organic vegetables upon which they lived. 'This was seen as very unusual and striking in those days,' says Tom Burke, who first met Teddy as a Friends of the Earth activist in 1973. 'He was a very influential figure, very energetic and very enthusiastic and not as monomaniacal as he became. He was always an obsessive. It was a sort of religious thing with him. He had a fantastically nihilistic, apocalyptic vision.'

Even in Cornwall it was not entirely possible to escape the Curtis syndrome, however. Mr and Mrs Curtis were the couple from Vancouver who, in search of a haven of peace in a changing world, sold up and moved to the Falkland Islands. They landed a week before the Argentinian invasion of 1982. Teddy and his companions were more fortunate but when the Central Electricity Generating Board announced plans to build a nuclear power station near the neighbouring village of Luxulyan they joined around 200 other environmentalists and locals in occupying the site and blocking off the entrances. The demonstrators held out for six months until the CEGB thought better of its plan.

It was in 1970 that Teddy was elevated from obscure, self-taught intellectual to radical seer through the establishment of *The Ecologist* magazine, backed with £4,500 of his brother's money. Its doom-laden editorials soon earned him a reputation as a brooding pessimist and reports of its more extreme positions gave him names like the Prophet of Loss. But in 1972 he became a figure of interest to a wider public with *The Ecologist*'s publication of *A Blueprint for Survival*, a 40,000-word critique of the way the world was heading. It warned of the exhaustion of food supplies and other resources and, naturally, 'the collapse of society as we know it'. It was taken seriously, however, because some of its predictions had the ring of truth and many of its recommendations appeared sound. No one took it more seriously than the *Sunday Times*, which compared it with Marx's Communist Manifesto and Abraham Lincoln's Gettysburg Address as a document of great moment which had been received with little fanfare. Indeed the Penguin Special edition of *Blueprint* carried the *Sunday Times*' words on the cover in even bigger type than the title: 'Nightmarishly convincing . . . after reading it nothing seems quite the same any more'.

It certainly did launch itself upon an unsuspecting world. The Britain of the early '70's was a very different place from the relatively environmentally conscious country we know today. CFCs were used with abandon in refrigerators and aerosols, manufacturers and consumers alike blissfully ignorant of the hole they were burning in the ozone layer. Recycling was a left field affectation and council-funded bottle banks were unheard of. Motorways, far from being seen as a blight on the landscape, were considered a brave attempt to create an efficient transport network, linking the cities of the nation. Meanwhile, popular literature on the environment was largely limited to *Silent Spring*, Rachel Carson's mould-breaking exposé of the effects of the indiscriminate use of chemicals on wildlife and the countryside, published in 1962.

Like Carson's book, elements of *Blueprint* were visionary and imaginative. On transport, for example, it recommended that Britain stop building roads and concentrate instead on restoring defunct railway lines and extending the use of canals on the basis that this would end the steady erosion of the stock of agricultural land. This is now a popular orthodoxy. A little more controversially, it argued for punitive taxation on the usage of raw materials from coal to gold on the grounds they were irreplaceable. Scientific opinion is split on this subject, with some arguing that industry reacts to the growing scarcity – and thus higher price – of materials by developing alternatives. One celebrated dispute between two American academics led to a large bet over whether the prices of a particular set of commodities would rise or fall by a set date some years later. In the event, instead of rising, as the Goldsmith school would presumably have us believe, they fell.

Much more radical was *Blueprint*'s approach to global population. Ever since the political economist Malthus divined population growth as the greatest challenge to the world's economies in the late 18th and early 19th centuries, the so-called Malthusian Devil has preyed on the minds of economic planners. It certainly preoccupied Teddy Goldsmith and his colleagues and it is in relation to the control of population growth that they are at their most sinister. In the A to Z of measures required to bring about their new order, the first recommendation had an Orwellian air: 'a) establishment of national population service,' it said.

The Ecologist's aim was to reduce the population of Britain from 56 million to 30 million over 150–200 years. After first ending population growth by bringing the birth rate into line with the death rate, Britain would then be expected to reduce its propagation of children still further – and ban immigration completely – so that the population actually fell. This would initially be achieved by employing the 'finest talents' in the advertising business on campaigns to 'inculcate' a socially more responsible attitude to child-rearing, including the 'great need' for couples to have no more than two children. The campaign would be backed by a programme of free contraceptives, free sterilisation and abortion on demand. *Blueprint*, which is nothing if not detailed, goes on to recommend that if a review – notionally timed for 1995 – found that the target of replacement-size families was not being met, 'socio-economic restraints' should be brought in.

Much of the above thinking is in tune with the times but it is references to undefined 'socio-economic restraints' and a total ban on immigration that give his views an unpalatably extremist flavour.

Although 33 academics put their names to this radical manifesto, including 17 professors, five of them fellows of The Royal Society, the authors themselves were a group of gentleman amateurs. Apart from Teddy, who was named first as the editor of *The Ecologist*, there were Robert Allen, his 29-year-old deputy; Michael Allaby of the Soil Association; and John Davoll and Sam Lawrence of the Conservation Society. Allen, for example, had not only failed to complete his degree in English Literature at Oxford but had performed so poorly in the sciences as a child that his school had refused to enter him for O-levels in that field. After a stint selling text-books to developing countries in Africa and South America, where he became interested in ecology, he left publishing to set up the Primitive People Fund, now known as Survival International. After meeting Teddy soon afterwards, he helped him set up *The Ecologist*.

Not surprisingly, *Nature*, the most prestigious scientific periodical of its day, recoiled at the contents of *Blueprint*. In a leading article, under the headline 'The Case Against Hysteria', it described *The Ecologist*'s polemic as an attempt 'to fan public anxiety about problems which have either been exaggerated or which are non-existent'. 'I think he's softened his views quite a lot since then,' says Tim Lang, professor of food policy at Thames Valley University. 'I think he's still got a genially apocalyptic view but he's one of those people who's got quite an interesting capacity to think the unthinkable.'

Two years after the success of *Blueprint*, which sold an

estimated 500,000 copies in 17 languages, Teddy even stood for election as an independent for his father's old seat in Suffolk, by now renamed Eye. The election campaign was fought like a low-budget version of his brother's Referendum Party push more than 20 years later. London's party set were roped in to help with the canvassing effort and John Aspinall even provided a camel from his zoo as a publicity stunt. But Teddy failed to capture the imagination of the voters, polling just 395 votes compared with the 23,486 gained by the Conservative victor, Sir Harwood Harrison.

Jimmy, meanwhile was showing little solidarity. 'He gave a party for 24 friends at his London home and then flew the majority of them to Santo Domingo in the West Indies for a week's escape from the embarrassment of the Eye poll,' reported the *Daily Express*.

By the late '70s, Isabel was not the only one to have tired of Teddy's unrelenting pessimism. Goldsmith had grown impatient too. 'You're boring me with all that,' he would say after a particularly intense session, and at one stage the brothers could go for months, even years, barely exchanging a word. All this changed forever in the '80s when three of Teddy's gloomy predictions came to pass.

He had long warned that one consequence of the widespread use of antibiotics would be the cultivation of a growing resistance to them in the population at large and the eventual emergence of a major epidemic against which modern medicine would prove powerless. The arrival of Aids appeared to bear him out. For years he said it was only a matter of time before there was a disaster at a nuclear power plant as use of the energy proliferated and, in 1986, the catastrophic explosion at Chernobyl in the Ukraine endorsed his judgement. In the same year, scientists discovered the first signs of a hole in the ozone layer, something that Teddy had forecast to the extent that he had voiced fears about the long term effect on the atmosphere of steadily rising pollution levels. This hit rate meant that his brother began to look on him with a new respect. And, for all their periodic frostiness and the gulf between the sizes of their respective bank accounts, it is said that Jimmy still sought his older brother's imprimatur.

Others, like Tom Burke, now a consultant to the multinational mining company RTZ, see Teddy as something of a busted flush. While acknowledging the pioneering work Teddy has done on the environmental damage caused by the construction of huge hydroelectric dams, Burke reckons his time has passed. 'I think his influence has waned as he's become more and more of an Old Testament prophet,' he says. 'He always over-claimed and, by the '80s, he was getting a reputation for crying wolf. As people learned more, his views resonated less. He was always very coherent but Teddy has spent his life exploring the problems. He is not interested in any solution that involves boring compromise. He is not interested in anything other than a pastoral agrarian paradise.

'Teddy is a nihilist, he really wants it all to fall down and for us to build something better out of the ashes. He wants to do heroics. It's Jesus Christ sort of stuff. Any attempt to disagree with Teddy became a personal attack on him, so you have a choice. You can submit, go away or strangle him. I didn't want to do the first or the third, so I disengaged. He's a loner, he's not a team player.'

Teddy is no longer in day-to-day charge of *The Ecologist*, concentrating instead on his writing and lecturing. Since the publication of *Blueprint*, he has written or edited ten books, including *5,000 Days to Save the Planet* and *The Way: an ecological world view*. He was awarded the Right Livelihood Award in 1991 and made a *chevalier* of the Legion d'Honneur in France later the same year. At 68, he remains a vital figure with a distinguished grey beard. His voice is so similar to his brother's that his wife used to confuse one for the other on the telephone. His gestures are as expansive as his speech. Arms flung wide as he speaks, his eyes crinkle behind his glasses as he searches for a phrase or discusses a matter which is distasteful to him.

Of the two Goldsmith brothers, if anyone seemed likely to produce tearaway children it was Jimmy. But his offspring appear tame beside Teddy's two oldest daughters, Dido and Clio. Renowned for their looks from an early age, they hobbled through their late teenage years in platform shoes and mini skirts. Like Jemima, Clio Goldsmith went to the Francis Holland School in west London. There, however, the similarity between the cousins ends. While Jemima studied hard for a university place, at a similar stage, Clio succumbed to the attractions of long days in the sun by Richmond swimming pool. If money was tight, she and her elder sister Dido would raise funds by selling designer frocks to a secondhand clothes shop at the wrong end of the Fulham Road. After all, life chez Teddy was not as gilt-edged as it was at Chateau Jimmy. It was not long before Clio's serial truancy and her foul-mouthed abuse of her teachers when she did turn up led to her being asked to leave. With no qualifications to her name, Clio decided to trade on her looks.

At 17, already a conspicuously attractive young woman, she left England for Paris. Her eyes were as compelling as her uncle's and her dark hair formed a striking jet black mane. In the French capital, the combination of her stunning looks and figure made her much in demand as a model, where her covers for French *Elle* established her as a '70s sex symbol. Behind the scenes, however, her fiery temperament soon earned her a reputation as the friskiest clothes horse of her day. 'I hated it. I hated it,' she told one interviewer. 'I arrived four hours late with last night's make up on and the most appalling hangover. The first thing I'd ask for was five cans of beer, then talk away like a lunatic and drive everybody mad.' Her behaviour at home was little better. Friends of her mother would be shocked to hear her scream for no apparent reason and then slide under the table. Another party piece was to tear her clothes off, something she did often enough for her easygoing father to take to greeting her with the words 'Hello Stripper' when he phoned.

Increasingly bored by modelling and the English social scene, Clio took to travelling widely with a group of wealthy foreign friends. At one stage she claims to have spent six months living naked in a commune in Ibiza. It was after a trip to Bali in 1982 that she decided on impulse to fly to Rome rather than London and become an actress. There she met her future husband, Carlo Puri, the heir to the Pirelli tyre fortune, in a night club. She was five months pregnant with her daughter Talitha Allegra when the couple married in Genoa in 1982. With her husband's encouragement, she embarked on a screen career which began promisingly. After her erotic debut in *La Cicala* (*The Gipsy*), the French and Italian critics hailed her as the new Maria Schneider, the German actress who had made her name in the controversial *Last Tango in Paris*. So explicit were the sex scenes in *La Cicala* that it even came to the attention of the Italian public prosecutor who ordered copies to be seized after complaints from the public that it was obscene.

But it proved the first in a long line of what one writer described as 'spaghetti porno' movies. Her follow-up role was in a film called *Honey*. The plot called on her to lose all her clothes at the beginning and spend most of the rest of the film looking for them. 'If I had to regret anything in life – which I don't – then I'd regret that one,' she said later.

Neither of these films was released in Britain but they did get Clio noticed in France where she became something of a star after a cameo role as a courtesan in *La Dame aux Camelias*, and her status as a sex symbol was confirmed by her appearance as a seductive mistress in *Plein Sud*. As her fame grew, she even outflanked Goldsmith himself. 'There was a time when Jimmy was referred to in France as Clio's uncle,' says Teddy with evident pride. He has several photograph albums devoted to his daughter's screen career and has no hesitation in showing them to visitors. His brother, however, saw nothing to admire in his niece's antics. 'Oh he won't speak to me,' she told the *Sunday Express* columnist Roderick Mann in 1983. 'He is furious. He claims I'm just a porn star who has made an exhibition of herself. My grandmother Marcelle, who is French, keeps telling me not to worry. She says the only reason he is furious is because nobody ever offered him money to take his clothes off.'

When her marriage ended after three years, she lost custody of her daughter to Puri and travelled to Mexico where she met a man who had been living in the jungles of Central America for ten years. She and her peripatetic lover – whom she has never named – spent two years touring the region in his car, collecting antiques and artefacts and sleeping on a mattress they kept in the back of the vehicle.

By 1987, relations with her uncle Jimmy had been restored to the extent that she was on the guest list for a party he gave at Cliveden, the grand country house where the Conservative cabinet minister John Profumo first met Christine Keeler, the call girl who was to prove his downfall. Also in attendance was Mark Shand, the brother of Camilla Parker Bowles. Shand was then one of the most eligible bachelors in town. His form included relationships with Princess Lee Radziwill, the sister of Jackie

Kennedy; her niece Caroline Kennedy; Bianca Jagger; and the model Marie Helvin. He had met Clio some time before but had been turned down when he asked her out to dinner. This time, however, it was different. 'We just clicked,' said Shand later. They married in 1990 and went to live quietly in a house comprised of four converted cottages near Bath with their daughter Ayesha. Today they live in Kew, not far from Teddy's home in Richmond.

The Clio Goldsmith-Mark Shand union is a typical example of the circular nature of the relationships that make up the extended Goldsmith family. Not only is Shand's sister Camilla a friend of Lady Annabel Goldsmith but he was Imran Khan's best man at his wedding to Jemima.

Clio's sister Dido had a similarly traumatic love life, which, again like Clio's, appears to have settled into middle-aged stability. When she married for the first time, at the age of 20, she was already pregnant by her groom, the Brazilian playboy Roberto Shorto, then 26, the brother-in-law of the fabulously wealthy Baron Heini Thyssen. When the marriage fell apart a year later she, her daughter, Maxine, and a nanny moved in with her mother, Gill, and brother, Alexander, who were living in Chelsea. Not that she had any intention of allowing motherhood to cramp her style. When the French night club queen, Regine, made an ill-fated attempt to expand her empire by opening a branch of the famous Parisian club in London in 1979, she paid the well-connected Dido £200 a week to rope in her society friends.

By this time she was living with the sporting baronet Sir William 'Piggy' Pigott-Brown but it was not to last. Within five weeks of their split at Christmas, 1979, she had met and married former film producer Peter Whitehead, a 43-year-old father of three, in the presence of witnesses Bianca Jagger and Oxford-educated drugs smuggler Howard Marks. It may have looked like yet another inauspicious Goldsmith pairing but Whitehead had found a lucrative new career as chief falconer to a Saudi prince and four daughters later the couple are still together. Today, they live in a village in Northamptonshire where Dido writes and illustrates books.

Compared with his sisters, Teddy's oldest son Alexander has led a quiet life. The only one of the children to share his father's obsession with ecology, he worked with Jonathan Porritt at a think tank called Forum for the Future where he edited a magazine called *Green Futures*. He is now a freelance journalist.

It was in October, 1990, that *The Sun* ran a six paragraph story under the headline, 'Tycoon quits to save the forests'. Up to then, Jimmy Goldsmith's philanthropy had been largely restricted to the Ecological Foundation whose charitable expenditure stood at £88,000 by 1992, according to *Millionaire Givers*, a study of the nation's benefactors published by the Directory of Social Change. In 1990, however, he set up the Goldsmith Foundation which supports a wide range of environmentalist causes. In a letter to *The Guardian* in May, 1994, Teddy claimed that the foundation handed out 'several million pounds a year'. Its beneficiaries have included *The Ecologist*, which received £50,000 to fund a campaign to discredit the nuclear power industry's claim to be the solution to the greenhouse effect, and Safe, the Sustainable Agriculture Food and Environment Alliance, which was launched with almost £100,000 of Goldsmith money in 1992. 'Making money took precedence over saving the world for the first two thirds of his life and it was in the final third, when he'd got the money, that saving the world became his priority,' says a spokesman for one group which benefited from his largesse.

But not everyone is happy to take the Goldsmith shilling. In 1991, Goldsmith addressed a cross-section of environmentalists assembled by Teddy on his plan for a series of court actions against manufacturers of CFC gases in a bid to bring forward the date when they would be outlawed. His audience was sceptical, however. One questioner raised the issue of his 41 per cent shareholding in Newmont Mining, a green bogeyman thanks to its strip mining of coal in North America. Goldsmith had acquired his stake a year earlier after striking a deal with his friend Lord Hanson whereby he and Jacob Rothschild swapped Cavenham Forest Industries for Hanson's stake in Newmont. Fortunately, Goldsmith was in a position to tell his detractors that Newmont's coal business had been hived off by Hanson and he absolved himself of any other guilt by association, arguing that he was merely a passive investor in any case. This failed to pacify his opponents, however. Friends of the Earth expressed an interest in his campaign but said they did not want to be publicly associated with him. When they followed this up with a request for a donation of $250,000, a piqued Goldsmith refused on the basis if he was not good enough for them, then neither was his money.

The representatives of Friends of the Earth did have a point, however. Even as they spoke, Newmont was a leading player in a consortium embroiled in a huge row in Australia over a proposal to dig for gold, platinum and palladium in an area claimed as sacred ground by a local Aboriginal tribe. Newcrest Mining, a tie-up between Newmont, Australia's BHP and others, had invested A$15 million in exploratory drilling and estimated that the mineral potential of the site known as Coronation Hill amounted to around £240 million. Then came the revelation that Coronation Hill was the resting place of an Aboriginal creator called Bula, revered by the 650 Jawoyn Aborigines of the region as the spirit who had roamed the area called the Sickness Country during the 'Dreamtime' creating people, animals and the landscape. 'The Jawoyn believe that if mining goes ahead Bula will physically shake the country and there will be an apocalyptic calamity, tidal waves and earthquakes,' said John Ah Kit, director of the Jawoyn Association. 'There will be no sun or moon, only wind and rain, and everything will be destroyed. Not just black fellas but white people in comfortable homes and offices.'

Fearful of incurring the wrath of the Aboriginal lobby, which had shown its might with mass demonstrations during the celebrations to mark 200 years of European rule in 1988, the then prime minister, Bob Hawke, caved in to the anti-mining pressure groups and called a halt to any further development. Many might see the Coronation Hill episode as confirmation that the world has gone mad but James Goldsmith is on record as a passionate supporter of the rights of indigenous peoples. Indeed, in *The Trap* he wrote sensitively on the subject. 'Harmony with natural processes is man's proper relationship with the world, not the imposition of human will upon it,' he wrote. He quotes approvingly and at length from a letter reputed to have been sent by the American Indian chief Seattle, chief of the Dwamish, Suquamish and allied Indian tribes, to President Franklin Pearce in 1854, in response to a request by the government to acquire its tribal lands. 'We know that the white man does not understand our ways,' it ran. 'One portion of land is the same to him as the next, for he is a stranger who comes in the night and takes from the land whatever he needs. The earth is not his brother but his enemy and when he has conquered it, he moves on. He leaves his father's graves behind, and he does not care . . . His father's grave and his children's birthright are forgotten. He treats his mother, the earth, and his brother, the sky, as things to be bought, plundered, sold like sheep or bright beads. His appetite will devour the earth and leave behind only a desert . . . Whatever befalls the earth befalls the sons of the earth . . . Man did not weave the web of life: he is merely a strand in it. Whatever he does to the web, he does to himself.' Almost 150 years later the Jawoyn could not have composed a more lyrical and appropriate open letter to the management and shareholders of Newmont Mining. For a man who prided himself on a lack of humbug, these were uncomfortable contradictions.

Nor was this the first time that Goldsmith had shown a willingness to allow commercial expediency to overcome a point of principle. One of his most memorable spats at his French news magazine, *L'Express*, occurred in the wake of the oil crisis of 1978. The magazine's energy correspondent, Jacqueline Giraud, who held strong ecological views, was a longstanding opponent of the French nuclear energy programme. On the face of it, this made her a natural ally of Goldsmith. But that was to reckon without the need to cultivate people in high places. According to Jean-François Revel, a former director of *L'Express*, Goldsmith had become friendly with the then French minister for industry, André Giraud (no relation to the *L'Express* correspondent), who had talked him round to a more pro-nuclear stance. For his part, Revel thought the magazine should be softening its stance on the nuclear industry and this provoked a showdown with Jacqueline Giraud, who claimed Goldsmith had assured her that she could decide the editorial line on energy issues. Revel responded to this gauntlet by writing to Goldsmith and saying he would be forced to resign unless he was given the authority to make policy on such matters and even succeeded in getting Goldsmith to come to his office and explain the situation to Giraud personally. Giraud's reaction was to accuse both men of servility to the pro-nuclear lobby and to storm out, sobbing. As she left, Goldsmith turned to Revel and said: 'Ah women! In situations like this they always end up in tears.'

Indeed, neither of the Goldsmith brothers was particularly good at practising what they preached. Teddy, after his brave attempt at living the dream in Cornwall, was brought into line by a force that few men down the centuries have succeeded in mastering: the mother-in-law in full spate. Mrs James objected to her daughter's primitive existence down on the organic farm and persuaded Teddy to decamp to a more metropolitan environment and to invest in a few mod cons. For years he had railed against the modern lust for consumer goods, arguing there was no real need for them. Today, Mrs James would be pleased to see her daughter's marital home in Richmond is equipped with modern appliances of every description. The man who campaigns for an end to pollution has a gas-guzzling Volvo in his drive and the revolutionary who once stressed 'the great need' for couples not to have more than two children has married twice and fathered five. Asked by a journalist how he justified the contradiction between his prescription for society and his own lifestyle, he replied: 'I'm part of it all. I've never suggested that I'm not. I depend heavily on the system I'm decrying. I'm not attacking it because I have a grudge. I came to my conclusions intellectually, not emotionally.' He added: 'What else should I do? I have a private income. I don't need to make money. I'm very bad at it in any case. I can't take to the bottle because I've got a bad liver. I don't like yachts. What do you want me to do?'

Chapter Eleven

Running for office

SIR James Goldsmith's first serious foray into British politics was made with characteristic extravagance. During a television interview with his old friend, Sir David Frost, in November 1994, he fulminated against the growing powers of the European Union and offered £20 million to anyone who was prepared to run candidates at the next general election who would advocate a referendum on the matter. One man viewing with particular interest was Dr Alan Sked, a senior lecturer in international history at the London School of Economics and former leading light of the Eurosceptic Bruges Group. The moment the programme was over he called Lord Harris of High Cross, the former chairman of the Bruges Group, to obtain a fax number for Goldsmith and fired off his proposal that the big-hearted billionaire back his nascent UK Independence Party (UKIP), which planned to contest the general election on a policy of taking Britain out of Europe. If he was expecting an immediate response, he was to be disappointed: it was to be more than a year before he got a reply, and then it was a *pro forma* response. By that stage, UKIP was in full swing and Goldsmith was at the helm of the Referendum Party.

Goldsmith's objection to UKIP, at the outset at least, may have been its commitment to full-scale withdrawal from the European Union which is something Goldsmith never advocated. Indeed, in the early days of the campaign he insisted his party was neutral on the European issue, merely fighting for the right of the 'people' to have a say.

Patrick Robertson had no such problem. Robertson was the

youthful founder of the Bruges group and an old sparring partner of Sked's. Unlike Sked – a highly articulate and assertive Scot – Robertson is well schooled in the arts of diplomacy and not a man to allow even the most obscure opportunity to pass unexploited. He had made it known to his circle of friends, including Dean Godson, a leader writer on the *Daily Telegraph*, that he was looking for someone to dog-sit his two Pekinese for a couple of months. Godson, a friend of the Goldsmith family for more than 15 years, told him that Goldsmith's stepson, Robin Birley, was keen to find himself a pet dog and would welcome the chance to test the responsibilities of dog ownership before committing himself. Robertson and Birley met and Birley duly agreed to dog-sit. But while Birley soon tired of Robertson's Pekinese and put them in boarding kennels for the last couple of weeks, Robertson himself was far from being in the dog-house. The two men got on well and Robertson was soon introduced to the great man himself. After that there was no turning back. Goldsmith may have had a fearsome reputation but Robertson is the consummate courtier. Few can match his talent for flattering and charming powerful men. And he had the additional attraction of being the man who had set up a limited company called the Referendum Company in 1992.

The two men set about creating a political party from scratch that would field up to 600 candidates in the general election of 1 May 1997.

Offices were found on Horseferry Road, near the Houses of Parliament, and a core group of activists installed. The man picked to run the party organisation was Malcolm Glenn, a former Goldsmith employee who went on to become chairman of Sketchley's, the dry-cleaning chain. He worked closely with Charles Filmer, the thirtysomething director of Stanhope Administration, the company that handled the Goldsmith family finances, who doubled as a director of the Referendum Party. These two aside, however, much of the administration of the party was in the hands of relatively young and inexperienced people, often with social links to the Goldsmiths. The party's head of research, for example, was Tim Williams, the son of Lady Marcia Falkender, a friend of Goldsmith for more than 25 years.

When one of the party's regional campaign managers, a former Conservative Party agent, jumped ship to join the UK

Independence Party, he described the organisation as an 'old boys network' run by amateurs. 'A lot of people that work for the Referendum Party are just jostling for position and favour with Sir James because they want jobs after the election,' said John Bostock, following his departure five months before polling day. He also said that the party had just 15,000 members but Glenn claimed in response that the true figure was 100,000.

Cash was clearly not a problem, but Goldsmith's stated intention of winding up the party after the 1997 general election was. It had the effect of putting off sympathisers with long-term political ambitions and it was clear from the party's earliest days that it would need the shrewdest operators in the business to compete effectively. Three opinion polls conducted by MORI on the party's behalf between April and August 1996 showed it had less than a half of one per cent of the popular vote. Goldsmith was furious and insisted the questions be framed differently in the hope of achieving better results. MORI refused and the relationship ended in mutual acrimony. The gravity of the row emerged in March 1997, when Goldsmith accused his pollsters on Radio 4's *Today* programme of being 'either a very, very inefficient or dishonest organisation'. MORI's chairman Professor Bob Worcester demanded an apology and retraction.

The party's evolution was not helped by the fact that doubts remained until March 1996 over whether the party would actually contest the general election, according to Lord McAlpine of West Green in his autobiography, *Once A Jolly Bagman*. He describes an elaborate game of thrust and counter thrust between the prime minister, John Major, and Goldsmith as Major sought to persuade his billionaire opponent not to enter the race. The two men had met once before soon after Major became prime minister but their first encounter after Goldsmith entered the electoral reckoning came at Margaret Thatcher's 70th birthday party at Claridge's on 16 October 1995. They met privately less than a week later and, according to McAlpine, a former Conservative Party treasurer who defected to the Referendum Party in October 1996, Major asked Goldsmith to hold back while he tried to persuade his party of the wisdom of a referendum, a strategy he personally favoured.

The two men spoke again at the end of January 1996, after an intermediary had arranged for the Downing Street switchboard to put a call through to Goldsmith in Cuixmala. Once again, McAlpine says, Goldsmith agreed to hold off so that Major could organise commitment to a referendum without appearing to capitulate to his threat. Advertising was postponed, and a plan to distribute millions of campaign leaflets was deferred.

By early March, word reached the Referendum Party camp that Major intended to offer a referendum on the single currency only, not the broader provisions of the Maastricht Treaty (which he had negotiated and promoted), and was to bill the Conservatives as the real Referendum Party. This proved to be the *casus belli*. On 11 March 1996, Goldsmith ran an open letter to his candidates and supporters in the form of full-page ads in the national press. Battle was joined in the most appropriate way possible, for advertising was to be more significant to the Referendum Party than any other. While its main competitors could rely on thousands of committed members on the ground to turn out to canvass for votes nationwide, Goldsmith's party, lacking an army of grassroots activists built up over decades, was heavily reliant on a media push. Unlike his maverick equivalents in the US and Italy, Ross Perot and Silvio Berlusconi, he was also prevented by law from advertising on television and had to restrict himself to newspaper and poster advertising and marketing direct to people's homes. In the circumstances, one agency stood out from the rest, Saatchi and Saatchi. It had produced the most effective political advertising ever for the Conservatives but the agency had lost that account to its founders, Maurice and Charles Saatchi, when they quit to set up a competitive shop. Goldsmith duly had a meeting with the management of Saatchi and Saatchi but an inspired intervention by a much smaller outfit, Banks Hoggins O'Shea, clinched the Referendum Party's account for them. In addition to spending more than £20 million through Banks Hoggins O'Shea, Goldsmith also produced a tabloid newspaper, *The News*, that was sent to every household in the country at a cost of £2 million A video featuring himself that went to eight million homes is estimated to have set him back a further £10 million.

On the stump, Goldsmith did not perform with distinction. He was a forceful rather than charismatic figure and lacked the common touch. But perhaps his greatest failing was that he was so rarely there to press the flesh. Indeed, sightings of him were so infrequent and fleeting that some of those in his chosen constituency of Putney, south-west London, awarded him the nickname the Loch Ness Monster. In hindsight, this was obviously unfair. Within weeks of election day, it emerged that Goldsmith had been suffering from cancer of the pancreas for four years and had been enduring regular scans and operations during the campaign.

The Referendum Party's push probably reached its apogee in October 1996, when, for one bright weekend, an English seaside town was transformed into a temperate Cannes during Film Festival week. Goldsmith chose Brighton Conference Centre as the venue for his party's first and last conference. The mood for the conference was set in the preceding week with a series of newspaper ads. One carried the line 'Meet the British government' above mug shots of 20 European Commissioners. Another showed pictures of John Major, Tony Blair, Paddy Ashdown and Screaming Lord Sutch above the line, 'Frankly it doesn't matter who you vote for. He won't be running Britain anyway.' The party's PR effort was given added momentum in the same week by the announcement that Edward Fox, former England batsman Geoffrey Boycott and Lord McAlpine had all signed up to the cause.

While some heed was paid to the conference speeches in the hall, more column inches appeared to be devoted to the social dimension of the whole affair. A party hosted by Lady Carla Powell, wife of Sir Charles Powell, Baroness Thatcher's former private secretary, on the Friday night preceding the conference attracted the most attention. The paparazzi were out in force as the family filed in. Isabel entered, trailed by Zak and Ben. The arrival of Jemima, then heavily pregnant, was presaged by security men shouting 'Make way, make way.' There were aristos: the Marquis of Worcester, Countess Maya Schonburg and Goldsmith's friend Lady Cosima Somerset. There were celebs: Edward Fox, the actor, Maya Even, the television presenter, and Adam Faith, the pop singer turned businessman turned actor. And there were even some with a political background: Lord McAlpine, Sir Alan Walters, a former economics advisor to Thatcher, and Charles de Gaulle, a French MEP and grandson of the late French president.

It was a different story in the conference hall the next

morning. As the golf courses of the south east lay empty and their members flocked to Brighton to cheer their spiritual leaders, Matthew Engel of *The Guardian* observed: 'There were rumours that the hall would be full of drop-dead gorgeous Sloanes. In fact, most of the audience looked more likely to drop dead.' This was a perspective denied to the authors as, on Goldsmith's instructions, they were refused accreditation to the conference itself.

It was, by all accounts, more of a rally than a conference with few, if any, dissenters among the estimated 4,000 supporters who overflowed into side rooms. The speeches, unrestrained by the traditional red light to warn speakers their time was up, frequently over-ran and an extra two hours had to be tacked on to the end of the day to ensure most of the scheduled 43 speakers had their say. There was precious little sign that this was a party for people who merely felt the voters should have a say in the direction of Britain's European policy. On the evidence of the speeches, the conference was a gathering of rabid Eurosceptics. John Aspinall excelled himself. 'We've been unconquered for 930 years,' was his message to Brussels. 'Come back in another 1,000 and we'll discuss it.' He went on to eulogise 'the five great tribes' that made up England – Angles, Saxons, Danes, Jutes and Normans – which would not only have marginalised the Celts in the party, like Lord Tonypandy and, to an extent, his Anglo-French-German-Jewish best pal, Goldsmith, but any Afro-Caribbean and Indo-Pakistani supporters.

So what did lead such an obvious outsider as Goldsmith to promote such a nationalist agenda? A clue to his thinking can perhaps be gleaned from comments he made as guest of honour at a lunch hosted by the *New Statesman* almost 20 years earlier. One journalist asked why he felt he was considered an ally of the left in France at that time but right-wing in Britain. One who was there, Bruce Page, recalls Goldsmith's answer as follows: 'The reason I like being in England is that whatever you may think about the French right, however they pretend, always somewhere behind them is the sound of the jackboot. In England, I find it much more relaxing because I can be my natural, right-wing animal. I don't have the same fears about the English right.'

On the face of it, this made his alliance with the French politician Phillipe de Villiers rather a surprising one. De Villiers is the right-wing leader of L'Autre Europe (The Other Europe), a Eurosceptic movement that confounded the pundits by sending 13 MEPs to Strasbourg after the European elections of 1994, including one James Goldsmith. Thanks to the French list system, which frees candidates from the necessity of campaigning in person, Goldsmith had to do little more than put his executive jet at the disposal of the party leader to ensure that he won a seat.

De Villiers' brand of right-wing populism has its roots not in Vichy – that is more the culture of Jean Marie Le Pen's National Front – but in God and the king. While the Vichy regime of the Second World War was collaborationist and anti-Semitic by its very nature, de Villiers' politics have more ancient roots. As a viscount, he draws his title from the area which rebelled against the Revolutionary forces in the eighteenth century and the worst massacres of royalists occurred in his constituency.

Anti-Semitism is not an issue that Goldsmith ever turned into a crusade. Strictly speaking, Jewishness is passed on only through the mother and while Goldsmith's father was the son of German Jews, his mother was a French Roman Catholic. But such a blood link would certainly have been enough to condemn him in the eyes of the Third Reich and may well have been enough to attract racist taunts at Eton. He certainly saw anti-Semitism at the root of *Private Eye*'s campaign against him. A columnist for the *Jewish Chronicle* wrote on 13 May 1977: 'Apart from an intermittent concern about Israel, Goldsmith was only vaguely aware of his Jewishness until *Private Eye* began what he regarded as a personal vendetta against him. Scratch a semi-Jew and one will discover a full one.' Right up to his death, Goldsmith made a point of visiting a synagogue once a year on the anniversary of his father's death to perform the *yahrzeit* ritual. This involves lighting a *ner zichron*, or candle of remembrance, which burns for 24 hours. At least one of his sons, Manes, was circumcised by a rabbi in a *brith-milah* ceremony.

Whatever the extent of his observance, sources close to Goldsmith during the 1997 election campaign testify to his despisal of the German chancellor Helmut Kohl and his suspicion of German domination. In many other ways, however, Goldsmith's Euroscepticism was strongly Anglo-Saxon. A proud island that has gone unconquered for more than a thousand years should not throw away its hard-won independence for a supporting role in an economic union dominated by one country it helped to defeat in the Second World War and another it freed from enslavement. On trade policy, however, his position could not be more French, that is to say, he was a protectionist. Global free trade is a recipe for wholesale unemployment in the West as less developed countries with low-paid work forces undercut European producers, he argued. The only way to keep the workers of the developed world in jobs was a system of tariff barriers against the tiger economies of the Pacific Rim to price their goods out of the market or, at least, limit their penetration.

The most obvious flaw in this argument is that it fosters complacency. Insulated from the cut and thrust of the global market, there would be an obvious danger – indeed, one might say inevitable tendency – that innovation would wane and that, in the long run, Europe would become the sick trading bloc of the developed world. It was a curiously socialist position for such an unfettered capitalist to take and one which marked him out from the Eurosceptic herd who saw even this limited proposal for pan-European co-operation as a perilous genuflection to the forces of federalism.

Indeed, as Goldsmith became more and more involved in the British brand of Euroscepticism he moved further and further away from the arcane principles laid out in his book *The Trap*. Take the wording of the referendum question itself. It appeared after much goading from political opponents and did not disappoint in its length and complexity. Published in the form of yet another full-page ad in the newspapers, it ran: 'Do you want the United Kingdom to propose and insist on irreversible changes in the treaty on European Union so that the UK retains its powers of government and is not part of a federal Europe nor of a European monetary union, including a single currency?' It was the final proof, if such proof were needed, that the Referendum Party was not an organisation for people who merely considered it important that the people be consulted before any momentous decisions were taken over Europe, but one for ardent anti-Europeans.

Britain's dealings with Europe have never run smooth. As far back as 1955, when Britain was grudgingly negotiating with the six members of the European Steel and Coal Community over whether to sign up to the Common Market, the discomfort was plain. Indeed, the British representative Russell Bretherton, our deputy secretary for foreign trade negotiations at the Board of Trade, pulled out of a meeting following the Messina conference on the instructions of Anthony Eden, then foreign secretary but to become prime minister shortly afterwards. Bretherton's parting shot must go down as one of the less distinguished contributions to the European debate: 'The future treaty which you are discussing has no chance of being agreed; if it was agreed, it would have no chance of being ratified; and if it were ratified, it would have no chance of being applied. And if it was applied, it would be totally unacceptable to Britain. You speak of agriculture which we don't like, of power over customs, which we take exception to, and institutions, which frighten us. Monsieur le president, messieurs, au revoir et bonne chance.'

Within two years, the Treaty of Rome had been signed and the EEC formally came into being on 1 January 1958. Three and a half years later, Harold Macmillan, the then prime minister, made the first of Britain's two unsuccessful attempts to join up. Charles de Gaulle, the French president, took great satisfaction from vetoing both and it was not until his resignation in 1969 that any meaningful headway was made. Britain eventually succeeded in joining up on 1 January 1973.

The parallels with the current situation are stark. The words of Bretherton could easily be put in the mouths of any number of today's opponents of a single currency, including Goldsmith himself.

The question for Goldsmith's successors is: can Britain, as a country which is steadily losing its power and influence in the world, prosper as healthily outside a well-functioning inner Europe as within it? Eurosceptics argue that a semi-detached Britain would have all the benefits of membership but none of the downside. But would it not test the patience of Britain's more committed neighbours? What would prevent them imposing substantial tariffs on goods manufactured in Britain thus pricing them out of the European market? How could London expect to remain the banking capital of the world in a global economy dominated by the euro and the dollar? Would not Frankfurt be a better base for European operations?

In the event, the Referendum Party, which had consistently indicated that a total of one million votes would be considered a 'respectable' performance, fielded 546 candidates and polled 810,778 votes. Goldsmith's reaction to his own defeat and to the words of the former heritage minister David Mellor, also defeated, proved to be one of the highlights of election night. As Mellor taunted his opponent during his speech after the count was announced, Goldsmith joined in the slow hand-clapping and chants of 'Out, out, out'.

He could take some solace from the fact that, partly as a consequence of his efforts, both the major parties were bounced into committing themselves to holding a referendum before signing up to a single currency. As we know from Goldsmith's increasingly irritable phone conversations with John Major, however, this result fell very short of his ambitions. His torch will continue to be carried by the Referendum Movement but as Goldsmith's press spokesman during the election campaign, Bernard Shrimsley, once said: 'It's like Hamlet without the Prince when he's not here.'

Chapter Twelve

The billionaire's way of death

GOLDSMITH'S call was typically conspiratorial. He wouldn't say where he was phoning from and explained that he was only calling to pre-empt a story that he knew was going to appear in the following day's papers. And yet he was not speaking to an aide about some business matter, but to his eldest daughter, Isabel, to serve notice of his impending death.

'He said you're going to read something in the papers tomorrow which is quite true,' recalls Isabel. 'So I thought it was probably something to do with girlfriends and I said, "Oh really, what?"' Goldsmith explained that he had cancer. Even this news did not particularly faze Isabel, who had long known her father as something of a hypochondriac. When she queried whether it was serious, there was silence at the other end of the line and when she asked whether he was going to be operated on he said that he already had been. Even at this stage, Isabel remained under the impression that it was a relatively minor form of illness, like skin cancer, but she made appropriately sympathetic noises before ringing off. In fact, Goldsmith was in the late stages of pancreatic cancer and was to die less than two months later.

Like anything under his direction, the manner of Goldsmith's going was planned to the last detail. Family members and friends were informed on a need-to-know basis. Unknown to Isabel – indeed, all the children – Goldsmith had first been diagnosed as having cancer a full four years earlier. His financial affairs were so well organised that there was never any question of dispute over the will. For most of the last three months of his life he persisted in talking things through with his lawyers for a few hours each day.

And, just in case anyone did decide to contest his legacy, the executors of his estate were instructed to defend his instructions to the full extent of the law.

One thing that Goldsmith could not legislate for, however, was the behaviour of his extended and riven family. When a powerful man dies, his nearest and dearest flock to his bedside. In Goldsmith's case this meant rather more visitors than most: one wife, one ex-wife, one mistress, and a total of eight children by four different women. As we have seen, whatever the public face put on Goldsmith's domestic arrangements, the feuds and petty jealousies between the women were legion.

Take Isabel's experience. The day news broke of her father's condition she consulted friends who told her how serious pancreatic cancer could be. After calling her half-sister Alix, Isabel discovered that her father was in a hospital in Paris. At the same time, the lease on where she was staying, the house in London's Wilton Place that Goldsmith had taken out for the general election campaign, was on the point of expiry and she was forced to pack her belongings and put them into storage as she waited for work to be completed on her own house on Tregunter Road.

The day after the story of Goldsmith's illness had appeared, Isabel left for Paris. 'I couldn't stay in the Rue Monsieur because Ginette wasn't calling me or being friendly, so I stayed in a hotel, from where I called the secretary in the Rue Monsieur to relay Get Well messages,' she says. 'I'd spend three days in Paris and three days in London to supervise the work. But I saw him very little. I saw him once at the Rue Monsieur. I'd write to him saying, If you're too tired or whatever, I quite understand but I'm thinking of you and I'm here. When you have the strength, I'll come over.' Nor was Ginette's hostility the only problem. 'Laure was even worse,' says Isabel. 'She's very hard and very tough.'

Meanwhile, Annabel had to cope with the trauma of telling her children that their father was beyond help. As Isabel flew to Paris, Annabel was staying at Torre Tramores, her estate in southern Spain. Apart from her children, the guests included the interior designer Kathryn Ireland, a friend of her eldest surviving son, Robin. 'The first week in June was when they were told there was nothing modern medicine could do,' says Ireland. 'Ben-Ben [Benjamin, 16, Annabel's youngest] was on that trip and she said, "You'd better help me. You've got to tell Ben-Ben this weekend about it."'

Among the first to be told of the seriousness of Goldsmith's condition was Balendu Prakash, a practitioner of Ayurvedic medicine, who went under the title 'Vaidya', the Sanskrit term for doctor. By this time, it was clear that the only thing that conventional medicine could offer Goldsmith was increasingly high doses of morphine to deaden the pain. He was losing weight with astonishing speed and was having difficulty eating. With the end approaching fast, it was Imran who suggested bringing in Prakash, 38, who runs a medical research foundation 140 miles north of Delhi. He was also known to Teddy Goldsmith, having successfully treated a friend of his who had been suffering from brain cancer. In Goldsmith, however, Prakash was confronted with a patient *in extremis*. Goldsmith had already been operated on no fewer than seven times in as many months But Prakash, who counted the president of India among his patients at the time, insisted that Goldsmith call him personally before agreeing to take him on as a patient and the two men eventually met in Paris in the last week of April 1997. 'Sir James Goldsmith, his wife, some of his children and his doctors were there and he narrated his story about how he'd got cancer four years previously and they'd operated on him to cut it out,' says Prakash. Goldsmith went on to explain that the cancer had returned, and chemotherapy and further surgery had failed to arrest it. 'He told me he had not passed a motion for seven days,' says Prakash. 'We had been talking for an hour and a half, when all of a sudden, he developed serious pain, acute pain, and he was rushed to hospital. The doctors operated and they found his intestine was blocked in many places.'

After promising to help prevent the cancer spreading, Prakash left on an urgent trip to Germany. He was in Israel when he received an anguished call from one of Goldsmith's children. Goldsmith had taken a turn for the worse and wanted to try Prakash's course of medicines. Prakash duly returned to Delhi to pick up the relevant preparations – bizarre-sounding concoctions produced from mercury, arsenic, copper, and gold – and returned to Paris where he was greeted warmly. A grateful Goldsmith, who had already handed over a cheque for £40,000 for Prakash's foundation in India, said he wished he had met him earlier.

It was widely reported that Prakash's treatment meant Goldsmith had to come off pharmaceutical painkillers as they were considered to counteract the effects of the Ayurvedic medicines, and that as a result, the man who had everything spent his final days writhing in agony and roaring in pain. But Prakash denies this and insists that Goldsmith's avoidance of painkillers at that stage was agreed between him and his conventional doctors. Indeed, Prakash says that Goldsmith, far from being in great pain, was merely 'uncomfortable'.

As June wore on, Goldsmith left hospital for Montjeu, his chateau in south-east France. 'Last time I saw Daddy was ten days before he died,' Isabel says. 'He was walking about the house in Burgundy, putting on as good a show as possible. It was Alix who told me that he had been mostly in bed before I came. Perhaps he had kept his illness secret so as not to admit that it was happening – to exert some kind of control over it. His illness may have been about to destroy him but if he didn't even admit its existence he still had the better of it in a way.'

John Aspinall visited Goldsmith in Burgundy several times, taking with him groups of Goldsmith's closest friends, to pay their last respects. 'Henry Kissinger [the former US Secretary of State] called him twice (while I was sitting on his bed) during the last few weeks, asking to come and see him,' said Aspinall. '"Henry," he said, "I can't receive you at the moment in the manner I would wish. When I am better, I will call you back."'

As the end drew near, a growing number of family members began to congregate at Montjeu and there was some dispute over the course the treatment was taking. Prakash claims 'some' family members or friends were pushing for more pain-relieving treatment. 'They wanted us to use unconventional things, like some narcotics,' he says. 'I said, "No, it's not fair to do that." You see what happens when we lose something. This sort of frustration is bound to come.' This did not prevent a friend later saying of Prakash: 'I'd like to wring his neck for the agony Jimmy went through. His final days were hell on earth.'

Although Isabel left ten days before Goldsmith's death on the understanding that her father was in no imminent danger, Laure was in residence with her children, Charlotte and Jethro. Ginette was visiting with Alix and her son Manes. And Jemima had just arrived with her baby Sulaiman. Goldsmith, obviously aware that he had little time left, conducted a touching ritual. Each member of the family was summoned to his bedside in order of seniority. He himself had always carried a piece of amber as a good luck charm and so his parting gift to each of his children was a piece of the semi-precious substance. Manes, his eldest son, received a pair of Goldsmith's father's cufflinks.

One person who was not present at either Montjeu or Torre Tramores was Lady Cosima Somerset. She had lived at Ormeley Lodge as a teenager when she was attending Glendower with Annabel's daughter India Jane Birley. But it was suggested in one newspaper that she had been kept away from his deathbed. Lady Somerset strenuously denied this, telling one of the authors: 'That's absolute rubbish, that really is untrue, that is very important.' When asked if she had seen him at the end, she replied, 'No, but it's nothing to do with Annabel, absolutely not. That's very unfair.' She would not be drawn further. Cosima had spent her early years believing she was Annabel's niece as her mother was married to Annabel's brother, the 9th Marquess of Londonderry. It was not until the age of 11 that Annabel took her aside to tell her that her real father was Robin Douglas-Home, the piano-playing rake who went on to have an extra-marital affair with Princess Margaret. He overdosed on pills and alcohol in 1968 and never met his daughter. It was not the only shock fate had in store for Cosima: her mother, Nicolette Harrison, who divorced Lord Londonderry and married '60s singing star Georgie Fame in 1972, also committed suicide in 1992.

Firm friends with Kathryn Ireland, Cosima moved into her house in Battersea. She married at the age of 20 but was divorced within a year and went on to date Viscount Linley, among others, before embarking on a serious relationship with playboy-turned-gossip columnist Taki Theodoracopoulos. She was his most frequent visitor when he was serving four months in Pentonville in 1984 for drug offences but the affair fizzled out. She married her second husband, Lord John Somerset, in 1990 at the age of 28 but was divorced again six years later.

Vaidya Prakash saw Goldsmith for the last time eight days before he died and says his patient had no fear of death. 'I am telling you, I never saw such a brave person in my life,' he says. 'Brave, honest, caring, and such an aristocratic person. I was there when he was in pain. But he was concerned about all the people around him, whether they were being fed and looked after properly. He was such a great man with so much money but he was attending to everybody like he was the housekeeper.' It was Prakash's understanding that his patient, who had professed a vigorous atheism throughout his life, was to die a believer.

On Friday, 18 July 1997, Goldsmith made what was to prove his final journey. He and his medical team were transported from Montjeu to Dijon, around 40 miles away, where his Boeing 757 waited to fly him, Laure and Annabel to Malaga. At Malaga airport, a helicopter was waiting to ferry Goldsmith and his medical team to the Spanish estate he shared with Annabel. Within hours of his arrival, Goldsmith had died – just after midnight on the morning of Saturday, 19 July.

When his body was cremated, the only mourner present was his personal assistant Charles Filmer. The whole family turned up for the scattering of his remains except for Annabel who sent Ben with a single white lily to cast on the water at the same time as Manes threw his father's ashes into the sea. It was the only flower at the ceremony.

Quite why Goldsmith should have chosen to make a pain-wracked journey from central France to the Costa del Sol at such a delicate stage has been the subject of much debate. Some say it was a desire to die in the bed he was born in. Others maintain it was because he wanted to feel the heat of the Spanish sun on his face and breathe the mountain air for one last time. But it is hard to avoid the conclusion that it was done out of rather less romantic motives. Tax authorities in both France and the UK cannot fail to have been watching his progress with interest. On the face of it, the French were favourites to benefit most from his death duties, though the Inland Revenue could make a good case based on the fact that he had spent a good deal of time in Britain as he spearheaded the Referendum Party's campaign. By bailing out to Spain at the last moment, however, Goldsmith certainly made life more difficult for the French who would have capitalised on the fact that he died on their soil to claim inheritance levies of up to £600 million.

His will was read to the family within days of his death. There were no surprises. Annabel got her beloved Ormeley Lodge and the Spanish retreat where she had once entertained Princess Diana; Laure – 'devastated' by Goldsmith's death, according to her friend the interior designer Robert Couturier – kept her magnificent chateau in Burgundy and both she and Ginette kept their joint interest in the Rue Monsieur mansion in Paris. If there was a controversial aspect to Goldsmith's will it was the way in which he chose to dispose of Cuixmala in Mexico. The estate which Annabel had initially refused to visit at all and then only when Laure was not in residence, was left for use by all members of the family under the management of Ginette's children, Manes and Alix, who were neutral observers of the ongoing *froideur* between his widow and his mistress.

A small financial management company with offices in Hong Kong, Geneva, New York and London administers his estate. It generates an income in excess of £100 million a year but Cuixmala alone is estimated to have annual running costs of £15 million. The family soon showed signs that it was prepared to live more frugally than Goldsmith himself had, however. Soon after his death, his airliner was put up for sale with a price tag of $50 million. It was always an expensive luxury, made even more so because the way it was registered meant it could not be put out to charter. The scope for bickering over who used it and when may also have been a factor in its demise.

There are signs that the family are beginning to throw off the spectre of 'Jimmy' and starting to enjoy life out of his shadow. At Ormeley, Annabel gave Kathryn Ireland the go-ahead to redecorate her late husband's bedroom. The walls were bright yellow and the bed was covered with a distinctly feminine patchwork quilt. 'I don't know that Jimmy would have approved,' says Ireland. 'It would not have been grand enough for him.'

In the business sphere, Goldsmith's heirs gathered at a series of functions for the president of Chechnya when he visited London in March 1998. Devastated by a battle for independence from Russia that had dragged on for years, the mineral-rich state was looking for enterprising investors to help rebuild the country and, in particular, its capital, Grozny. It was just the sort of venture Goldsmith himself would have relished: a high-risk proposition with the prospect of rich returns but sanctified by an air of do-goodery. The promotional tour was organised by a company set up by Patrick Robertson, the Referendum Party's former leading light, and Goldsmith's step-son Robin Birley. Annabel and Jemima mingled with the likes of Baroness Thatcher and Lord McAlpine, chairman of the Goldsmith-backed oil company, the Trans-Caucasus Energy Company, to market Chechen oil and a Caucasus Investment Fund.

But is there more to Goldsmith's legacy than sumptuous homes, trust-fund babes and the future of Grozny? There is no multinational corporation employing thousands of people. There are no Referendum Party MPs sitting in the House of Commons moulding the course of Britain's policy on Europe and the single currency. Imran Khan shows no sign of becoming a force in the politics of his native Pakistan. There is no great charitable institution bearing his name. Instead, a vast fortune lies tied up in a portfolio of investments around the world supporting the lifestyles of his inner circle of wives, lovers, and children, both legitimate and illegitimate.

As a young man, Goldsmith worked long hours to build a pharmaceuticals business in France. He showed flair and ingenuity in the creation and marketing of products but the organic growth of a business based on modest capital was never going to be enough to contain the aspirations of a man fiercely conscious of a generations-long rivalry with the Rothschilds. When he decamped to the UK, he built an empire by acquisition. Critics argued that he was a financier rather than an industrialist, a man who would pare costs by removing the string tail from a sugar mouse but who rarely showed the flair to create lines of his own.

Without the gambling instinct he first showed at Eton, however, he would never have been able to reach a point where the City pages would point with exquisite piquancy to the fact that Jacob Rothschild was a member of his 'fan club'. He repeatedly staked everything he had on bigger and bigger bids, multiplying his fortune each time. Goldsmith always justified his approach by comparing himself to the predator who kept the herd healthy. There is, indeed, some truth in this. A number of the companies he took over were moribund and inefficient but to make him out to be some sort of altruistic industrial force is to ignore what he gained from these adventures. He rarely built businesses and created jobs, his approach tended to revolve around rationalising enterprises and then getting out while there were bucks to be made. Even his authorised biographers can find few instances of meaningful long term investment and growth. All too often Goldsmith was the predator who was left licking his chops after a mouthwatering stock market coup.

Goldsmith pursued social cachet via the bedroom as well as the boardroom. As a husband and lover, he collected women of wealth and position who could ensure that his friendships and influence touched the highest tables in the land. In taking the former Annabel Birley as his mistress he acquired one of the most aristocratic women in Britain. After marrying Annabel, the woman who replaced her in the post of mistress was a niece of the Comte de Paris, the pretender to the French throne.

In politics, he achieved strictly limited success. A plain MEP in France, in Britain he walked a bigger stage as leader of the Referendum Party. It failed to win a single seat in the 1997 general election and was disbanded after his death to be replaced by a glorified talking shop, the Referendum Movement. Even as an ecologist – the cause for which he was knighted – he sacrificed principle for self interest, losing credibility along the way. His green image was not helped by the fact that he used an airliner built to carry 233 passengers as his private plane, which burned two tonnes of fuel with every take off.

The field in which he excelled was, purely and simply, the accumulation of personal wealth and he had a talent for spending it stylishly. In that sense he added to the gaiety of nations. For that, at least, we should be grateful.

One motivation that remained with him throughout his life was a desire to overcome a sense of being an outsider: a Jew at Eton, a gentile at the synagogue; a Frenchman in England, an Englishman in France; a billionaire in the boardroom but a commoner in the drawing-room. And that required a ruthless streak. Much has been said and written about his undoubted courage and his almost self-effacing charm. Almost everyone who admired him testifies to his generosity and lavish hospitality. But without a studied ruthlessness he would have achieved only a fraction of what he set out to.

Kathryn Ireland has a telling anecdote in this regard. 'I was staying in Barbados, with Annabel and Jimmy when my father died,' she recalls. 'I was due to play tennis as Jimmy's partner against Evelyn and Victoria Rothschild. I go on the court, I play tennis and, after the game, I remember walking up to the house and Annabel taking me aside and saying, "Darling, I've got some bad news. Your father's died." And I remember thinking that's very weird, why would she tell me now? The point was, of course, that Jimmy knew before the game and he had said, "Don't tell her. It'll ruin our game of tennis if you tell her before."

'So he knew and I had to play doubles with him. But he said, "Oh tell her after tennis because it would ruin our game. It would ruin our foursome." That for me puts Jimmy in a nutshell.'

Index